Changing the Subject

Changing the Subject
Writing Women across the African Diaspora

K. Merinda Simmons

THE OHIO STATE UNIVERSITY PRESS
COLUMBUS

Copyright © 2014 by The Ohio State University.
All rights reserved.

Library of Congress Cataloging-in-Publication Data
Simmons, Merinda, 1981–
  Changing the subject : writing women across the African diaspora / K. Merinda Simmons.
    pages cm.
  Includes bibliographical references and index.
  ISBN 978-0-8142-1262-2 (cloth : alk. paper) — ISBN 978-0-8142-9366-9 (cd rom)
  1. American literature—African American authors—History and criticism. 2. American literature—African American women—History and criticism. 3. West Indian literature (English)—Women authors—History and criticism. 4. African American women in literature. 5. African Americans in literature. 6. Slave trade in literature. 7. Collective memory in literature. 8. Culture in literature. I. Title.
  PS374.N4S45 2014
  810.9'928708996073—dc23
2013050843

Cover design by Mia Risberg
Text design by Juliet Williams
Type set in Adobe Sabon

Cover image: Willie Cole. *Female Hothead Dancer in a Scorched Skirt*, 2005. Iron scorches and varnish on plywood and found wood. 62 1/2 x 62 1/4 / 159 x 158 cm. Image courtesy of Alexander and Bolin, New York.

∞ The paper used in this publication meets the minimum requirements of the American National Standard for Information Sciences—Permanence of Paper for Printed Library Materials. ANSI Z39.48–1992.

9 8 7 6 5 4 3 2 1

For Phil, and for Houston, for all of it.

CONTENTS

Acknowledgments   ix

INTRODUCTION   When Literature and Identity "Get Real"   1

CHAPTER 1   Sites of Authentication: Migration and Subjectivity in *The History of Mary Prince*   23

CHAPTER 2   "Different with Every Shore": Women, Workers, and the Transatlantic South in *Their Eyes Were Watching God*   49

CHAPTER 3   Familiar Ground: The Rhetoric of "Realness" in *Mama Day*   78

CHAPTER 4   "Recuperating" the Subject in *I, Tituba, Black Witch of Salem*   111

CONCLUSION   Writing Women across the African Diaspora   137

Notes   145

Works Cited   157

Index   163

ACKNOWLEDGMENTS

SO MUCH of the scholarly writing process is inevitably confined to library stacks, piles of articles, and long hours at a computer screen. I am lucky to have had the kind of support system that drew me out of the library and motivated me back into it at intervals and that kept me bolstered on both academic and personal levels.

The late and brilliant Robert Young was a crucial sounding board at this book's inception. When what would later become this project was just a handful of thoughts, he asked the right questions, offered the right suggestions, and helped me ultimately turn our conversational brainstorming sessions into the very first drafts of some of the earliest work that would ultimately form this book's basis. The seminars he led on Marxism and African American literary theory shaped my intellectual interests early in my graduate study, and his sharp critical edge motivated the theoretical questions that laid the foundation for my own work. His life exemplified the very best and most important implications of the work that he did, and I am honored to have known—let alone worked—with him. I am also grateful to his spouse, Nirmala Erevelles, whose own presence in the University of Alabama's College of Education and in the academy in general is a gift. She forces scholars to think about race, class, and disability, and she makes better thinkers of those who have the good fortune to cross her path.

This book is dedicated to two people, both of whom have been instrumental to my development as a scholar. First, I extend deep thanks to Phil Beidler at the University of Alabama—a trusted advisor, mentor, and friend for years—who motivated me through the writing process, helped me hone my arguments, and offered a sounding board when I needed it most. He has been my compatriot and my ally, especially when the writing process felt isolating, and I have relied on his encouragement every bit as much as his savvy work on nationhood and identity. Next, when this book was just a pile of rough ideas, it managed nonetheless to introduce me to Houston Baker at Vanderbilt University. Working with him has been one of the great pleasures of my life, and I have come to rely on his calm insight and uncompromising feedback. His is the voice in my head, and this book would not be what it is without him. Indeed, my own understanding of myself as a scholar would not be what it is without him.

There were many who read countless drafts of various sections of this project. I am especially grateful to Tony Bolden, who spoke early on with confidence about the book that would eventually come from my chapter drafts; Yolanda Manora, who helped me see the light at the end of the tunnel and whose expertise in African American women writers proved invaluable at so many points; Micki McElya, whose sense of humor and conversations about scholarship in Southern Studies over countless cups of coffee were a thing I treasured; and Heather White, my friend in knitting and in academe who is without question the best reader I've ever come across.

The course of this work saw my incorporation of the academic study of religion into my range of scholarship. For this and so much more, I have my incredible colleagues in the Department of Religious Studies at the University of Alabama to thank. My professional life would look entirely different were it not for Russell McCutcheon, who helped me find my footing in a new discipline, who consistently and with encouragement challenges my ways of thinking, who helped me navigate the stages of book publication, and whose own work is among the clearest and most effective critiques of authenticity claims I have read. I am privileged to call him my colleague and even happier to call him my friend. Very special thanks also go to Ted Trost, to whom I owe my earliest introduction to the Department. His kindness and support have been so important to me, and I have found the phrase "Thanks, Ted" to be one of my most oft-repeated during any given day. Steven Ramey helped make my transition into a new department a smooth one, and he remains my go-to for so many things. He graciously provides an extra set of eyes on the things I write, a trove of knowledge about all things logistical, and a general presence from whom I derive daily conversation and encouragement. Steve Jacobs has been kind enough to check in on me consistently, asking about the status of the book, talking with me about the writing process, and cheering me on. I am also grateful to the late Tim Murphy, who was always eager to talk with me about my work.

The academic study of religion has presented me with all sorts of wonderful opportunities, and I have most recently appreciated the addition of the Culture on the Edge research group into my professional life. This past year has produced some tremendous exchanges, and those conversations have been extremely useful in my own work, including this book. Thanks to my colleagues Leslie Dorrough Smith, Craig Martin, Russell McCutcheon, Monica Miller, Steven Ramey, and Vaia Touna for the remarkable way in which they all keep my critical edge a sharp one.

Very special thanks go to Sandy Crooms, editor extraordinaire at The Ohio State University Press, whose expertise and sustained interest in my work throughout the review process have been tremendously important to me. I am very appreciative of the efficiency and commitment to excellence shared by the OSUP team that saw the book through its production process; thanks especially to Malcolm Litchfield, Lindsay Martin, Tara Cyphers, Kristen Ebert-Wagner, and Linda Patterson Blackwell. I am also grateful to the anonymous readers who made this a better project with their attention to detail, careful critiques, and thorough feedback. I am exceedingly fortunate to have benefited from their insights.

Particular people in my life should not go without mention for all of the kindness they showed while I was working on the book, especially in its final stages. Sarah Kane was there not only to talk through my ideas in the beginning but also to help motivate me as I got closer to the finish line. Elizabeth Wade, Bonnie Whitener, and Craig Martin were essential conversation partners through the process, both professionally and personally. Pete Schulte reminded me of how important it is to step back and look at one's work with a fresh pair of eyes. He was an integral part of the completion of this book, and I will never be able to thank him adequately or enough. Finally, Christina Frantom, Meredith Bagley, Alex Davenport, David Deutsch, and Kirk Walter kept present for me the importance of community when my mind was totally consumed with my work. For their perspective and generosity, I will remain forever so very grateful.

My brilliant family has been an endless source of support. John, Kathy, Aaron, Evan, Nathan, Vanessa, and Atticus inspire even as they motivate. All of the work I do is thanks to their insistence on analytic inquiry and their continual energy to question. Finally, gratitude and so much love go to Nathan, my partner in the profession and in parenthood. This book comes into the world the same year as our child, and I am so thankful for the timing of both in my life.

INTRODUCTION

When Literature and Identity "Get Real"

LOCATING THE "NEAR"

Just outside the Biology building at the University of Alabama in Tuscaloosa, there is a small freestanding marker with a plaque that reads as follows:

> BURIED NEAR THIS PLACE ARE JACK RUDOLPH AND WILLIAM "BOYSEY" BROWN, TWO SLAVES OWNED BY UNIVERSITY OF ALABAMA FACULTY, AND WILLIAM J. CRAWFORD, A UNIVERSITY STUDENT WHO DIED IN 1844. RUDOLPH WAS BORN IN AFRICA ABOUT 1791 AND DIED MAY 5, 1846, FROM "BILIOUS PNEUMONIA." BROWN WAS BORN APRIL 10, 1838, AND DIED NOVEMBER 22, 1844, FROM "WHOOPING COUGH."
>
> JACK RUDOLPH AND BOYSEY BROWN WERE AMONG THE SLAVES OWNED BY THE UNIVERSITY OF ALABAMA AND BY FACULTY. THEIR BURIALS WERE HONORED AND RECOGNIZED BY THE UNIVERSITY OF ALABAMA ON APRIL 15, 2004. THE FACULTY SENATE APOLOGIZED FOR THEIR PREDECESSORS' ROLE IN THE INSTITUTION OF SLAVERY ON APRIL 20, 2004. THIS PLAQUE HONORS THOSE WHOSE LABOR AND LEGACY OF PERSEVERANCE HELPED TO BUILD THE UNIVERSITY COMMUNITY SINCE ITS FOUNDING.

Both Jack and Boysey were owned by Basil Manly Sr., the second president of the university and namesake of Manly Hall (where the departments of Religious Studies and Gender and Race Studies are now housed, and where my own office resides).[1] The plaque commemorating their unmarked graves is right in front of a small group of headstones, where members of a white family—the Pratts—are buried, their graves enclosed by an iron fence.

The image that appears is striking in its representation of various attempts at "recognition." Initially, there are the marked graves for the white family. It was not until 2004 that the UA administration officially recognized its role in the buying and selling of human bodies and its reliance on slave labor to build many of its own walls. So, now there is a twenty-first-century counternarrative to the "original story" (at least, the first one given any visual signifier) of the family who is buried there. Interestingly, many passersby confuse the marker about Jack and Boysey with the dingy headstones, thinking those are the slave graves that had just gone unnoticed. The line between the counternarrative and the narrative against which it is situated (literally, right in front of, in this case) becomes blurred and confused. These two graves (whether marked or unmarked) provide a striking visual for those who are interested in histories and narratives about race and labor in the South. Worth mentioning, of course, is that the bodies were never *buried* at all. There were certainly (and many) more than two slaves on campus, after all. How many bodies were simply left, how many bones were scattered and separated by animals and weather, is not known.

What becomes clear in the attempt to "get right" the story of who's where and how they came to be there is that there is no "real" history, no true story that we can access with careful scholarly work. The attempt to play academic excavator and go digging to uncover "what really happened" is potentially well-intentioned but ultimately ineffective. Whatever history we might reveal is a highly manipulated thing, understood and edited differently by a variety of agents. In the cases of Jack Rudolph and Boysey Brown, the administration that subsidized the monument has a decidedly different role to play from the faculty who critiqued the timing of its commemoration, for example. On the level of scholarship, there are still other and varying interests represented in relation to the issues of historical narratives and forgotten people. Depending on what kinds of concerns are at the table, scholars will perhaps emphasize personal narratives or civic records, journals and letters or contracts and bills of

FIGURE 1. Marker commemorating the role of slave labor at the University of Alabama, specifically noting the lives and deaths of Jack Rudolph and William "Boysey" Brown. University of Alabama, Tuscaloosa. Photo by author.

sale. These different approaches, however, tend to share an emphasis on the idea of historical accuracy and on the personal stories of the peoples themselves. Herein lies the rub. Scholars attempt to offer a history of this or that, pretending that they can stand removed and apart from the particular curiosities and expectations they bring to a text or community. Further, there is implicitly present the idea that these texts or communities are "things in themselves," as if they exist nondiscursively or as *a priori* subjects. The phenomenological descriptive efforts, however, are their own brick monuments, metaphorically speaking. Many might approach the stories they tell as objective histories that tell a contemporary audience about this or that part of the transatlantic slave trade. But just like the marker that commemorates the lives and representative experiences of Jack Rudolph and Boysey Brown, these histories have inevitable erasures and inclusions of very particular sorts. In this way, they corroborate Hayden White's understanding of histories—that they are only ever and inevitably fictions[2] and that, as such, they rely on and indeed come into existence through the discourses that name them.

Rather than the object of study (in this case, slave histories) being the starting point for critical inquiry, then, I locate the starting point in the interests and theoretical approaches taken in identifying what stories get told and how. The scholarly approach that has become pervasive within postcolonial and feminist readings of African diasporic histories is one that would bring light to counternarratives and alternative histories (at UA alone, there is an annual and successful symposium called "Recovering Black Women's Voices and Lives," as well as a popular "African American Heritage tour" of the campus). This approach aims to chip away at the seeming monolith of colonial discourse, telling the stories of those who are left out of the narrative. As such, those of us working in these fields of identity studies try to follow in the narrative vein that has manifested brilliant works from *Clotel* to *The Wind Done Gone*. However, while these novels have the convenience of genre to keep the constructed nature of history at the fore, scholars doing so-called recuperative work in strands of race and gender theory too often forget that our ethnographic, historical, and literary studies are projections of present interests. Our recovery or recuperation efforts presume to identify (through a Nietzschean "myth of immaculate perception") the intentions and investments of a particular subject, forgetting that critical analyses of texts say less about the object of study (the various themes, characters, contexts—i.e., the text "itself") than they do about the scholars discussing it.

Changing the Subject looks at just a few of the ways in which slave narratives and first-person novels about women of color resist critical appeals to "authentic" histories. The textual entree is *The History of Mary Prince, A West Indian Slave, Related by Herself* (1831). This story of a Caribbean slave who moves from place to place with her owners, joins the Moravian church, and finally "relates" her story in England under the patronage and guidance of the Anti-Slavery Society has received more critical attention in recent years after Henry Louis Gates Jr. "legitimized" it by including it in his volume *The Classic Slave Narratives* (1987, reprinted in 2000). This book seeks to put the 1831 narrative in conversation with novels in which slavery remains a pivot point for negotiations of women's migrations, of diasporic identities that are in literal, geographical flux. Specifically, I offer readings of how the constructions of "gender" and "labor" come into relief—for both the protagonists and those in the communities they encounter—in such contexts of migration. These constructions and migrations suggest that the notion of "authenticity," often used in feminist and postcolonial readings of women's narratives, is too narrow a classification to be as productive in literary scholarship as has been commonly assumed.

APPROXIMATING THE AUTHENTIC

In scholarly and historical recuperation efforts, there is often the implicit suggestion that "They told it wrong. Here's the *real* story." As appealing as this logic is, the closest we can get to something "authentic" is to say that the stories and bodies we are trying to recuperate—in the case of the marker commemorating the unmarked slave graves—are "buried *near* this place." We can only approximate. Thus, there is no "coherent past" as such, no "stable memory" that points to an authentic story of what "really" happened. Tara McPherson makes a similar claim in *Reconstructing Dixie: Race, Gender, and Nostalgia in the Imagined South* regarding tourist sites:

> [There is] . . . an overarching concern with the "authenticity" of history: each structures its historic account as a series of tangible locations, displays, or artifacts that truthfully and accurately represent History (albeit in air-conditioned comfort). History's "realness" here depends on spectacular display and immersive experience, on structuring an encounter with "excellent relics" and "exceptional details." There is an overwhelm-

ing emphasis on authenticity and accuracy as the keys to some "real" History rather than an understanding that our only contemporary access to history (as the actual past) is through the stories we tell about it. (101)

Indeed, the *re*construction of a subject is a new construction. Too many times, a stable and linear history is confused for legitimacy. In making a claim for a real story granted by experiential authority, scholars project their own interests backwards, attempting to recreate marginalized identities in their own image and, by extension, granting "authentic" narratives to stories that have not been told.

While academic conversations about identities and personal narratives have made a habit of critiquing appeals to individual and collective essences, scholarly discussions of race and experience often remain strangely invested in the notion of "authenticity." Accessing the supposed "truth" of a tale is an obsession of not only the reality-TV-drenched pop culture but also the essentialism-wary communities within academia. As J. Martin Favor notes in *Authentic Blackness: The Folk in the New Negro Renaissance,* "the definition of blackness is constantly being invented, policed, transgressed, and contested. When hip-hop artists remind themselves and their audiences to 'stay black' or 'keep it real,' they are implicitly suggesting that there is a recognizable, repeatable, and agreed upon thing that we might call black authenticity" (2). In postcolonial theory, this emphasis on the authentic has taken shape in the ways in which cultures are situated as cohesive wholes around which scholars and activists might rally for progressive ends. Even when promoting a focus on creole or hybrid identities and cultures, as Stuart Hall does in "Créolité and the Process of Creolization," there remains an identifiable geographical and imaginative region called "the Caribbean" and, what's more, a Caribbean possessing of a distinctive character: "I would argue that the process of creolization in this sense is what defines the distinctiveness of Caribbean cultures: their 'mixed' character, their creative vibrancy, their complex, troubled, unfinished relation to history, the prevalence in their narratives of the themes of voyaging, exile and the unrequited trauma of violent expropriation and separation" (29). Leaving alone the irony of suggesting a "distinctive" mixed-ness or complexity, I find reason to pause at the notion of the Caribbean as a cohesive and self-evident region possessing a distinctive character in its own right. The Caribbean, as such, might be instead viewed as a manufactured product of those discourses that identify "it" as a specific place or thing.

All of the texts that I discuss in this book have two thematic elements in common. First, each is a first-person account—a woman telling her own story about moving from one place to another. This framing structure is often what invites critical responses that emphasize the "authenticity" of the voice telling the story. Second, they all sustain a focus on migration as the reason for and motivation behind much of the events that drive the plot. Ultimately, these texts are *about* migration, as the changes in context force the characters to rethink signs like gender in particular ways. This second element complicates the first—or, at least, the simplistic readings that emphasize first-person vocality as a subversive end in itself. My own contribution to literary and migration theory, then, comes in an alternative to analyses that, in the name of legitimizing diasporic women's voices, lend experiential authority to their narratives. Reading diaspora narratives through simultaneity discourse—that is, through an analysis of the mutually constitutive but ever-changing constructions of gender, race, and work—destabilizes authenticity as the ideal to which the women in these narratives aspire. My approach changes the subject of literary criticism about diasporic identities—or, more aptly, identifications—as it provides close readings of how these subjects in the narratives change.

Within the academy, attempts to "recuperate" or unearth a previously ignored past often take shape as descriptive data-driven analysis operating within a framework of standpoint theory. We will talk about this or that group of women, this or that diaspora, and so on, as a piece of *sui generis* data that is interesting or compelling in its own right. This not only (and inevitably) ignores particular communities—we cannot discuss *everyone,* after all—but also avoids more substantive analytical critique. More directly, such an approach reduces ideas like "race," "blackness," "diaspora," "women," and so forth to a single subject position. While "the personal is political," identity theorists would do well not to engage autobiography solely on its face. The personal is *only ever* political. Thus, the subject or "person" of the personal comes into being as such only through the contextual (political) lenses used to discuss that subject. A more useful project involves asking questions about contexts and classifications—what kinds of stories are told by whom in what venues and why? Specifically, I problematize classifications of race and gender within culturally specific contexts that broaden the scope of inquiry regarding autobiography. As Frances Smith Foster notes, "Not only is autobiography the most democratic genre in American literature, it is also one of the oldest and offers the best opportunity for examining a variety of particular confrontations of culture by particular people in particular settings" (26).

By traveling from one social and societal sphere to another where "race," "gender," "sexuality," and "class" freight with them different meanings for the bodies to which they are ascribed, bodies in motion allow for an interrogation of the very categories that would label and essentialize them. Indeed, to talk about bodies as if they can somehow be removed or held in isolation from notions like "race," "gender," or "nation" is problematic. At issue here is how bodies in motion help to underscore the instability of these signs by presenting characters for whom categories simply do not work. They productively shift critical focus, making the "subject" not the women "themselves" but rather the discourses about them. What is more, they are examples of bodies *becoming,* and they signify not only spatial but also classificatory flux, always coming in and out of contact with other bodies and societal expectations or definitions of their own. As such, they represent the corporeal interpretation that Judith Butler articulates in *Undoing Gender:* "[the] body is not . . . a static and accomplished fact, but as an aging process, a mode of *becoming* that, in *becoming* otherwise, exceeds the norm, reworks the norm, and makes us see how realities to which we thought we were confined are not written in stone" (29, emphasis mine).[3] Elizabeth Grosz gives a similar reading in *Volatile Bodies,* suggesting, "Presence and absence are coupled in and to the same framework. In place of plenitude, being, fullness or self-identity is not lack, absence, rupture, but rather *becoming*"[4] (165, emphasis mine).

An argument may be made that would see the academic quest for authenticity like any other search for "truth"—a mainstay that, while perhaps misguided, is not ultimately a cause for serious critical concern. As marginalized identities and diasporas become the focus of more scholarly discourses, however, the kind of attention we give them is itself a piece of data worth study. In other words, there is no black female body without *discourse* on black female bodies. Likewise, there is no African diaspora or narratives coming out of it so much as there are *discourses* on the African diaspora and its literary tradition. This book is an example of how we might look at the conversations of gendered and working bodies in migration as our object of study more than the ostensible bodies themselves. In examining the terms of engagement in identity theory, we might start to let go of the pressure of trying to get at and recuperate identities themselves (the authentic story of this or that woman of color) and more productively discuss what is accessible in the realm of academic analysis: discourses on identity and on narratives by women of color.

DEFINING THE CATEGORIES

I am using terms in this study that are familiar in academic conversations about identities and diaspora: terms like "migration," "gender," and "labor."[5] It is worth spending time to explain how I define and deploy these terms in relation to the specific contexts of the narratives I discuss in the following pages. Among the various unifying threads of the narratives in my study, the most important are migration and a so-called diasporic community. The women in all of the narratives I analyze are travelers. They are moved variously by coercion, force, or choice. An easy and appealing scholarly move in the face of such foregrounded travel in diaspora narratives is to trace a sort of heroine's journey as an epic quest for self-discovery and self-governance. Such critical tracking is not an uncompelling enterprise. Indeed, a central argument in the following chapters is that so much of what we often understand as "identity" does *change*—sometimes radically—with shifts in geographical (and it would follow: social, national, and economic) contexts. What require more careful attention than they have received, then, are the often-inexact mappings of geosocial diasporas and the critical assumption that clear and identifiable starting points mark them.

This book rejects such triumphalism and attempts more productively to approach texts about women, migration, labor, and identity in the office of a more thoroughgoing Diaspora Studies. The analyses in the following chapters attempt to resist both an easy synonymity and a reductive critical impulse to confine works categorized as "women's narrative" to a closed trajectory. I am in complete agreement with Anne McClintock when she writes in *Imperial Leather: Race, Gender and Sexuality in the Colonial Contest* as follows: "gender is not synonymous with women . . . feminism is as much about class, race, work and money as it is about sex. Indeed, one of the most valuable and enabling moves of recent feminist theory has been its insistence on the separation of sexuality and gender and the recognition that gender is as much an issue of masculinity as it is of femininity" (7).[6] I would add to this claim, however, that masculinity and femininity are just two classifications within a spectrum of gendered categories.[7] In the same way that class, race, work, and money (and surely nation-state and migration) are constitutive elements of feminism, sexuality and gender are not so easily teased apart.

The ways that gender identity becomes performed and understood in the texts I analyze are not uncomplicated products of a steady-state exploitation leading indubitably to gifted empowerment. In fact the narratives are visible in a relational field of multiple practices. Masculinities and migrations are the matrices, and both of these are themselves contextualized by structures of race, work, and sexuality. Diaspora is a gender-complicated business. How womanhood is presented and manipulated in changing geographies is affected by the kinds of work women do—from place to different place, in physical contexts of labor that are ever-varying, comprising a diachronic panorama that yields prospects of cross-temporal theorization and more exacting accounts of diaspora.

In discussing "labor" I am talking about systems of exchange. Specifically, in the narratives I discuss I am interested not only in physical "work" but also in economies of classification.[8] For example, along with the material ways that Mary Prince's body is bought and sold in her narrative, "womanhood" serves as its own currency in negotiations between the respective legal endgames of Prince's slave owner and proponents and members of the Anti-Slavery Society. "Womanhood" is thus complexly traded and given varying degrees of *value* governed by competing orders of trade. Gender and labor, one might say, are presented in the narratives I analyze as transient properties. They scramble across literally shifting sands, transmogrifying with social contexts that regulate both "womanhood" and "work."

IDENTIFYING THE SUBJECT

The classifications of various identity signifiers become particularly beleaguered in the realm of autobiographical literature, where individuals are quickly and easily cast as archetypes. Frances Smith Foster makes this point in specific reference to slave narratives: "Though ostensibly individual life stories, these narratives create a protagonist who was not an individual but a type" (31).[9] Discourse, then, constructs types—and, indeed, subjects—that then are read as naturally occurring states of being. Françoise Lionnet takes these questions about discourse and subjectivity into productive arenas by casting them in relation to cultural convergence in *Autobiographical Voices: Race, Gender, Self-Portraiture*. She cites Edouard Glissant from his *Le Discours Antillais,* wherein he suggests that

"This practice of cultural creolization [practique de *métissage*] is not part of some vague humanism, which makes it permissible for us to become one with the other. It establishes a cross-cultural relationship, in an egalitarian and unprecedented way, among histories which we know today in the Caribbean are interrelated" (qtd. in Lionnet 4). For Glissant, as well as for Lionnet and many contemporary scholars of identity and diaspora, the domain of creolization (*métissage* for Lionnet) has "led to the recovery of occulted histories" (4). *Autobiographical Voices* is worth quoting at some length here:

> In the effort to recover their unrecorded past, contemporary writers and critics have come to the realization that opacity and obscurity are necessarily the precious ingredients of all authentic communication . . . Since history and memory have to be reclaimed either in the absence of hard copy or in full acknowledgment of the ideological distortions that have colored whatever written documents and archival materials do exist, contemporary women writers especially have been interested in reappropriating the past so as to transform our understanding of ourselves. Their voices echo the submerged or repressed values of our cultures. (4–5)

For Lionnet, then, these writers are tapping into values that were suppressed by colonial rule. The cultural pasts and ancestries seemingly lie in wait for contemporary women writers to discover and use for their own purposes. This "reappropriating the past," as Lionnet sees it, is the recuperative project of a communal paradigm.[10]

Within literary studies, scholars offering critical readings of slave narratives often state their purpose using the familiar rhetoric of "recuperating" a "lost" story, unearthing *the* heretofore unknown, and so forth. Foster discusses the resulting connection that many readers make between black autobiography and slave narratives:

> Scholars of ethnic studies and of women's studies have been especially quick to exploit the treasures that the personal narratives' combination of history and discourse provides. In black studies the research has focused upon the testimonies of slaves and ex-slaves concerning their lives in slavery and their determination to be free. However, the enormous popularity of the slave narrative, both in the nineteenth century and at the present time, has contributed to a perception of the Afro-American experience prior to the Civil War as a monolithic oppression, differing in detail, perhaps, for the house and the field slave, but generally contoured by daily

struggle for survival. The slave narrative becomes for most people the voice of our Afro-American ancestors. The slave narrative becomes synonymous with early Afro-American autobiography; and the prototypical autobiographer, then, is the slave. (26)

This phenomenon offers an inroad into scholarly dialogues about gender, race, and diaspora.[11] The route that *Changing the Subject* takes is, thus, an analysis of first-person narratives and autobiography alongside one another. "Voice" and the issue of experiential authority (such that one might have a real story to recuperate after the fact) are laden with the politics of external and intersubjective discourse. As Houston Baker points out in *The Journey Back: Issues in Black Literature and Criticism,* "Egotism, self-consciousness, and a deep and abiding concern with the individual are at the forefront of American intellectual traditions," and as such, the limits of autobiography as a narrative methodology and genre were not particularly concerning to white authors (27). "The question of autobiography's adequacy," Baker suggests, "entails questions directed not only toward the black voice in the South, but also toward the larger context of the American experiment as a whole" (27–28).

Complicating the "master narrative" by adding more voices and stories has been and continues to be an important pursuit. Also important, however, is not seeing the addition alone as an "add-narrative-and-stir" end in itself. What results in such projects is ideological imperialism in the name of progressive politics. The notion of a "self" that might speak, as Baker points out, is endlessly imbricated with issues of societal classifications of and expectations made on individual agency. Speaking specifically of the *Narrative of the Life of Frederick Douglass,* Baker notes, "One can realize one's humanity through 'speech and concept,' but one cannot distinguish the uniqueness of the self if the 'avenue towards areas of the self' excludes rigorously individualizing definitions of a human, black identity" (38). Thus, as conceptions of the subject change as she travels from place to place, so too might the subject of scholarly discussions that would describe "her" identity as a stable or self-evident end in itself.

There are certainly important exceptions to the critical trend that purports to recuperate a lost but stable subject. One of the most notable is the work of Hortense Spillers. With essays like her classic "Mama's Baby, Papa's Maybe: An American Grammar Book," accompanied by collections such as *Black, White, and In Color: Essays on American Literature and Culture; Conjuring: Black Women, Fiction, and Literary Tradition;* and *Comparative American Identities: Race, Sex and Nationality in the*

Modern Text, Spillers's writing is an example for those of us in fields of literary theory and cultural studies who want to engage seriously the blurry lines between history and text. The category of "black women" (or, broadly speaking, "gender" itself for that matter) is not at all an irreducible given for Spillers. She has offered vital critiques of the way that categories of black womanhood have come into relief through systems of slavery and plantation economics, and many scholars duly note the importance of her work to analyses of race, gender, and class. Nonetheless, too much work on race and identity has nodded at the heterogeneity of subjectivity without keeping close the lessons that thinkers like Spillers articulate. Namely, while emphases on notions like creolization and hybridity have become more and more the order of the day in academic circles, they nonetheless imply a self, a subject, to which the creolized hybridities refer. In this manner, creolization comes too often at the price of contingency, such that dominant spaces of power and white supremacy are not *also* understood as creolized, fluid, and subject to reinvention. We thus keep stable the very systems we seek to deconstruct by our unwillingness to frame all identities as contingent and not at all self-evident.

MAPPING THE TEXT

In relation to Prince's *History,* subsequent chapters focus on Zora Neale Hurston's *Their Eyes Were Watching God;* Gloria Naylor's *Mama Day;* and Maryse Condé's *I, Tituba, Black Witch of Salem.* These texts demonstrate that gender and labor mutually constitute, even as they struggle against, each other. Further, the narratives expose authenticity as a trope nostalgically appealing to the presumed origins of the women to whom the trope is attached and operating based on the social interests of those making the judgments of what counts as authentic and the social worlds those judgments help to create. The migrations and displacements in the texts that follow keep categories of gender and work within diasporic contexts in constant flux and degrees of interaction. To put it another way, the question this book answers is: "How might scholars of literary and identity studies change the subject of our analysis in relation to women of the African diaspora?" We would like to presume that identities exist apart from that secondary discourse, when in fact "they" are contingent upon it. What is at stake in recognizing this relationship? Self-reflexive scholarship that takes seriously our own roles in constructing the subject of analysis involves a reworking of the notion of "authenticity" not in terms of its value or potential but in terms of its stasis. That is, a critical call for "authenticity" is not invalid as such, but it is quite limiting when taken as an end in itself.

Whether the context of their migrations is a traveling slave owner's motion in the world, or a more self-actualizing and affective hope for a new beginning, the narratives I analyze literally navigate shifting senses of *place* as their female protagonists confront shifting structures of economic subjugation and racial and sexual disparity. True, these texts present visions of imagined refuge and return. Mary Prince dreams of a return to the Caribbean; Janie Crawford strolls confidently through the center of a Southern town oblivious to the porch talkers' envious disdain at her return. Cocoa makes a point of returning to Willow Springs. In each case, however, the "home" or place of supposed *return* is not cast as something enduringly stable, or even uniquely identifiable. "Home" is endlessly contextualized as a site of multiple players and unceasingly shifting histories. Critiques suggesting that the narratives I analyze are products of some cosmogony of personal struggle and liberation—one marked by singularly knowable origins and signally heroic self-actualization—are, I think, misguided. They are undone by their commitment to a myth of discernible origins, usually conceived as *national*.

Ironically, these texts (and many others whose generic company they share) are held in great esteem by virtue of their inclusion in a canon of black women writers precisely as a result of the valorization of origins. And this valorization, rather than enlivening the interpretive and theoretical fields, tends toward intellectual rigor mortis. The texts are categorically "conserved" within the specific parameters of national, racial, and gender narratives with prescribed origins and ends. Their diasporic complexity is subsumed by a low-voltage critical impulse to conform them to a closed trajectory: oppression's *origin,* and its triumphal conquest by a radiant community of self-empowered women warriors. More productive is a reading that emphasizes the ways in which subjectivities change as women move from place to place. Critically foregrounding how these subjects change, I find quickly apparent a need to change the subject of our discourse in relation to women and African diasporas.

An easy point of access for such a project may be thought to lie in texts that deal with the Great Migration. Certainly the mass exodus out of the South is a key moment for those who wish to analyze migration within the African diaspora. Farah Jasmine Griffin's *"Who Set You Flowin'?": The African-American Migration Narrative* is a compelling example of the fine work being done in this genre. For this specific project, however, I am interested in travel that is not focused in one specific direction. Thadious Davis addresses slavery in relation to constructions of "the South" as a region and "Southern identity" in her essay "Reclaiming the South." She suggests that, as signifiers, "slavery" and "slave-economy" allowed for "cultural outsiders to define the region and for cultural insiders to justify both self-perception and social order" (58). In Davis's view, difference rather than diversity became the issue in describing the South. "The result," she notes, "has been curious: whites in the South became simply 'southerners' without a racial designation, but blacks in the South became simply 'blacks' without a regional designation" (58). Rather than escaping *from* an oppressive South and heading *to* an opportunistic North, the women in the texts I discuss find themselves within complex webs of coercion, retreat, escape, and return.[12] I am suggesting, then, a focus on the moves that the narrative subjects make not only geographically but also socially and politically. In such moves that change the classificatory rubrics of gender, race, and work, the North and South do not represent isolated spaces of freedom and oppression.

STARTING THE JOURNEY

In chapter 1, "Sites of Authentication: Migration and Subjectivity in *The History of Mary Prince,*" I read Mary Prince's *History* as a work that subverts a singular quest for authenticity. Specifically, I focus on Prince as a less stable figure whose text is inevitably freighted with nineteenth-century British cultural ideologies and persuasions. Her story, while certainly only one of many slave narratives that arose out of European colonial expansion in the Caribbean, is distinctive not because of an isolated series of events unfamiliar to other slaves (though certainly her specific set of circumstances should not be too quickly universalized) or because of some special, essential quality to what many read as Prince's own "voice" (though her own specific ethos should not be undermined by a reading of Prince as a would-be representative for the whole of nineteenth-century enslaved subjects). Rather, her narrative deserves more attention because of how it manages to subvert the charges made for and against her "authenticity" as a woman of a certain kind of character—both by her editor and former owner, and by many modern scholars who continue to make similar appeals to her "authentic" and universalizing voice.

Prince's *History* as an analytical framework is compelling specifically because the narrative encourages critical attention to be not on "her" text, implicated in and produced by a series of contextual particularities as she is, but rather on the interests with which we as readers and critics might approach her text. The *History* calls attention to our roles as readers. In her role as "speaker," that is, as author of her own experiences, Prince remains nonetheless ambiguous; she is out of her master's house but working in her patron's, she is free in England but still enslaved in Antigua, she is an exotic outsider as well as a respectable British subject. The triangulation of gendered respectability, work, and migration that is present in her narrative offers a productive lens through which to approach twentieth-century novels that present the same triangulation in different genres. In making the *History* relatable to more recent texts, I hope to suggest an approach that ceases to view the slave narrative as exceptional. If we dislodge it from a "special" space, we can find it useful in more expansive dialogues on narrative, genre, identity, and migration. Explaining her own project which examines texts from Augustine and Nietzsche alongside twentieth-century women writers, Lionnet encourages readings of "the interconnectedness of . . . various traditions," as such a practice "would teach us far more about the status and function of our own subject positions in the world" (*Autobiographical* 7). The result of this approach, as she sees it, is liberating: "the renewed connections to the past can emancipate us, provided they are used to elaborate empowering myths for living in the present and for affirming our belief in the future" (7). Thus, her focus is on what kind of journey various authors are on and what kind of pasts they unearth. In reference to the autobiographies of Hurston and Condé, Lionnet suggests that, for these writers, "writing is an unrelenting search for a *different* past, to be exhumed from the rubble of patriarchal and racist obfuscations" (21). My own contribution to readings of first-person narratives is one that disavows a return to a clear or identifiable past as a possible endgame in the first place.

Chapter 2, "'Different with Every Shore': Women, Workers, and the Transatlantic South in *Their Eyes Were Watching God*," examines the gender and labor expectations projected by both the communities in and critical responses to Hurston's novel. Slave histories and diasporic Caribbean workers make significant appearances in Zora Neale Hurston's *Their Eyes Were Watching God* (1937), a novel that finds a strong textual parallel in Mary Prince's narrative. Once again, a woman of the African diaspora must navigate social impositions and ideologies of gender and work that change as she moves from place to place. What initially seems to be solely the personal quest for liberation and autonomy is in fact a much more layered narrative that rejects a single understanding of an "authentic" experiential tale.

Hurston's framing of Janie's story with its transference to Pheoby, even as she aims to protect that same story, is a key part of what makes an understanding of Janie as an "authentic" feminist hero a faulty identification. I see the impossibility of such a label, far from being a failure of Hurston's vision, as exactly what allows Janie's story to be so instructive and useful for Pheoby and for scholars of literary criticism. Even though the tale is coming from Janie's own mouth, it necessarily moves through various filters in its relation to Pheoby. As Janie externalizes her memory, she, of course, makes choices about what details to include and exclude, how long to linger on this or that description of her experience. It is, necessarily, an edited thing that serves her interests. The degrees of separation that exist between the narrator and her journey are revealed through the act of narration. Pheoby, meanwhile, serves as a framing filter—the receptive audience to Barthes's dead author. In this way, "Janie," then, is just as much a text as anything else, and just as much a construction.

Significantly, Janie ends her tale with the difficult knowledge that comes with migration: "you got tuh *go* there tuh *know* there" (192). Her story arises out of her own displacement, and it ends likewise in flux. Like with Mary Prince, a reading of the migrations within *Their Eyes* reveals slippages in the constructions of gender and labor that leave both unstable instead of fixed or categorical. All of the novels that I discuss in this project can be described in the way that Gordon E. Thompson characterizes *Their Eyes* when he suggests that the text "can be thought of as a 'fictionalized autobiography'" (741). In this way, they offer constructive readings to accompany a discussion of Mary Prince's slave narrative, an "autobiography" nonetheless intercepted in many instances by editorial revisions. Indeed, Zora Neale Hurston's *Their Eyes* is a key—perhaps unavoidable—text to consider when looking at the implications of migration for the signs of gender and labor or at the convergences of the Caribbean and a transatlantic American South. It is also an important text in its presentation of African American travel patterns that are not as well known or as well documented as the Great Migration.

Chapter 3, "Familiar Ground: The Rhetoric of 'Realness' in *Mama Day*," likewise reads the South as an extension to and from the wider Atlantic, with an analysis of the migrations and displacements in Gloria Naylor's *Mama Day*. Set on the island Willow Springs off the coasts of Georgia and South Carolina, *Mama Day* tells a story of a place, which, in turn, offers the story of a community. Like in Prince's *History* and Hurston's *Their Eyes,* women are telling their own stories, though not attempting to prove an "authentic" voice.

Early on, Naylor makes very clear that her agenda has little to do with establishing an accurate historical account: "It ain't about right or wrong, truth or lies; it's about a slave woman who brought a whole new meaning to both them words, soon as you cross over here from beyond the bridge" (3). Through textual manipulations of history and memory, Naylor engages the story of a nineteenth-century slave woman. While *The History of Mary Prince* receives editorial and legal arguments for and against its textual veracity, the history of Sapphira Wade (whose name remains unknown to protagonist Miranda and the rest of Willow Springs for much of the book) is shaped by the island community that transmits her story orally. The summary of *Mama Day* on the back cover describes it as "Timeless yet indelibly authentic"; however, Naylor sustains a critique of the very rhetoric of "realness" that she includes. This rhetoric takes different shapes in accordance with geographical context— we hear interpretations of "realness" from George and Cocoa in New York, for example, which begin to change once they arrive in Willow Springs. Naylor's articulation and simultaneous critique of the "real" is key to the subversion of "authenticity" that runs throughout the novel. Such subversion shapes the way we read the figure of Sapphira and the forces at work in Willow Springs, to name just two important examples. Like *Their Eyes Were Watching God, Mama Day* presents the South as a space where ideologies and identities are both constructed and destabilized. While this concurrent construction and destabilization can be said to be true of all places, such ambivalence is particularly key to a study of the transnational South, where multiple and diverse histories of power and oppression converge.

Chapter 4, "'Recuperating' the Subject in *I, Tituba, Black Witch of Salem,*" brings the textual framework back to the Caribbean and back to a genre of slave narrative with a revision of the story surrounding Tituba, the slave who was the third person to be accused of witchcraft during the 1692–93 Salem witch trials. Tituba presents a particularly noteworthy figure to study alongside Mary Prince's *History.* Like Mary Prince's narrative, which was subjected to ideological and editorial revision depending on who was characterizing Prince, the details of Tituba's story are fodder for historical and anthropological debate. She thus quite literally represents the sort of rejection of sociohistorical and literary "authenticity" that I trace throughout this book. Even her race remains in question. Condé sets her squarely within Barbados, even as the self-identifying title allows Salem to lay at least a contextual claim to her. Meanwhile, scholars like Elaine Breslaw specifically suggest she was an Arawak Indian, and other historical accounts refer to her as a "Spanish Indian" (which then would have set her place of origin in the very contexts of *Their Eyes* and *Mama Day:* Florida, Georgia, and the Carolinas). With details about her life that are less than specific, *I, Tituba* is an attempt to resituate and recuperate a narrative that was never able to be written. Accordingly, the many critical appeals to the "authentic voice" that Tituba exercises within the text are at best misplaced. Combining fiction and first-person slave account, Condé offers Tituba's story as something of a mock slave narrative. As such, it resonates with the major strands of slavery, migration, labor, and oppression found in Mary Prince's account. It also presents Tituba's story through an authorial lens that plays a role not so entirely dissimilar to that of Mary Prince's amanuensis, Susanna Strickland. Once again, we are able to see authorial agendas and emphases subtly manipulating the narrative that aims to recuperate a woman's experience. While Mary Prince's narrative is a traditional example of the slave narrative genre, written as a contemporary text of Afro-Caribbean slave experiences, Condé's is a "fictionalized" exercise in telling a similar story. The migrations and displacements in each narrative shape the constructions of gender and labor identity. In the case of Tituba, migration frames her thoughts on womanhood, desire, and her "work" as an alleged witch.

The conclusion, "Writing Women across the African Diaspora," offers analysis on how "writing women" is often a practice of "righting women." As narratives purport to bring their stories into the analytical light of day, an emphasis comes with getting the story right and doing right by "the woman herself." Insistence on "the real story" of "the real woman" implicitly suggests a "Mary Prince" or a "Zora Neale Hurston" existing outside the criticism and analysis about her—a claim I find well-intentioned but ultimately naïve. It evades the responsibility that scholars have in creating our own narratives and speaking "the truth" about this or that author or text into existence. By this, I do not mean to suggest an exceptional creative omnipotence for academicians. I only mean to draw our attention to the simple fact that discourse—endlessly mediated and politicized and contingent—is all we have when approaching the ostensible real story about someone or something. There is, additionally, another mode of "rightness" working here. Even as the narratives I discuss subvert efforts at identifying authenticity, they nonetheless conserve a certain notion of gender and the self and its relations to others, making these texts ironically more conservative than they might appear. While I will not go as far as to call them narratives from the political right (not because I do not think that that case cannot be made but simply because it is outside of my primary interest in this project), I emphatically reject the notion that these texts herald categorical feminist and racial progressivism. The hybrid or creolized constitution of the identities narrativized is not a reformist or progressive end in itself and does not necessarily do the work that critics might want it to on its own. Suggesting otherwise amounts merely to rhetorical radicalism that nonetheless conserves a reliance on a stable subject. I look briefly to an example in the conclusion that illuminates this vein of inquiry in relation to women and diaspora—from two scholars writing on recently uncovered work by Zora Neale Hurston.

Changing the Subject suggests that the shifting geographical and social locations of the women in these texts are not geographical and social transitions alone. They uncover fluctuating dynamics of gender performance and class identifications that expose the notion of an authentic narrative as an impossible endgame. Even when scholarly efforts employ rhetoric of creolization and hybridity, there are too often thought to be bodies and subjects behind the descriptive classifications we apply to them. What I hope to show in this book, however, is that there *is* no subject sans those classifications, and that we would be well served to talk about the scholarly moves that create the conditions/interests for such labels. Katharyne Mitchell's "Different Diasporas and the Hype of Hybridity" is likewise skeptical of scholarly projects that tout hybridity as its own progressive strategy. Interestingly, Mitchell is a professor of geography, and the important moves she makes are not ones that have necessarily become part of identity theory, where there is something more at stake in retaining a stable subject even in the focus on hybridity. However, while her case studies in the essay are located in Hong Kong and Vancouver and are presented through a specific methodology vis-à-vis geographical analysis (the essay was originally published in *Environment and Planning D: Society and Space*), her critique of hybridity discourse is instructive for identity theories. She discusses her project as follows: "Without denying the *potential* for resistance, I critique the notion that the diasporic, the liminal and the hybrid can *always* be equated with a politically progressive agenda" inasmuch as "liminal and partial sites can be used for the purposes of capital accumulation quite as effectively as for the purposes of intervention in hegemonic narratives of race and nation" (258). "The overuse of abstract metaphors," Mitchell suggests, "often leads to thorny problems of fetishization": "As concepts such as hybridity become disarticulated from the historically shaped political and economic relations in which identities and narratives of nation unfold, they take on a life and trajectory of their own making" (258).

Thus, this book is meant to open several discussions or considerations. It asks, for example, about what role slave narratives might be able to play in and what they might offer to literary criticism surrounding more recent—specifically twentieth-century—novels. Too often, slave narratives are housed in an isolated realm of literary and historical analysis, as if they speak solely to the authentically experiential, without any editorial intervention or subterfuge. One aim of this book is to bring slave narratives into a more active exchange and conversation with other literary genres that do not make the same appeals to "truth" but that continue to frame and rework some of the very issues that a text like Prince's navigates. The chapters are bookended with texts that arise out of the Caribbean—Prince's *History* and Condé's so-called neo-slave narrative *I, Tituba*, both of which present women telling their stories within the context of enslavement. Couched between them are examinations of Hurston's *Their Eyes* and Naylor's *Mama Day*, where slavery remains central in the manufacturing of race, womanhood, and work. The chapters on *Their Eyes Were Watching God* and *Mama Day* look at the particular case study of the cultural convergences between the Caribbean and the South. Expanding the South beyond American borders creates opportunities for complicating notions like a woman's work, as *Their Eyes* reveals, and southern womanhood, in the case of *Mama Day*. Violence, time, and trauma interrupt the attempt to get the story right, as scholars seek to uncover, only to bury again differently, the tortured pasts of their subjects.

Uncomplicated and ascribed cosmogonies that tend to accompany discourses on diaspora often appeal to authenticity: a *woman's voice* that is both home origin and fecund place of communal redemption. But surely "diaspora" as it is inferable from the texts I analyze in the following pages is not bound by such honorifics. Like all else in Diaspora Studies, "authenticity" is a shifty classification that must be subjected to critique and inquiry for its various significations. I hope to productively respond to the irony often present in scholarship that discusses diasporas in relation to origins, hybridity, and, of course, authenticity. My goal is to rigorously follow the migratory and laboring course of the narratives and narrators I analyze and arrive at critical and theoretical protocols that provide a more capacious understanding of the registers of identification surrounding African diasporas. In so doing, I offer a change of "subject" in studies of narrative and diasporic subjectivity.

Sites of Authentication

Migration and Subjectivity in *The History of Mary Prince*

CONTEXTUALIZING MARY PRINCE

The History of Mary Prince, As Related by Herself (1831) gives an account of a West Indian slave who, after being forced to move from place to place in and around the Caribbean, tells her story in England to the Anti-Slavery Society.¹ Her story begins in Bermuda, where she is bought by a Captain Darrel for his granddaughter Betsey Williams. Upon her mistress Mrs. Williams's death, she is sold to the cruel Captain I—. She is separated from her mother and sisters, endures brutal physical labor and punishment, is sexually exploited, and somehow manages to remain economically resourceful and make a small amount of money in her own right by buying and selling goods in the public square. Her narrative, while certainly only one of so many others that arose out of European colonial expansion in the Caribbean, deserves attention for the way it manages to subvert the charges made for and against her authenticity as a woman of a certain kind of character by her editor and former owner, as well as by modern scholars who continue to make similar appeals to her "authentic" and universalizing voice.

Questions of authenticity are nothing new in studies of slave narratives, of course, as often the ones relaying the experiences had to "prove" their own good character and the veracity of their stories. In their volume *Early Black British Writing,* Alan Richardson and Debbie Lee suggest that "Prince . . . writing after the abolition of the slave trade in 1807, attempt[s] . . . to bring colonial slavery home to the metropolitan center" (11). In this sense, her attempt at appearing authentic to British citizens becomes all the more important: "[She] presents her own dilemma—technically free in England, but doomed to re-enslavement if she returns to her home and husband in Antigua—as a study in imperial contradiction and British hypocrisy" (Richardson and Lee 11). Thus, from a "dilemma" of ambiguity, Prince must pass a threshold of authenticity and moral character in order to have at least some version of her story told. Further, Prince presents a certain kind of image to the readers of her narrative that is "utterly sentimentalized and in need of pity and salvation" (234). Her position and presentation as a slave are in a constant state of construction and revision. So, too, then, is her narrative separated from a notion of authenticity that would impose a fixed understanding on her subjectivity.

It is important to foreground Prince's narrative context of England in the early nineteenth century. Both textually and emphatically, British societal norms and expectations are present. Indeed, Prince's narrative was published for the first time only two years before England put its 1833 Emancipation Bill into effect. Thus charged politically, Prince's narrative was both laden with the Anti-Slavery Society's editorial agenda and subjected to legal scrutiny that questioned the text's veracity as well as Prince's own feminine moral character.[2] This series of textual and sociohistorical impediments demonstrates the way agency is simultaneously created and decentered in Prince's text. The formation and disruption of agency is of particular significance, as arguments for and against the authenticity of Prince's experience shaped the editorial strategies as well as the reception of her text.

Richardson and Lee point out the significance of Prince's narrative alongside other slave narratives: "Mary Prince (c. 1788–c. 1833) occupies a singular place in the history of Black British writing: not only was she the first black woman to escape slavery and publish her narrative but her work remains the only known English-language narrative written by a West Indian slave woman" (233). That Henry Louis Gates includes Mary Prince's *History* in a volume entitled *Classic Slave Narratives* (1987) speaks to the increasing critical attention paid to her text. Richardson and Lee go on to provide a useful summary of the critical response to Prince's *History:*

Scholars regard Prince's *History* as a unique cultural production. Sandra Pouchet Paquet (1992) holds that despite the constraints placed on Prince and her text, her narrative nevertheless retains a "qualitative uniqueness," one that is "distinctly West Indian, distinctly a black woman's and distinctly a slave's," while Sukhdev Sandhu and David Dabydeen (1999) remark that against other Black British slave writings, Prince's narrative stands out for its visceral quality. They rightly contrast the monosyllabic, "witness stand simplicity" of Prince's account with the long-winded, moralistic tone of polemic that creeps into some other British slave narratives. (233)

Of particular interest to me is the critical emphasis on the "qualitative uniqueness" and the "visceral quality" of Prince's narrative. This focus is echoed in criticism of *Their Eyes Were Watching God, Mama Day,* and *I, Tituba, Black Witch of Salem*. A consistent, essentialist examination of these texts maintains that there is such a "qualitative uniqueness," preserved by what is thought to be an authentic voice projected in each novel. Unveiling this sustained critical lens reveals that a search for a "visceral quality" is the wrong quest; however, these novels share more interesting and productive elements with *The History of Mary Prince* than misguided critical readings. My reading of Prince's *History* attempts to subvert not only a linear reading of her narrative but also a clear reading of Prince "herself" as a stable subject.

In his preface to the narrative, abolitionist and secretary to the Anti-Slavery Society Thomas Pringle discusses the circumstances under which Prince's words were recorded and the cares taken to ensure their accuracy. He states, "No fact *of importance* has been omitted . . . It is *essentially* her own," going on to note the "requisite" changes made to make the narrative "intelligible" (185, emphasis mine). After the initial writing process, Pringle and Joseph Phillips "went over the whole, carefully examining her on every fact and circumstance detailed: and in all that relates to her residence in Antigua" (185). Mary Prince herself, then, is only one of several voices that constitute "her" story. My reading of the narrative takes its cue from Jenny Sharpe's claim in "'Something Akin to Freedom': The Case of Mary Prince" that "we must acknowledge the limitations of a model of subjectivity based on notions of self-autonomy and/or free will" (53). Such a reading, according to Sharpe, allows for an account "of the slave rather than the ex-slave" (53). She offers Mr. Wood's threats to sell Prince as an example of Prince's complicated would-be autonomy, as

Prince answers Wood with others' requests to purchase her. Sharpe understands that "A simple and linear plotting of the slave's quest for emancipation is inadequate for explaining such negotiations, whereby the slave woman's sale is not the sign of her status as property but of her will" (53). In that vein, I submit that linear understandings of the way in which Prince employs "voice" are likewise inadequate. Prince speaks both with rebellion to masters and with internalized acquiescence to the moralistic conventions of her British audience. Her voice is by no means singular or consistent.

For the purposes of this discussion, I maintain Sharpe's emphasis on the subject in the context of slavery instead of post-emancipation. However, I want specifically to take up the figure of the slave *in motion*. Thus, my reading of Mary Prince focuses on how the elements of volition and repression are manifested in her migrations, both geographical and textual. These latter textual migrations of *The History* come in the form of the English patronage and printing of Prince's narrative and subsequent legal fallout.[3] First I look at discursive handlings of gender and sexuality, particularly the admissions and omissions of sexual experiences, and then I move into a discussion of the significant relationships engaged with and by other women in Prince's *History*.

Directly following Prince's first-person account of her experiences, Thomas Pringle publishes a "Supplement to *The History of Mary Prince*" in which he explains the legal feuds surrounding Prince's freedom. Significantly but not surprisingly, the supplementary material is laden with rhetoric and allegations having to do with character—especially the character of John Wood, Prince's master upon her arrival in England, and of Mary Prince herself. Place is at the heart of these discussions. Specifically in question is whether Prince should legally be allowed to travel back to Antigua as a free woman, having left Wood and his family in England and living free under British law. Wood fought back and remained steadfast in his refusal to give over his legal hold on Prince. Pringle's description of the legal fallout and his own argument regarding the case's relevance to the Anti-Slavery Society's ideals are important to consider on two levels. First, this material solidifies the powerful rhetorical position that Pringle holds over the narrative. It casts Mary Prince as the object of intellectual analysis, certainly not as intellectual agent in her own story. Inasmuch as discourse creates identity, Prince as a subject is not only economic but also intellectual property. This is not to suggest that Pringle was purely self-motivated. I mean only to foreground his editorial volition that disrupts what is often read as Prince's identifiable and autonomous voice. Second, the supplementary material proves key to a reading of gender and labor as complementary and conflicting forces that receive meaning(s) based on and through geographical situation. In her role as speaker, or as author of her own experiences, Prince remains nonetheless ambiguous—out of her master's house but working in her patron's, free in England but still enslaved in Antigua, exotic outsider but respectable British subject.

In his depictions of Mary Prince and her case, Pringle emphasizes qualities that are particularly important to the cultural context. Important for him is a portrayal of Mary Prince as a lady that contrasts with the depiction that John Wood gives of her as a licentious, promiscuous miscreant. Pringle initially writes up Prince's case with the solicitor George Stephen to determine whether "her freedom could be legally established on her return to Antigua" (216). Pringle describes her reaction to their work in such a way that presents her as a doting wife:

> On this occasion, in Mr. Stephen's presence and mine, she expressed, in very strong terms, her anxiety to return thither if she could go as a free person, and at the same, time, her extreme apprehensions of the fate that would probably await her if she returned as a slave. Her words were, "I would rather go into my grave than go back a slave to Antigua, though I wish to go back to my husband very much—very much—very much! I am much afraid my owners would separate me from my husband, and use me very hard, or perhaps sell me for a field negro;—slavery is too too bad. I would rather go into my grave!" (216)

We see here an expressed conflict between gender and labor concerns. Prince articulates her predicament as one of a wife who wants to see her husband before immediately following that desire with the one to remain free. Her fears of slavery are cast in terms of being "use[d] . . . very hard" and working as a field slave.

Gillian Whitlock suggests the efficacy of reading Mary Prince's *History* in relation to "other colonial autobiographic subjects," as "Prince's story foregrounds those visceral processes which determined who might speak; how, when, where and why; and how they might engage a 'believing' reader" (10). I see this as the case, too, for what Prince's narrative has to offer to women's stories more generally in which migration plays an integral part in subject formation. While many readers of her text, such as Whitlock and Sharpe, discuss the stylistic ambiguities and complexities in the narrative, I want to emphasize the role that the geographical and societal shifts themselves play in the often conflictual presentation of Prince's voice.

HEARING VOICES: CRITICAL CONTEXT

Much of the literary criticism on Mary Prince's *History of Mary Prince, A West Indian Slave* explores the issue of "voice," looking at where and how the central figure of each narrative "speaks."[4] There are particularly striking possibilities and limitations of two manifestations of this vein of criticism. First, scholars point to voice as an authentic and identifiable thing, a representation of empowered and unfettered autonomy. Second, many use the seeming presence of such voice in each text to signal a representative envoy for a broad collective. The critical trend that focuses on voice, presumably, has to do with important questions of subject formation and the ways that marginalized women of color reject abject status in relation to their societies. Thinking of how identity is constructed offers extremely useful readings of the relationships between the authorial or editorial voices and the "I"s in the texts. However, such a focus also relies on the idea of authenticity, a trope upon which these very narratives cast doubt. Rather than insisting on the authentic voice or authority of a woman speaking from coercive contexts in which the writing is not her own, feminist and postcolonialist thinkers should approach such voice in the manner that Gillian Whitlock suggests we read. In *The Intimate Empire*, Whitlock states that the narrative "alerts us that autobiographic texts in the field of colonial and postcolonial cultures will raise issues of power and privilege, marginality and authority, truth and authenticity in ways which may disqualify them as autobiography as it is conventionally understood" (15). If we are willing to investigate the other voices and dynamics at work in Prince's text rather than classify *The History* simply as "autobiographical slave narrative," we will invite more options with which to explore and understand the importance of her life and work. Such a reading is particularly key for enabling a comparative analysis setting Prince's work in relation to novels such as *I, Tituba*, which also present women of African diasporas in coerced patterns of migration that leave them speaking and telling their stories, but ultimately displaced.

In her *Writings on Black Women of the Diaspora: History, Language, and Identity*, Lean'tin Bracks situates her reading of Mary Prince's narrative at a nexus of ancestry, family, and African memory. Emphasizing the role of Prince's relationship with and separation from her family as well as the role of Africa in establishing identity, Bracks seeks to identify Mary Prince the individual even while establishing her in the broader context of the African diaspora. While Bracks notes the influences of European editorial and cultural contexts, she nonetheless retains a focus on Prince's "unique voice": "Much of what Mary Prince tells in her narrative is tempered by religious and abolitionist goals, but Mary's unique voice can still be heard" (41). Similarly, Brenda F. Berrian suggests, "Although *The History of Mary Prince* was structured and edited for use as propaganda for the Anti-Slavery Movement in Britain, Prince attempts to assert herself and to reflect her presence and her place" (200). For Bracks, evidence of this voice comes through in depictions of the tortures suffered under slavery: "There are passages recounting atrocities done to others as well as to Mary, for instance, that appear consistent with Mary's behavior toward exposing inhumanity and brutality in securing black people's freedom" (41–42). These passages are, as Bracks suggests, significant to Prince's project of condemning the horrors of slavery. However, decrying the slavery institution was the Anti-Slavery Society's agenda as well. In relaying scenes of brutality, Prince does not speak alone but as a representative example of what the Society was trying to bring to English citizens' attention. Accordingly, the voice in her narrative does not constitute half of an either/or dichotomy with "religious and abolitionist goals" on one side and her own "unique voice" on the other. Rather, they mutually and simultaneously construct and complicate each other.

Another tendency in the appeal to voice in the *History* is to generalize its implications and relegate an individual voice to platitudes. There is an attendant nod to the editorial and cultural layers of influence on the text; however, these are seen as secondary to what is considered to be a woman's "true" voice. For instance, in "The Heartbeat of a West Indian Slave," Sandra Pouchet Paquet admits that "issues of voice and identity are complex" in Prince's *History* and that "religious prohibitions . . . and legal liabilities . . . placed further constraints on Mary Prince's individual voice" (131). "Yet," Paquet continues, "her narrative retains a qualitative uniqueness that is distinctly West Indian, distinctly a black woman's, and distinctly a slave's" (131). Paquet further appeals to a notion of Prince's "distinct voice" and suggests that "In the context of the region's historical quest for freedom and independence, [Prince's] contextualized and transformed literate voice emerges as a gender-specific, all-inclusive ancestral voice" (131–32). Paquet is right to call attention to the "circumstances governing the textual production of Mary Prince's narrative"; nonetheless, the idea of "distinctly" singular and identifiable ethnic and gendered categorizations (e.g., "West Indian," "black woman," and "slave") is limiting (131). To insist upon an individual voice and simultaneously use that voice to speak for an entire collective is to reduce dynamic signs like "race," "gender," and "work" to fixed categories. Speaking as a slave certainly does not suggest that Prince somehow speaks for a universal African diaspora or a general slave experience. While Prince's narrative undoubtedly carried far-reaching implications for nineteenth-century British society, it remains instructive as *one woman's journey* across societal expectations and faulty identity constructs that such expectations employ.

In her essay "'I Will Say the Truth to the English People': *The History of Mary Prince* and the Meaning of English History," Kremena Todorova provides a useful overview of critical emphasis on voice:

> Most of the *History*'s contemporary critics focus on the ex-slave's agency in the proliferation of voices in her narrative. "A delightful book that should be widely used in schools etc., as well as women's history classes," announces Joan Grant (1988) who hails Mary Prince unconditionally as "a spokeswoman for Black people in Britain and the Caribbean." "The heteroglot voices compete with but do not dominate Mary Prince's fully integrated sense of self," declares Sandra Paquet in her 1992 article, emphasizing the connection critics usually draw between the authenticity of the ex-slave's voice and the success of the book as an anti-colonialist piece of writing. Moira Ferguson calls her introduction to the 1987 and 1997 reprints of the book "The Voice of Freedom: Mary Prince," even though she is not quite as straightforward in her praise of Prince's autonomous voice as Grant. (285–86)

Departing from such emphases and focusing instead on the sociohistorical implications of the text's publication, Todorova argues "that the *History*'s publication event does not simply suppress or authorize the ex-slave's voice, but manifests cultural anxieties about Britain's imperial project that became particularly intense by 1831, shortly before slavery was abolished" (287).

While my own interests lie more in the consequences of movement and migration than in historicized "cultural anxieties," I do think that Todorova's critical shift away from personal authenticity in the narrative is a productive one. Certainly the *History* marks a significant moment in British society, especially as it was published only two years before passage of the Emancipation Bill. My focus on the cultural influences and surroundings conditioning the *History* is limited to the ways that contexts provide layers of separation between Mary Prince and her story. Sharpe rightly notes that a fuller portrait of Mary Prince comes from intersections and interrogations of not only Prince's narrative but also pro-slavery documents and court proceedings regarding her manumission and character. Such legal archives speak more directly to issues this chapter takes up, namely the ways in which the rhetorics of character and respectability imbue discussions of gender and work.

Whitlock addresses the historical and critical calls for Prince's authentic voice with a comparative look at two editors of her story, Thomas Pringle, who oversaw the first printing, and Moira Ferguson, who revisited the narrative in 1987: "As Pringle desired Prince to speak as an authentic subject for abolitionist rhetoric, so Ferguson desires to return to the *History*, to 'Mary's own lips,' and exhume the independent, authentic subject pursued by late twentieth-century feminism" (32). Whitlock very rightly notes that the Mary Prince of contemporary readerships is just as much a contrivance as the one "stage-managed by Pringle" (32). She describes the conventional Mary Prince as follows: "This subject has agency; this subject is able to surmount all the prefaces, introductions, apologias, diatribes that encrust the text and establish her own domain, autonomous and independent, an essence free of the text" (32). Uncritically reading the narrative of this authentic subject, according to Whitlock, "is less restricting only if we accept that it is the implications of sexual abuse, the installation of a sexual history, which lend truth to the *History* and amplification to the self" (32).[5] While female subjectivity should not be thought to be produced solely through sexual roles, such "amplification" nonetheless allows for a more inclusive reading that would invite comparative analyses of Prince's *History* and twentieth-century texts that present women in various spaces of gender and labor.

CONSTRUCTING "CHARACTER": EXPECTATIONS OF GENDER PERFORMANCE

While in the Caribbean, Prince experiences a series of important migrations. She begins in Bermuda with the Williams family, but is then sold to Captain I— at Spanish Point. She runs away and returns to her mother, but her father returns her to her owner. Five years later, "to [her] great joy," she is sent to Turk's Island and sold to Mr. D— (197). There she works in salt ponds shoveling and harvesting salt. While she hopes the migration would signal a positive shift, she "found it was but going from one butcher to another" (198). She draws attention to the relationship between labor and place, suggesting "Work—work—work—Oh that Turk's Island was a horrible place! The people in England, I am sure, have never found out what is carried on there" (199). She makes a rhetorical nod here to British sensibilities, suggesting that the good people of England would never have let these practices continue if they had only known about them. After ten years working in the salt ponds, she returns home to Bermuda when Mr. D— goes back to a house he owns.

Prince is again hopeful: "I was sick, sick of Turk's Island, and my heart yearned to see my native place again, my mother and my kindred" (201). Mr. D— is so intolerable, though, that she asks to be sold to Mr. Wood so that she can travel with him to Antigua. It is in Antigua that she meets and marries her husband Daniel James and joins a Moravian church. It is also where she ultimately departs for England with the Woods. She casts the migration to England in terms that would appeal to English respectability: "I was willing to come to England; I thought that by going there I should probably get cured of my rheumatism, and should return with my master and mistress, quite well, to my husband" (208). She attempts to prove herself a devoted worker and wife, wanting only to get well so that she might be of use to her master and husband.

Sharpe uses the idea of one's contradictory status, referencing Frederick Douglass's statement of being at once a slave and not a slave, to "offe[r] an alternative to addressing the slave woman as either a victim to be saved or an enlightened individual" ("'Something'" 36). Certainly the discussions of gender and sexual labor, both in Prince's disruptions of masters' power through relationships with white men and in her deliberate silences to retain a sense of feminine integrity, showcase her contradictory status between liberation and repression. Specifically, Mary Prince's migrations and how they complicate her subject "position" raise several important questions about the ways that categories begin to get disrupted.[6]

Whitlock notes that all documents dealing with Prince's sexual exploitation at the hands of white men or relating to her sexual character are supplementary and are placed outside her actual narrative. In this sense, there are two stories of Mary Prince, one that attends to the nineteenth-century societal call for a certain feminine appropriateness, and one that reveals a different extent to which sexuality played an important role for slave women. Significantly freighted with any discussion of her body and how it was used sexually is a rhetoric of shame, a rhetoric that suggests an appreciation of a very specific audience, and code of conduct.

Sexuality, in the case of Prince's narrative, has much to do with the status of a discourse on work. Thus, another way that categories are destabilized as singular entities is the degree to which sexuality and labor mutually construct each other and figure Prince's narrative ethos. Lean'tin Bracks notes that "Caribbean slaves had more opportunities for participating in their own maintenance than did North American slaves and had access to forming more self-contained societies" (30). She goes on to refer to what Michael Mullin calls "the dynamic internal markets dominated by slave women" (qtd. in Bracks 30). Thus, Prince's buying, selling, and trading in town, as well as her portrayals of specific tasks she performed for her owners, are instructive to a reading of how labor and autonomy work to construct and complicate each other. Bracks points out that "Prince's narrative . . . is reflective of the working slave woman's experience, which broadens our understanding of the variety of individual responses to oppression, the wide range in acts of slave resistance, and the complex processes women slaves engaged in to achieve self-definition" (30).

Once in England and able to leave her master's home, Prince speculates on her potential freedom, decidedly obscuring the word's very meaning. The new country confronts her with overlapping societal constraints. She states, when Wood present her with a false option, "I also said . . . that I was sorry I had come from Antigua [to England], since mistress would work me so hard . . . Mr. and Mrs. Wood, when they heard this, rose up in a passion against me. They opened the door and bade me get out" (209). Prince's anxiety is not merely about hard work. Locative anxieties factor as key elements of her fear. She continues, "But I was a stranger, and did not know one door in the street from another, and was unwilling to go away" (209). The slavery/freedom dichotomy does not fit Prince's framework. She is unable to dwell as *either* enslaved *or* emancipated. She *hovers,* instead, in a both/and context of duality and flux. She is a slave in the Woods' household, yet is nonetheless "unwilling to go away." Being turned out into free society presents its own risks and limitations. The move away is one she resists as long as she can until she is left with virtually no choice. Significant to my own analysis is how Prince's migrations serve to destabilize a transcendent concept of freedom. For Prince, her would-be freedom is not simply a matter of being or not being enslaved.

CONSTRUCTING FEMININE RESPECTABILITY

The supplementary material provided by Prince's editor shapes a particular vision of gender performance that sells Prince with all the best traits of nineteenth-century femininity—she is well behaved, mild mannered, and of good character. Pringle, who describes himself as "her advocate with the public," cannot effectively relay his emancipation agenda without presenting a *woman* worth emancipating (225). Thus, alongside the smatterings of post-Enlightenment appeals to the corruption of institutions and qualities of individuals, he rhetorically focuses on conventions of womanhood. Letters from Prince's past master, John Wood, uses the same rhetoric but with a different slant. Wood depicts Prince as unruly and unmanageable—a "wild woman" effectively stripped of any "ladylike" qualities. In order to provide a reading of the ways in which something called gender is at work in the narrative, therefore, a dual analysis is necessary, one that first looks at how supplementary material projects a category, and then looks at how the shape of a text dismantles this projection.

Throughout the supplementary text, Pringle refers to Prince with some form of the phrase "the woman" (e.g., "the bondwoman," "the Negro-woman," "the poor woman") approximately twenty times. These references present Prince as a representative of the most appealing kind of woman to male-centered Anglo society—a woman in need. However, Pringle works to make his audience understand that she is not simply needy—she is also *worthy* of help and compassion. He emphasizes Prince's religious faith, her dutiful compliance, and her humility. After providing written accounts of other people's experiences with Prince and her master, Pringle offers his own insights, his "own testimony in behalf of this negro woman" (230). He introduces their association as follows:

> Independently of the scrutiny, which, as Secretary of the Anti-Slavery Society, I made into her case when she applied for assistance . . . and the watchful eye I kept upon her conduct for the ensuing twelvemonths, while she was the occasional pensioner of the Society, I have now had the opportunity of closely observing her conduct for fourteen months, in the situation of a domestic servant in my own family; and the following is the deliberate opinion of Mary's character, formed not only by myself, but also by my wife and sister-in-law, after this ample period of observation. We have found her perfectly honest and trustworthy in all respects. (230)

While Pringle attests to his ability to keep Prince under "watchful eye," his wife and sister-in-law are the ones who give credibility to his judgment. They are key arbiters, as male assessment is seen as tenuous or questionable. He keeps the same order in his description of Prince's character. He first outlines how she handled domestic duties placed in her care, then moves to a depiction of her feminine attributes. Focusing on her abilities, he states, "She had the entire charge of the house . . . and conducted herself in that charge with the utmost discretion and fidelity. She is not, it is true, a very expert housemaid, nor capable of much hard work, (for her constitution appears to be a good deal broken) but she is careful, industrious, and anxious to do her duty and to give satisfaction" (230). Here, the emphasis is on industry and duty rather than "inner qualities" that receive feedback from his wife and sister-in-law. He goes on to describe the feminized qualities of Prince's character:

> She is capable of strong attachments, and feels deep, though unobtrusive, gratitude for real kindness shown her. She possesses considerable natural sense, and has much quickness of observation and discrimination of character. She is remarkable for *decency* and *propriety* of conduct—and her *delicacy*, even in trifling minutiae, has been a trait of special remark by the females of my family. (230, emphasis mine)

The focus here is on innate properties, a so-called natural sense that feeds an emotional, grateful, and delicate presentation of Prince.

John Wood, Prince's master when she arrives in England, has much to say in response to Pringle's requests that he grant her manumission. In keeping with conventional nineteenth-century views on female subjectivity, much of his rhetoric treats the same foci as Pringle's—the *character* of Mary Prince. In a letter offering his rationale for maintaining his legal hold on Prince in Antigua, he casts the general situation in moral and place terms. It is not merely a question of Prince's freedom—it is a question of her return to Antigua as a free woman. He makes the distinction thus:

> There are many and powerful reasons for inducing me to refuse my sanction to her returning here in the way she seems to wish. It would be to reward the worst species of ingratitude, and subject myself to insult whenever she came in my way. Her moral character is very bad, as the police records will shew; and she would be a very troublesome character should she come here without any restraint. (220)

Wood follows this critique by noting, "She is not a native of this country, and I know of no relation she has here" (220).

Exposing Prince as a foreigner, an outsider who has no "real place" in England, Wood submits place as a key agent in deciphering Mary Prince's character. Depending on her geographical and cultural context, the codes of conduct and racial expectations, gender, and work shift. The very constructions of gender and labor for a diasporic slave woman are revealed as slippery formations that must be constantly reiterated and corralled in order to maintain place. Prince is a figure who begins to reshape and unsettle notions of fixed, authentic, moral character determined by gender and work.

"Appropriate" gender is not isolated in its performance, however. It occurs in combination with other facets of identification that unavoidably make their way even into Pringle's supplement. In describing his desire that John Wood free Prince, Pringle notes, "Some faint hope was still cherished that this unconscionable man would at length relent, and 'in his own time and way,' grant the prayer of the exiled negro woman" (219). By invoking the "prayer of the exiled negro woman," Pringle speaks to Prince's Christian piety, place, race, and gender. All of these play a role in shaping Prince as both a paradigm of British respectability and a symbol of slavery's consequences. Thus, Prince is neither fully one nor the other, yet she is both. What are the authorial and vocative implications for a woman's self-story when caught between male interlocutors?

"VOLATILE COLLECTIVITIES": GENDER ALLIANCES

A significant space of contradiction lies in the companionship established on gendered bases. Prince transgresses boundaries of power by forming close bonds to one of her mistresses, but she also develops deep ties with other marginalized women who help her read her experiences. As she destabilizes racialized power discrepancies, she also comes closer to "understand[ing] rightly [her] condition" through the stories of other women likewise enslaved or ostracized.

Important to note before a discussion of relationships seen within the text itself is the association between Mary Prince and her amanuensis, Susanna Strickland. This tie is critical. It offers a certain Anglo-authenticity to Prince's otherwise unseemly experiences. It also suggests a revised voice for Prince—her story heard, but put through a very specific filter to make it appealing and appropriate to English audiences. In *The Intimate*

Empire, Gillian Whitlock examines this relationship with an eye to its effects on Prince's text as "autobiography." Whitlock identifies the major culturally racialized and gendered distinctions between the two women: "[Strickland] is . . . in every sense Prince's foil: the white English woman who is able to embody the precepts of femininity, domestic respectability and innocent womanhood, an Englishness that casts Prince as 'the other woman'" (17). Thus, the very conduit for Prince's voice is also what indelibly stamps its otherness. Whitlock goes on to explain the symbolic representations of differing ethos:

> The amanuensis embodies at the scene of writing the epitome of English womanhood as it was understood in terms of the cult of domesticity. As a young, unmarried woman recently converted to Methodism, Strickland is an innocent scribe. On the other hand, Prince has to tell a story of degradation and punishment, a history about things of which she herself has been "too ashamed to speak" on occasion. (20)

The question for Whitlock is, "How is decency preserved here?" (20). With all of the editorial tensions and limitations, she wonders, "where does Prince find room for maneuver in the text?" (20). One way, she suggests, comes in the form of Prince's description of Strickland at the end of her narrative as "my good friend" (Prince 214). "Here," writes Whitlock, "the scribe works to and for Prince; the allusion to friendship . . . stresses the sense of equality and alliance in their relationship" (20). Of course, there remains only a *sense* of equality, as this gendered alliance is both constructed and complicated by race and class. Whitlock continues, "no simple equation can be made . . . on the basis of . . . gender alone" (26). However, she goes on, "Nor can we establish a relationship . . . by recourse to terms of doubled, tripled colonizations of women. Race, gender, class and nation have imprinted their bodies in very different ways" (26). Whitlock employs Denise Riley's notion of a "volatile collectivity," which she summarizes thusly: "Female persons . . . can be very differently positioned so that the apparent continuity of the subject 'women' isn't to be relied on" (26). She applies this, then, to Prince and her relationship with Strickland:

> Riley's idea of the volatile collectivity of women alerts us to instability and change not only across the range of women's experiences but also within the life of the individual. Characterizations of women vary historically and socially between women and within the life history of one

> woman. Mary Prince and her amanuensis are forceful examples of how women are positioned very differently synchronically, and how carefully they must negotiate access to the public at any one time. They also remind us . . . that women's access to the status of autobiographer is negotiated through a passage from which subjectivity emerges bearing the imprints of experience and culture, self and society. The body is always embedded in history. (26)

The notion of a volatile collectivity is certainly, as Whitlock suggests, at work within Mary Prince's relationship with Susanna Strickland. It is also present in analogous ways, as I argue throughout this book, in *Their Eyes Were Watching God, Mama Day,* and *I, Tituba*. Tracing the ways that gendered collectives navigate multilayered concerns of class and race is key to understanding voice as a process rather than a fixed entity in autobiographical and first-person migration narratives.

This sort of mutilayered relationship between women can be found within Prince's narrative itself as well, and it signals an important role that gender camaraderie plays in highlighting the ways in which categories might be complicated. Prince's relationship with and feelings for her first mistress, Mrs. Williams, works to forge a close bond. Mrs. Williams is terrified of her husband, forming alliances with Prince on a level of shared gender oppression. Prince describes her master as "a very harsh, selfish man," noting that "during his stay at home, [his wife] seldom dared to shew her usual kindness to the slaves" (188). Here again is an instance in which Prince refers to not only the cruelty but also the licentiousness of her master. After her description of him as "a very harsh, selfish man," she adds, "He often left [his wife], in the most distressed circumstances, to reside in other female society, at some place in the West Indies of which I have forgot the name" (188). His own sexual behavior—his "residing in other female society"—suggests a certain degree of danger for Prince. Nonetheless, her rhetorical focus is directed toward Mrs. Williams. She suggests that "all her slaves loved and pitied her," Prince herself referring to Williams as "my poor mistress" (188). Prince is quick to position her gendered connection to her mistress in contradistinction to racial alterity:

> I was truly attached to her, and, next to my own mother, loved her better than any creature in the world. My obedience to her commands was cheerfully given: it sprung solely from the affection I felt for her, and not from fear of the power which the white people's law had given her over me. (188)

In this sense, Mrs. Williams fashions a familial bond with Prince. In her discussion of Mrs. Williams, Prince thus admits devotion to the very system of gendered companionship and devotion that would reject her on the level of race and station. She does not focus on her own danger, deferring to the prototype of respectable, white womanhood that society recognized as worth protecting. This gender negotiation reappears in a sort of volatile collective with the novels to be discussed in the chapters that follow, with deliberate usages of tropes like "a woman's work," in the case of *Their Eyes*, "southern womanhood" in *Mama Day*, and "witchcraft" in *I, Tituba*.

Jenny Sharpe discusses the politics of Prince's relationship to Williams. Certainly the emphasis on the kindness of a mistress "demonstrate[s] that they are not inherently cruel; rather, it is the system of slavery that corrupts them" ("Something" 39). It also "reassures readers that slaves will be loyal and obedient servants so long as they are treated well" (39). In addition to this compliance with both abolitionist and pro-slavery emphases on appropriate behavior, however, is a significantly gendered alliance that unsettles fixed constructs of race and gender within slavery contexts. Significantly, Prince's discussion of Williams appears beside that of her removal to another master and the separation of her family. Thus the productive disruption of racial power relations occurs within the very migrations that mitigate it.[7]

Here, and in the various novels I discuss, these telling relationships among women likewise occur on levels where power differentiations are not quite as obvious. For Mary Prince, an important example lies in Hetty. An important parallel gendered alliance occurs in Condé's *I, Tituba*, where Tituba shares a prison cell with Hester Prynne. In both cases, the women connect not only in terms of a mutual or shared oppression but also on important levels of gender performance. Hetty dies prematurely, leaving an extremely powerful mark on Prince. When she newly arrives on Captain I—'s plantation, Prince forms a quick closeness with "a French Black called Hetty" who cares for Prince, offering her food and bedding (193).[8] Prince responds with intrigued observation of Hetty's work, remembering, "She was the most active woman I ever saw and she was tasked to her utmost . . . I liked to look at her and watch all her doings, for hers was the only friendly face I had as yet seen, and I felt glad that she was there" (193). When Captain I— beats Hetty, Prince cannot help but fear for her own life, their relationship forming on the levels of both gender and corporeality. She states, "I sat up on my blanket, trembling with terror, like a frightened hound, and thinking that my turn would come next" (193). The abuses inflicted on Hetty's body necessarily transfer at least imaginatively to Prince's.

Hetty, like Hester, is pregnant, and meets an early death. When a cow gets loose, Captain I— whips her severely. Her child is stillborn, and she never fully recovers. Prince describes how her reaction differed from that of the other slaves when Hetty dies soon after:

> Ere long her body and limbs swelled to a great size; and she lay on a mat in the kitchen, till the water burst out of her body and she died. All the slaves said that death was a good thing for poor Hetty; but I cried very much for her death. The manner of it filled me with horror. I could not bear to think about it; yet it was always present to my mind for many a day. (195)

After the death, Prince again aligns herself with Hetty, this time on the level of labor. Prince becomes responsible for all of Hetty's work, leading her ultimately to desire another connection with her lost friend: "After Hetty died all her labours fell upon me, in addition to my own . . . There was no end to my toils—no end to my blows. I lay down at night and rose up in the morning in fear and sorrow; and often wished that like poor Hetty I could escape from this cruel bondage and be at rest in the grave" (195). Prince does not end on this desire for death. She instead goes on to say, "But the hand of God whom then I knew not, was stretched over me; and I was mercifully preserved for better things" (195). This reference to God's mercy is another appeal to her audience, as most Christian readers would certainly not have responded to suicidal thoughts with sympathy.

THE WORK BODIES DO: LABOR AND CORPOREALITY

The enforcement in the text of particular kinds of feminization often occurs in the context of "a woman's work," a notion that reappears dramatically in the novels I discuss in the chapters that follow. Therefore, a substantive analysis of gender in Prince's narrative should be coextensive with a discussion of women's labor. Like the emphases on femininity and character that arise in the supplementary material as fixed monoliths but move through the narrative as fluid constructs, work is an ambivalent presence in the text. In the supplement, Prince's work appears as an uninterrogated (but certainly gendered and subject to critique) fact of the circumstantial matter; however, it is a volatile force in her narrative. First of all, her discussion of domestic duties alongside her portrayal of hard manual labor offer a complex portrait of what she, as a woman and as a slave, is expected to *do*. She sells and trades outside her hours of slave labor in order to save her own money and gain a small sense of autonomy. Even with regard to her own position, she makes use of her masters' views of her as property, mentioning who has offered to buy her and for how much in order to manipulate attitude and outcome. What I wish to emphasize, however, is the ways in which sexuality and work coalesce in the text, despite—and even through—the deliberate omissions of material deemed inappropriate by editorial prudence. I turn first to Thomas Pringle's supplement, followed by a reading of the narrative itself.

Pringle makes frequent mention of slave labor as a key part of the destructive nature, or what he calls the "spirit," of slavery. Prince's narrative, Pringle suggests, is "a most instructive illustration of the true spirit of the slave system, and of the pretensions of the slaveholders to assert, not merely their claims to a 'vested right' in the *labour* of their bondmen, but to an indefeasible property in them as their 'absolute chattels'" (233). Pringle follows with how such claims of property rights play into concerns of gender and place in Wood's personal resentment, noting that Wood "prefers losing entirely the full price of the slave, for the mere satisfaction of preventing a poor black woman from returning home to her husband!" (233).

It is no small matter that the legal documents and the letters between Pringle and Wood are the most ready sources of information and speculation about Prince vis-à-vis sexuality. Pringle spends a great deal of time refuting what become key in Prince's legal battles, namely John Wood's allegations of Prince's sexual immorality. Significantly Pringle's rebuttals are often aligned or justified with matters of domestic labor. He refers, for instance, to Wood's accusations of her promiscuity:

> [Wood] alleges that she was, before marriage, licentious, and even depraved in her conduct, and unfaithful to her husband afterwards. These are serious charges. But if true, or even partially true, how comes it that a person so correct in his family hours and arrangements as Mr. Wood professes to be, and who expresses so edifying a horror of licentiousness, could reconcile it to his conscience to keep in the bosom of his family so *depraved*, as well as so *troublesome* a character for at least thirteen years, and confide to her for long periods too the charge of his house and the care of his children. (223)

Prince's *work* and her place in his *domesticity* are facts that run counter to Wood's charge. Accordingly, Pringle uses the work that Prince does in his own home as proof of her good character. He derives his knowledge of her integrity from his own scrutiny of her work abilities and ethic: "convinced from a twelvemonth's observation of her conduct, that she was . . . a well-disposed and respectable woman; I engaged her . . . as a domestic servant . . . I am thus enabled to speak of her conduct and character with a degree of confidence I could not have otherwise done" (219). Her work provides him with evidentiary support for his recommendation, without which he "could not have otherwise" spoken for her.

Another line of defense for Pringle against allegations of sexual impropriety is context and place. Having been sent Prince's narrative and Wood's letter by Pringle and asked for a measured response, Joseph Phillips writes to Pringle from Antigua. He brings up rumors of Prince's relationships and goes on to provide the rationale of context. He writes:

> I have heard she had at a former period (previous to her marriage) a connexion with a white person, a Capt.——, which I have no doubt was broken off when she became seriously impressed with religion. But, at any rate, such connexions are so common, I might almost say universal, in our slave colonies that except by the missionaries and a few serious persons, they are considered, if faults at all, so very venial as scarcely to deserve the name of immorality. (227)

Thus, Prince is a product and member of two environments—the base context of slavery in the West Indies and a redemptive England. This spatial dichotomy, I suggest, is a key element allowing Pringle to use the rhetoric of character and morality in order to identify Prince as a person worth the British people's time and thought. Certainly the Anti-Slavery Society had its political and philosophical sights set on emancipation. The conflation of this humanitarian ideal with a sociocultural ideal of appropriateness, however, requires a shift in emphasis. For Mary Prince to be not only the victim of brutal slave masters but also an example of upright womanhood, place must be at work. Educated British sensibilities must help "this poor woman," as Pringle so often refers to her, by lifting her into a new stratum of social respectability. Mary Prince herself maintains an intense concentration on fulfilling societal expectations of how a woman should behave. This focus plays important dual roles. First, her assertion of feminine ideals efficiently contrasts with nineteenth-century stereotypes of Caribbean women as oversexed savages. Second, her deployment of the expected rhetoric works on a more subversive level to disrupt stable ideas of authentic gender and labor performance espoused by white society.

In keeping with this depiction of Mary Prince on the right side of feminine conduct, Pringle includes an excerpt from Walsh's "Notices of Brazil," a work that he suggests "has vividly illustrated the true spirit of Negro Slavery" (235). Within this excerpt is an anecdote that uses rhetoric similar to John Wood's in order to cast Prince as a sexually base "wild woman." However, Walsh uses such rhetoric to describe a slave mistress, inverting the usual characterizations. His story proceeds as follows:

> In the rear of our house was another, occupied by some women of bad character, who kept, as usual, several negro slaves. I was awoke early one morning by dismal cries, and . . . I saw in the back yard of the house, a black girl of about fourteen years old; before her stood her mistress, a white woman, with a large stick in her hand. She was undressed except her petticoat and chemise, which had fallen down and left her shoulders and bosom bare. Her hair was streaming behind, and every fierce and malevolent passion was depicted in her face. She . . . was the very representation of a fury. (236)

Here, the woman is not merely "the very representation of a fury," but a strikingly sexualized representation at that. She appears in her underclothes, with her chest exposed and her hair "streaming behind" undone. The dehumanizing features of "bad character" here are overtly steeped in terms of unmanageable sexuality. For Pringle's purposes, Prince represents a contrast to the corrupting influence of slavery. Pringle's post-Enlightenment sensibilities lead him to focus on the institution rather than the individual as source of corruption—what he calls "the unquestionable tendency of the system . . . to vitiate the best tempers, and to harden the most feeling hearts" (234–35). The rhetoric of "character" thus carries on to Pringle's thoughts on slavery itself. He notes that, while "the system of coercive labour" may be more or less extreme depending on where it is located—proving "more destructive to human life in the cane culture of Mauritius and Jamaica, than in the predial and domestic bondage of Bermuda or the Bahamas"— "the spirit and character of slavery are every where the same" (234). Work and place, then, shape the very "spirit and character of slavery" for Pringle; this is an equation that appears in the narrative itself. However, within Prince's text, the most provocative discussions of work occur in what is edited and reworked even as it appears on the page—the role of sexuality as coerced corporeal work.

As Prince is caught in a triangulation of gender, property, and slavery, her body often becomes the site of sexualized labor. In "'Don't Let Nobody Bother Yo' Principle': The Sexual Economy of American Slavery," Adrienne Davis suggests, "enslaved women, and only enslaved women, were forced to perform sexual and reproductive labor to satisfy the economic, political, and personal interests of white men of the elite class" (107). While it is important to note the role that slave women played as sexual chattel, Davis's is largely a heterosexist and gender-blind statement. That "*only* enslaved women" were sexually exploited is a claim that paints a very specific picture of what danger looks like. White women remain sexually innocuous and obsolete, as if black men were never threatened by their mistresses. Whether her sexuality is manifested in contexts of pleasure or coercion, Prince has telling inclusions and exclusions in her text that help interrogate a notion of authentic narrative voice. With an English audience and a specific societal notion of feminine respectability in mind, Mary Prince's narrative elides the sexual abuse inflicted by her owner John Wood as well as her monetary earnings through her sexual relationships with white men like Captain Abbot (Sharpe, "Something" 32). Thus, Prince's voice is necessarily linked to her sexuality, as there are omissions at the hands of Thomas Pringle, who agreed to publish the text, Susanna Strickland, who served as an amanuensis, and Prince herself.[9]

As I have shown, much of the discussion surrounding sexuality comes in the form of accusations made by her pro-slavery antagonists and the responses that Pringle gives in the supplementary material.[10] However, there are also telling silences in her narrative that allow for an interrogation of not only complicated sexual constructs within the institution of slavery but also the role of textual production in the imaginative transference of such constructs. These factors are important when read in the context of the nineteenth century, in which stereotypes of appropriate femininity or womanhood abound even as women are, to use Hortense Spillers's words, "ungendered" within slave societies.[11] Sharpe points to the "paradoxical position of the slave woman as one who existed outside the structures of domesticity but had to uphold its ideals" (*Ghosts* 121). She suggests that such a position reveals "an inherent contradiction in the speaking subject of *The History of Mary Prince*": "While having no self-autonomy as a slave, she was expected to exercise a sexual autonomy over her body" (*Ghosts* 121). Such "inherent contradiction" is what makes appealing to Prince's authentic voice counterintuitive.

When Prince does offer some indication of sexual labor, it is laden with a severe sense of shame, again catering to an audience for whom her validity rests with an indication of appropriate female sexual behavior.[12] This is the case, for instance, when she discusses the disgust she felt when bathing Mr. D—. She states, "He had an ugly fashion of stripping himself quite naked, and ordering me then to wash him . . . This was worse to me than all the licks. Sometimes when he called me to wash him I would not come, my eyes were so full of shame. He would then come to beat me" (202). Significantly, Prince relates his harsh (and in this case sexualized) demands in the broader context of their migration. She tells him as he is about to beat her, "Sir, this is not Turk's Island," finding the geographical change to be sufficient foundation from which to stand up to and critique his actions (202). She goes on to explain to her readers, "He wanted to treat me the same in Bermuda as he had done in Turk's Island" (202). Critics of Prince's narrative use her description of and reaction to her abuse as another opportunity to examine her voice.

Lean'tin Bracks suggests that instances in which Prince directly confronts her masters are evidence of the power of her voice. Bracks suggests, "While some forms of covert resistance among slaves consisted of stealing, dissembling, and arson, Mary moves beyond those responses to a more overt and politically aggressive stance. She progresses swiftly to a position of confrontation" (36). Immediately following her description of Mr. D—'s baths, Prince recalls a time that she is beaten for dropping dishes. This is the example that Bracks uses to signal Prince's "position of confrontation." Prince states her response to Mr. D— as follows: "He struck me so severely . . . that at last I defended myself . . . I told him I would not live longer with him, for he was a very indecent man—very spiteful, and too indecent; with no shame for his servants, no shame for his own flesh" (202–3). I hesitate at Bracks's notion that Prince "moves beyond" other means of resistance simply because hers is apparently more overt. Rather than exhibiting a moment of transcendence, there is a more particular significance to Prince's confrontation in her emphasis on modesty and good moral behavior.

From the passage above, I would call attention to Prince's description of her master as "a very indecent man—very spiteful, and too indecent; with no shame for his servants, no shame for his own flesh" (202–3). Thus, the reason she gives for her uprising is not a call for human rights or a recoiling against basic mistreatment. Rather, it is a rebuke against what would classify to European sensibilities as "indecency" and a lack of "shame." However, I do not believe that such a rebuke is, as Bracks suggests, simply or necessarily a "shrewd use of the politics of British colonial society" (36). She does not speak into a vacuous nondiscursive space, untouched by her surrounding societal influences. Important here is that Strickland is likewise silent about Prince's untoward sexual encounters. Whitlock rightly points out that any information about sexual impropriety is kept from the text and left for the supplementary inclusions:

> It is in Pringle's supplementary materials that the issue of Prince's relationship with a white man in Antigua is discussed and rationalized. It is there that Wood's allegations of depravity and licentiousness are presented edited, given that they are "too indecent to appear in a publication likely to be perused by females." The amanuensis does not copy these sections of the text. The section which Prince and Strickland do produce together is a strictly policed first-person narration, with no sexually compromising material. What we see here is "acceptable." (20)

Whitlock suggests, then, that "this history of a slave is marked by race not gender" (20). That Strickland is not allowed to write such passages is important to a discussion of how and when Prince is capable of and stymied from manipulating rhetoric. What we see here is a broader societal imposition of "proper" codes of conduct and conversation for women in general. Rather, her travels make her a product of these same influences, and her political and rhetorical savvy do not necessarily preclude the possibility of her actually believing her master to be morally repugnant.

British society held not only sexual abuse but also broader physical violence in contempt as examples of immoral behavior.[13] Even so, beatings in slavery contexts were nonetheless freighted with sexual undertones and implications: "Flogging, in a word, was anti-Christian. Worst of all, it was a public act, involving an exposed nakedness and an unsolicited male gaze sometimes even attracting spectators and enthusiasts" (qtd. in Whitlock 23). Chronicling her beatings serves another function as well: it provides her story with a certain degree of truth or seeming authenticity.[14] Doing so speaks to the constructed nature of such notions, as Prince (or, more accurately, her amanuensis) literally creates the truth of her story in her relaying it. Using her abuse as a marker of narrative authenticity still takes her audience into account, of course. Furthermore, as Whitlock rightly notes, the interesting thing about Prince's voice, in this case, is its absence. Discussing examination of Prince's body conducted by Strickland, Mary Pringle (Thomas Pringle's wife), and others, Whitlock brings to the fore issues of what is able to be spoken and by whom with regard to racial and gendered oppression:

> Here is a final grasp to assert truth on Prince's behalf through a white reading of her body, through recourse to the marks of her history on her back. . . . Ultimately the inscriptions of flogging on the body of the Caribbean woman, a body made grotesque and painful by abuse, are what speak authentically to the good people of England. These marks are not spoken of by Mary herself, but by the amanuensis. (23)

Even in her authenticity here, however, Prince is resigned to an unavoidable alterity. Her "grotesque" difference is what proves the veracity of her story.

CONCLUSION: BEYOND "AUTHENTICITY"

Near the end of the *History*, Prince states, "The truth ought to be told of [the horrors of slavery]; and what my eyes have seen I think it is my duty to relate; for few people in England know what slavery is. I have been a slave—I have felt what a slave feels, and I know what a slave knows" (200). Bracks argues that, in this quote, "Mary claims her right to speak as coming from her experience of great suffering. The authority of her own claims and her possession of truths regarding slavery are evident in her language and an emphatic use of 'I'" (42). More is at work in her first-person rhetoric than the firm establishment of empowered voice, however. Important in her quote is that she sees her experiences and the "truth" about slavery as "my *duty* to relate." The "I" here is made of various and shifting subject positions. What is firmly entrenched is Prince's tie to a sense of duty even at the end of her narrative. Considerations of Prince and her narrative, therefore, cannot be teased apart from analyses of gendered, labor, and sexual positionalities.

Twentieth- and twenty-first-century novels in which women navigate identifications of race, gender, labor, and sexuality constructs in migratory societal contexts have an important literary conversation partner in *The History of Mary Prince*. For Mary Prince, something resembling an "authentic" voice is one of contradictions and ambiguities. Her text resists singular constructions of gender and corporeal labor dynamics.

She struggles throughout her narrative to "understand rightly [her] condition," as she moves from slave to political representative. Presenting more options with which to enact and describe a marginalized female subject in migration, Mary Prince's narrative offers much to contemporary dialogues that investigate hybrid female subjectivities, in the sphere of literary criticism as well as in feminist and postcolonial theories.

2

"Different with Every Shore"

Women, Workers, and the Transatlantic South in *Their Eyes Were Watching God*

EVEN THOUGH Zora Neale Hurston's *Their Eyes Were Watching God* (1937) is often read as Janie Crawford's journey of self-discovery and expression, the contingency of her identity is evident early on, as she knows herself only through the descriptions and projections of others. As she explains to Pheoby when talking about her experience as a child not recognizing herself in a picture with white children, "Miss Nellie . . . pointed to de dark one and said, 'Dat's you, Alphabet, don't you know yo' ownself?' Dey all useter call me Alphabet 'cause so many people had done named me different names" (9). While Janie speaks on her own behalf, telling her story to Pheoby, her status as speaking subject is cast in necessary relation to the people and places that figuratively "name" her. In this regard, subjectivity in the novel is like Janie's description of love near the end of the book:

> Ah know all dem sitters-and-talkers gointuh worry they guts into fiddle strings till dey find out whut we been talkin' 'bout. Dat's all right, Pheoby, tell 'em. Dey gointuh make 'miration 'cause mah love didn't work lak they love, if dey ever had any. Then you must tell 'em dat love ain't somethin' lak uh grindstone dat's de same thing everywhere and do de same thing tuh everything it touch. Love is lak de sea. It's uh movin'

thing, but still and all, it takes its shape from de shore it meets, and it's different with every shore. (191)

Categories throughout the novel are moving things, taking their shapes from the classifications that they encounter in different social and geographical contexts.

Their Eyes finds a strong textual parallel in Mary Prince's narrative. Once again, a diasporic woman must navigate social impositions and ideologies of gender and work that change as she moves from place to place. What initially seems, as evidenced by much of the critical focus, to be solely the personal quest for liberation and autonomy is in fact a much more layered narrative that rejects a single understanding of a presumably authentic experiential tale. Hurston's novel tells the tale of Janie Crawford, who returns from the Everglades to Eatonville and relays her story of migration and loss to her best friend, Pheoby. Someone else, then, is immediately given charge of her story, shown in this case by Pheoby's promise to Janie upon hearing her story that "Nobody better not criticize yuh in mah hearin'" (192). Houston Baker rightly suggests that this moment presents a "clearly figured success of poetics," as Pheoby rethinks her own role in her marriage and "alter[s] expected relationships, transforming the black woman from worker (mule) of the world to a participant in male, ludic rituals that provide leisure and a space for spiritual growth" (63).[1] Hurston's framing of Janie's story with its transference to Pheoby, even as she aims to protect it, is a key part of what makes an understanding of Janie as an authentic feminist hero a faulty identification. The impossibility of such a label, far from being a failure of Hurston's vision, is exactly what allows Janie's story to be so instructive and useful for Pheoby and for scholars of literary criticism. Her story arises out of her own displacement, and it ends likewise in flux. Like with Mary Prince, a reading of the migrations within *Their Eyes* reveals slippages in the constructions of gender and labor that leave both unstable instead of fixed or categorical. Hurston focuses on what Louis Kyriakoudes calls "highly mobile rural southerners" moving throughout the agricultural South. Such a focus offers a new way to read her novels, "elucidating her profound understanding of rural migration within and between the Southern states" (qtd. in Bone, "(Extended)" 761). It is in the contexts of these migrations that I want to examine negotiations of gender and labor in *Their Eyes Were Watching God*.

I first offer a reading of the ways in which notions of gender and labor conflate to form fixed ideas about "a woman's work." Specifically, I look at the projections of Janie as a "lady" and the attendant understandings of what she deserves and what she should do according to conventional male codes. Second, I consider the often overlooked, quite specific presence of the Caribbean migrant workers whom Janie encounters in the Everglades in order to foreground how the context of an expanded, transatlantic South reveals new relationships between work and migration in Hurston studies. Affiliation with transatlantic spaces brings Hurston's work into the province of a "New Southern Studies" that read the South not as a cohesive or distinct end in itself but rather as a global context. Tara McPherson's *Reconstructing Dixie* is a prime example of this new direction, as McPherson tracks discourses on the South "beginning from an appreciation of the impossibility of speaking of the region in isolation, concluding with an exploration of the South's role in the national imaginary" (2). Along the way, McPherson takes to task the vision of the South projected by thinkers like Coleman Coker, who suggests that the South maintains an "authentic regionalism" (McPherson 257).[2] My dual emphases on the slippery formations of gender and labor as well as the need to foreground the role of the Caribbean in Hurston's novel call for a more nuanced approach to Janie's story.

In placing Hurston in the context of Southern Studies, many locate her work in a nostalgic, agrarian South, full of the so-called folk culture that, even as it is celebrated, is often patronized in its characterization. Martyn Bone offers a few such descriptions from critics like Wright, Carby, and Leigh Anne Duck, who call Hurston's portrayal of the South "quaint," "nostalgic," and "allotemporal" (767).[3] Hurston's depiction of the 1928 hurricane not only offers historical specificity to a text that might otherwise warrant the above characterizations but also "helps to bring into focus another rarely considered aspect of Hurston's representation of black life and labor in the Everglades: the presence of Caribbean migrant workers" (Bone 767–68).[4] While scholars have provided extensive looks at Hurston's own relationship to the Caribbean—her travels to Nassau in 1929 and 1930, for instance—such a focus rarely translates to the appearance of Caribbean migrants and culture in the novels themselves.

Worth mention, of course, are also the well-documented and oft-discussed anthropological interests Hurston pursued in Haiti and Jamaica in 1936 and 1937, culminating in her book *Tell My Horse: Voodoo and Life in Haiti and Jamaica* (published in 1938). The book received tepid and broadly innocuous praise, but the criticism from some of her renowned contemporaries is well known. Langston Hughes saw her anthropological endeavors as pandering before white patronage, while Alain Locke panned the specific text of *Tell My Horse* as "anthropological gossip."[5] Locke's voice joined the chorus of others dismissive of Hurston's narrative efforts, and the link between her work in the Caribbean and what she was up to in novels like *Their Eyes* was quick and easy (though not necessarily explicit). That is, they saw her as doing little more than, to use the words of Richard Wright in his review of *Their Eyes*, "catch[ing] the psychological movements of the Negro folk-mind in their pure simplicity."[6] Wright's stinging rebuke includes the sentiment that "In the main, her novel is not addressed to the Negro, but to a white audience whose chauvinistic tastes she knows how to satisfy. She exploits the phase of Negro life which is 'quaint,' the phase which evokes a piteous smile on the lips of the 'superior race.'" In his 1938 review of the novel in *Opportunity,* Locke gives a more developed nod to her folkloric sensibilities but, like Wright, bemoans that the novel does not warrant company with the more serious literature that was also coming out at the time among other African American writers: "But when will the Negro novelist of maturity, who knows how to tell a story convincingly . . . come to grips with motive fiction and social document fiction? Progressive southern fiction has already banished the legend of these entertaining pseudo-primitives whom the reading public still loves to laugh with." Later, Ralph Ellison would go on to register a similar complaint about "Recent Negro Fiction" in general, but calling *Their Eyes* out specifically as "calculated burlesque" and as a "story of a Southern Negro woman's love-life against the background of an all-Negro town into which the casual brutalities of the South seldom intrude."[7] Thus, the "authentic" treatment of so-called folk life in the Caribbean and in the South that many now have come to revere was, for Hurston's contemporaries, what kept her from being a mature writer.

The renewed critical interest in Hurston's work has, of course, brought with it a change in emphasis. In readings of *Their Eyes Were Watching God,* scholars like Robert Stepto, Mary Helen Washington, Hazel Carby, Gordon Thompson, and others often sustain a focus on Janie's voice, or lack thereof—her silent role as the wife of a mayor who likes to do all the public speaking, her inability to speak for herself in the courtroom scene, her voice as it compares to that of the men and/or folk culture in the text.[8] This is certainly an important strain of Hurston scholarship, but there is a space left open for criticism of how migration from place to place, context to context, disrupts fixed spheres of gender and labor and removes the telling of an authentic story as a motive. When Janie tells her grandmother about all the things that her first husband Logan Killicks does for her (chops all the wood she wants, keeps both water buckets full), Nanny responds with a mild rebuke that she casts in terms of perception and gaze: "Humph! don't 'spect all dat tuh keep up. He ain't kissin' yo' mouf when he carry on over yuh lak dat. He's kissin' yo' foot and 'tain't in uh man tuh kiss foot long. Mouf kissin' is on uh equal and dat's natural but when dey got to bow down tuh love, dey soon straightens up" (23). Nanny's point speaks directly to Janie's struggle not merely to attain voice but to negotiate others' expectations and impositions. The multiple demands of her husbands and her communities set up insider and outsider positions of power as well as images of Janie as a certain type of woman who should do or should not do a certain kind of work.

While men throughout the novel offer fawning condescension in depictions of Janie as a queen or as above the likes of other classes and "kinds" of people, Janie herself begins to reclassify and rearticulate what it is to be a lady and what work she should be able and allowed to do. The gaze directed at Janie by her community and her male counterparts offers a fixed definition of what it is to be a lady—a definition that ties itself to the kind of work such a lady engages in. Meanwhile, Janie's travels present her with different social contexts and, thus, different opportunities for and expectations of work in a text that Sondra Guttman calls "embedded in the cultural politics of the Depression" (92). Janie moves from domestic servant to high-society lady to worker and lover, all the while working through her own understandings of place. These shifts in place offer implications on the level of both gender and labor, disrupting a single construction of either. She is neither fully trapped nor fully liberated; in this space between, she does not easily conform to the strong feminist prototype that many readers would impose on her. Rather, her story has more to do with a journey than with a single epiphany. As Leigh Anne Duck suggests, "In her search 'for far horizon . . . change and chance,' Janie's story seems to follow the traditional pattern of the *bildungsroman,* in which protagonists must overturn their early belief-systems as they discover that the communities of their youth were unaware of the changes affecting the larger world" (278). In that pattern, it is important to keep in mind Barbara Johnson's reading, however, which claims that "the very notion of an 'authentic voice' must be redefined" in relation to Janie: "Far from being an expression of Janie's new wholeness or identity as a character, Janie's increasing ability to speak grows out of her ability. . . to assume and articulate the incompatible forces involved in her own division. The sign of an authentic voice is thus not self-identity but self-difference" (50). In Janie's case, what gets overturned are constructions of what "real" women need to do to earn their livings and remain of high moral character.

"AIN'T GOT NO PARTICULAR PLACE": FROM DOMESTIC TO "DESERVING"

The "far horizon" that serves as the vanishing point for Janie's self-discovery is not fixed. As she moves from place to place, Janie encounters varying social and societal contexts, each with its own perception and set of rules for how she should enact both her gender and her work. Some scholars read Janie's travels as a productive means to an autonomous end. In "Projecting Gender: Personification in the Works of Zora Neale Hurston," for example, Gordon E. Thompson sees travel as a powerful means of escape and exploration:

> [Hurston] uses travel to contrast the negatives of domesticity with the benefits of exploration and its self-affirming powers, be such exploration fanciful and psychological or literary and geographical. Consequently, throughout her works, but particularly when using metaphors of travel, Hurston uses personification as a device to make new locales appear strange and wonderful and therefore desirable, or contrarily, she makes various places appear uncanny, frightening, and undesirable. (738)

Here, place is a diametric space of fancy or fear. I suggest a reading of travel that is more complicated than Thompson allows. To understand domesticity as a necessarily reductive space is to limit the possibilities for slippage and ambivalence available in such spaces. Furthermore, travel in *Their Eyes* is not comprehensively representative of either nostalgia or anxiety. Rather, it is a process of becoming. Importantly, work is, whether in subtle or obvious ways, at the heart of all of Janie's migrations—from her grandmother's house to Logan Killicks's, to Eatonville with Joe Starks, to the Everglades with Tea Cake, and back to Eatonville again. Thus, the travels themselves have broader implications than available in the archetype of a hero's journey—even a feminist or working hero.

On just this point, in "The (Extended) South of Black Folk: Intraregional and Transnational Migrant Labor in *Jonah's Gourd Vine* and *Their Eyes Were Watching God*," Martyn Bone offers an extremely useful overview of how Hurston has been read within the field of Southern literary studies. Specifically, he notes two camps. One attempts to make Hurston, in Jan Cooper's words, "always a Southerner too," while the other resituates Southern Studies—and, by extension, Hurston—in a "transnational rather than regional context, particularly in relation to the Caribbean" (Bone 755).[9] Bone's emphasis is placed largely in a critique of Hazel Carby's contention that "Hurston's writing discursively displaces the northward trajectory of the Great Migration" (Bone 754). However, the novel need not be read as *either* emphasizing a transnational context *or* displacing a North/South dichotomy. With the series of migrations that productively interfere with strict formations of gender and labor, *Their Eyes* likewise disrupts a geographic solidarity or focus to which both Bone and Carby refer as a firmly entrenched drive of Hurston's.

Janie migrates of her own volition, but she is later displaced by a hurricane that sweeps through and devastates the Everglades. Thus, it is important to see her journey not only as a quest, as many suggest, but also as a set of displacements that force Janie to rethink her situation, what it is to be a worker and a certain kind of woman. She leaves her first husband, for instance, by flinging off her apron in an act of rebellion of her place as well as her domesticity. The two are inextricably linked. After an argument that ends with Logan threatening to kill her, Janie answers her thoughts about his cruelty with kitchen chores: "Logan was accusing her of her mamma, her grandmama and her feelings, and she couldn't do a thing about any of it. The sow-belly in the pan needed turning" (32). Quickly after returning to her cooking, however, she decides to leave: "Turned the hoe-cake with a plate and then made a little laugh. What was she losing so much time for? A feeling of sudden newness and change came over her. Janie hurried out of the front gate and turned south" (32).

As Janie keeps moving south, she experiences what many consider to be her redemption—she ultimately leaves Eatonville to work alongside Tea Cake in the Everglades. As she explains to Pheoby when she moves, rather than stay and deal with the inevitable comparisons between Tea Cake and Joe Starks, "us is goin' off somewhere and start all over in Tea Cake's way. Dis ain't no business proposition, and no race after property and titles. Dis is uh love game" (114). She goes on to suggest that her grandmother's endgame that would have her sitting still on a "high chair" was one that she achieved with Joe, but she "nearly languished tuh death up dere" (114). Climbing down from the stationary chair, Janie pursues a more dynamic path with Tea Cake. In her new space, she seems to reside on a relatively equal level with him and other workers.

However, these moments are not facile signifiers of would-be liberation. Rather, they reveal themselves as moments in which the very notion of liberation is thrown into flux. After all, she is "start[ing] all over in Tea Cake's way." The interest in looking a certain way for Joe does not disappear with Tea Cake. It just goes through a change of wardrobe. As she tells Pheoby, "Wait till you see de new blue satin Tea Cake done picked out for me tuh stand up wid him in. High heel slippers, necklace, earrings, *everything* he wants tuh see me in" (115). In the Everglades, Janie not only learns to shoot and hunt but also picks beans alongside Tea Cake, telling him, "It's mo' nicer than settin' round dese quarters all day. Clerkin' in dat store wuz hard, but heah, we ain't got nothin' tuh do but do our work and come home and love" (133). With no real self to find or cling to that is unattached to male desire, Janie initiates a more productive endeavor that rejects a limited or fixed identification of her gender or work. Furthermore, the shifts in place and situation point to a broader South that avoids regional or colloquial singularity, a South that becomes positioned in a transatlantic context. Thus, because readings of *Their Eyes* often understand the South to be a specific and identifiable region of the United States, scholars often resign Janie's migrations to pedestrian travels in and around this fixed region and characterize her journey as one significantly detached from the Great Migration that took so many African Americans north.

Hazel Carby's work is perhaps the most notable to read an absence—or neglect—of the North as a necessary counterpart to the South in *Their Eyes*. Bone offers a persuasive critique of her reading of *Their Eyes* in "The (Extended) South of Black Folk," suggesting instead that Hurston has a more transnational South in mind that is not restricted to movement in and among the states alone.[10] John Carlos Rowe is another who "explicitly challenges Carby's theory of discursive displacement" (Bone 772). Rowe suggests, "Rather than treating this quest as an alternative to or escape from the urban experiences of African Americans in the North after the great migration of the post–World War I period, Hurston links urban and rural, northern and southern, U.S. and Caribbean cultural practices" (qtd. in Bone 772). While Bone uses *Jonah's Gourd Vine* as a companion to his reading of *Their Eyes,* his emphasis on "rural and intraregional migrant labor patterns" that, he suggests, gets "overlooked" in scholarly rubrics of travel and work within the text is one that my own reading shares (763).[11]

Significantly, Hurston's novel begins with a trope of travel that speaks both to migration and to gender difference.

> Ships at a distance have every man's wish on board. For some they come in with the tide. For others they sail forever on the horizon, never out of sight, never landing until the Watcher turns his eyes away in resignation, his dreams mocked to death by Time. That is the life of man. Now, women forget all those things they don't want to remember, and remember everything they don't want to forget. The dream is the truth. Then they act and do things accordingly. (1)

Truth is an ambiguous prospect here, with a dubious nature attached exclusively to women. *Their Eyes* does not present truth and reality as fixed signs. Rather, they are subject to the flux that characters like Janie represent with her travels. In this way, the novel is like *Mama Day,* which suggests, "It ain't about right or wrong, truth or lies; it's about a slave woman who brought a whole new meaning to both them words" (Naylor 3).

Parentless and newly removed from her grandmother, Janie begins the novel and her first marriage without an identifiable place, a fact Logan Killicks uses to assert his authority. When he tells her to help him move a manure pile, ironically pulling her away from a domestic role (saying to her, "T'ain't no use in foolin' round in dat kitchen all day long"), she responds with mild defiance: "You don't need mah help out dere, Logan. Youse in yo' place and Ah'm in mine" (31). In this instance, Hurston plays with the divvying out of specific places—notably, Janie has her own ideas of who should be in what gendered sphere, with Logan in the fields and her in the kitchen. However, Logan rejects this, suggesting, "You ain't got no particular place. It's wherever Ah need yuh" (31). Later, in Eatonville, Joe Starks positions Janie squarely back into the domestic sphere when the townsfolk compliment an impromptu speech Janie gives. He tells them, "Ah never married her for nothin' lak dat. She's uh woman and her place is in de home" (43). It is neither surprising nor insignificant, then, that Hurston uses a metaphor of travel to describe Janie's relationship with Joe as their marriage begins to disintegrate: "The years took all the fight out of Janie's face . . . No matter what Jody did, she said nothing . . . She was in a rut in the road. Plenty of life between the surface but it was kept beaten down by the wheels" (76). Meanwhile, she looks to migration as an escape, but Hurston rejects the pedestrian reading of travel as necessarily liberating: "Now and again she thought of a country road at sun-up and considered flight. To where? To what? Then too she considered thirty-five is twice seventeen and nothing was the same at all" (76).

Thus, refusing to characterize migration as always and essentially empowering, as Gordon Thompson and others suggest she does, Hurston instead presents what Patricia Yaeger calls "an incredible instability of place [as] she sends her African American characters southward" (qtd. in Bone 765). Rather than reading the South in an agrarian, isolationist way that would suggest the region as separated from and untouched by transatlantic crossings and convergences, Bone suggests instead that "Over the course of [*Jonah's Gourd Vine* and *Their Eyes Were Watching God*], Hurston depicts the South—especially south Florida—not as a nostalgic site of rooted rural community but as an unstable, liminal locus increasingly defined by intraregional and transnational flows of capital and labor" (758). In this sense, a reading of Janie's migrations within the South should also be a reading of her work, her negotiations of labor. First, however, I discuss such a reading's implications on Janie's gender performance and identification.

"AIN'T NO REAL 'OMAN YET": IMPOSING AND REVISING GENDER EXPECTATIONS

Hurston presents gender experience throughout the text in terms of patriarchal expectations as well as Janie's own attempts at accessing a sort of authentic womanhood. Early on, Janie's sexuality and gender obligations conflict as her desire threatens her virtue. When Janie's grandmother finds out about Janie's kissing Johnny Taylor at the gate, she explains to Janie, "youse uh 'oman now," to which Janie replies, "Naw, Nanny, naw Ah ain't no real 'oman yet" (12). The notion of being a "real" woman is important here, as it distinguishes different views of what being a woman means, especially in terms of sexual development. The prospect of real womanhood is what makes for the possibility of other expressions of womanhood that are interpreted as less valid. Also key to this discussion of her womanhood is temporality, as Janie suggests that she is not a real woman *yet*. While Nanny identifies a "real woman" in the moment one desires or is desired by a man and is marked by his kiss, Janie rejects that definition temporally. She may or may not adopt her grandmother's definition of what a real woman is, but she refuses to consider the implications or consequences of that particular meaning for the time being.

Another key description of what being a woman means for Janie occurs, again, at a gate and leads Janie's thoughts simultaneously to travel and gender experience: "The familiar people and things had failed her so she hung over the gate and looked up the road towards way off. She knew now that marriage did not make love. Janie's first dream was dead, so she became a woman" (25). Although *Their Eyes* receives a ubiquitous association with texts dealing with gender liberation and feminist ideals, it nonetheless presents womanhood in very specific relation to patriarchal power structures. Janie's liberating journey is largely tied to the men who shape Janie's gender and labor identification. Important here, too, is Janie's optimistic insistence on looking beyond the gate and on imagining a more productive horizon. In this way, she looks to the power of migration to change context and, thus, how she would be perceived.

Throughout the novel, the shifts in perception, whether coming from her grandmother or her husband or the community itself, hinge on a conflation of gender and labor. At the beginning of the book, Janie's grandmother, "Nanny," is insistent that Janie marry Logan Killicks to protect not only her virtue but also her status so as to avoid becoming the wife of Johnny Taylor, who her grandmother calls "trashy" and who would be "usin' [her] body to wipe his foots on" (13). As she speaks to these issues of Janie's gender identity, however, she simultaneously makes her point through the rhetoric of work with her often-quoted "mule of the world" metaphor. Borrowing from Houston Baker, Judie Newman notes that "Nanny's history under slavery dictates her strategic maneuvers in the wars of property and propriety" (820).[12] Nanny speaks to this history directly as she tells Janie about her dreams for her:

> You know, honey, us colored folks is branches without roots and that makes things come round in queer ways. You in particular. Ah was born back due in slavery so it wasn't for me to fulfill my dreams of whut a woman oughta be and to do. Dat's one of de hold-backs of slavery . . . Ah didn't want to be used for a work-ox and a brood-sow and Ah didn't want mah daughter used dat way neither . . . . Ah wanted to preach a great sermon about colored women sittin' on high, but they wasn't no pulpit for me. Freedom found me wid a baby daughter in mah arms, so Ah said Ah'd take a broom and a cook-pot and throw up a highway through de wilderness for her . . . But somehow she got lost offa de highway and next thing Ah knowed here you was in de world . . . Ah been waitin' a long time, Janie, but nothin' Ah been through ain't too much if you just take a stand on high ground lak Ah dreamed. (16)

There are several important considerations here. First, the metaphor of branches without roots and the description of Janie's mother getting "lost offa de highway" speak to what Nanny sees as the importance of a grounded and stable sense of place, hoping ultimately for her granddaughter to be able to "take a stand on high ground." Next, she casts "de hold-backs of slavery" in terms of gendered work, referring to her being used as a "work-ox and a brood-sow." Finally, the progress narrative is tied to generation here. Context and social order are prioritized over personal experience or comfort level.

An attempt to console Janie, Nanny's "mule of the world" lecture describes for her granddaughter the plight of African American women in terms of labor: "So de white man throw down de load and tell de nigger man tuh pick it up. He pick it up because he have to, but he don't tote it. He hand it over to his womenfolks. De nigger woman is de mule uh de world so fur as Ah can see" (14). The mule is an important trope, as it represents the very in-between space that Janie inhabits. Along with the references to labor that Nanny makes, it carries both racial and sexual implications, as the animal is hybrid, asexual, and sterile. For the light-skinned Janie, the metaphor her grandmother offers speaks directly to her work and her sexuality.

After marrying Killicks, Janie expresses her concern to Nanny about not loving him. Significantly, class status forms the basis of Nanny's chastising reply. She refers Janie to the status that marrying Killicks has given her, offering this new position as a sound reason for desire: "If you don't want him, you sho oughta. Heah you is wid de onliest organ in town . . . Got a house bought and paid for and sixty acres uh land right on de big road . . . !" (23). She bemoans the problem of romance for women and complains, "Dis love! Dat's just whut's got us uh pullin' and uh haulin' and sweatin' and doin' from can't see in de mornin' till can't see at night" (23). Here, the emphasis lies in Janie's new status that has accompanied her marriage. Nanny reminds her about what she owns and suggests that love leads to hard labor—pulling and hauling and sweating. This emphasis on work and how it corresponds to gender performance, however, is also at the heart of Janie's responses to the rhetoric of Joe Starks and Tea Cake when they try to win her affection. They each, in turn, appeal to her on a level of what she should have, how it is different from what "common" women deserve.

The transitional space between Janie's time with Logan Killicks and Joe Starks is met with its own attention to duty. When she considers the accusatory and condemning speech Logan gives her, Janie follows thought with domestic chores: "When the throbbing calmed a little she gave Logan's speech a hard thought and placed it beside other things she had seen and heard. When she had finished with that she dumped the dough on the skillet and smoothed it over with her hand" (32). As "[a] feeling of sudden newness and change came over her," Janie decidedly "turn[s] south," a shift marked by a simultaneous rejection of domesticity and embrace of traditional femininity: "The morning air was like a new dress. That made her feel the apron tied around her waist. She untied it and flung it on a low bush beside the road and walked on, picking flowers and making a bouquet" (32). Janie thus casts aside the domestic duties that were her only recourse before.

Upon meeting Joe Starks, Janie pairs her self-introduction with a description of her work. This is an important combination because it shows Janie conflating identity and labor, like Nanny and the community that uses Janie's work to identify her character or moral standing: "Mah name is Janie Mae Killicks since Ah got married . . . Mah husband is gone tuh buy a mule fuh me tuh plow. He left me cuttin' up seed p'taters" (29). Joe persuades her to leave Killicks and marry him with his appeal to a gendered status: "You ain't never knowed what it was to be treated lak a lady and Ah wants to be de one tuh show yuh" (29). Part of Joe's ironic appeal is his use of rhetoric that patronizingly touts the figure of woman as queen. When Janie tells him her husband has left her cutting potatoes and has gone to buy a mule so that she can plow, Joe replies, "You ain't got no mo' business wid uh plow than uh hog is got wid a holiday! You ain't got no business cuttin' up no seed p'taters neither. A pretty doll-baby lak you is made to sit on de front porch and rock and fan yo'self and eat p'taters dat other folks plant just special for you" (29). Janie's gender role, according to Starks's form of patriarchy, is something of a patronized privilege, sitting silently and waiting on others to provide. While the status of her work shifts, she remains objectified from her first husband to her second. She simply moves from workhorse to "doll-baby."

With similar references to her status as a lady, Tea Cake woos Janie once she is widowed. At one point, he tells her they need to buy groceries, and when she reminds him she sells groceries at the store Joe owned, he says, "You sells groceries for ordinary people. We'se gointuh buy for *you*" (108). Again, male gaze sets her apart as something other than ordinary.[13] Rather than setting up an easy rejection of this construct, Hurston complicates the boundaries and implications of status as Janie accepts and returns their advances. Janie is just as smitten with the idea of being taken care of by the drifting transient Tea Cake as she is when Joe Starks approaches her on a carriage. However, even though Tea Cake does not have the same political agenda that Starks reveals about needing a wife to be his "first lady," he is not the relational savior that some would suggest. Shawn Miller is right to note the critical focus and frustration surrounding the ambiguities present in Tea Cake—even though he is what many consider to be the redemptive relationship for Janie, he embodies many of the characteristics that make Killicks and Starks intolerable. This is one important way that Hurston disrupts a stable understanding of Janie's journey on the level of gender and sexuality. As Miller notes, "we must locate a different rationale for the failures and achievements of Janie's quest . . . [and come] to the conclusion that Janie is more dynamic than we have previously realized" (76). Tea Cake may have traits that offer the chance for a positive and productive romance, but he should not be mistaken for a redemptive masculine hero any more than Janie should be read as a purely feminist hero on a righteous quest for voice.

The ambivalence in Janie's relationship with Tea Cake is apparent in her own words to Pheoby when she tells her about clothes he picks out for her: "Wait till you see de new blue satin Tea Cake done picked out for me tuh stand up wid him in. High heel slippers, necklace earrings, *everything* he wants tuh see me in. Some of dese mornin's and it won't be long, you gointuh wake up callin' me and Ah'll be gone" (115). Tea Cake's gaze dictates, not so differently from that of Joe Starks, buying for her the things "he wants tuh see me in." Significantly, Janie follows her adulation with the prospect of travel. The process, as she relays it to Pheoby, is one in which Janie has had to reorganize and restructure her relational nomenclature: "So in the beginnin' new thoughts had tuh be thought and new words said. After Ah got used tuh dat, we gits 'long jus' fine. He done taught me de maiden language all over" (115). While she is specifically responding to a question about their age difference, I find this notion of being "taught . . . de maiden language all over" key to a reading of productive revisions in systems of meaning-making. Even here, however, Hurston does not allow for an easy moment of Janie's own self-identification. Rather Tea Cake is the one to teach her "de maiden language."

Even before Tea Cake wins Janie over, though, she must navigate numerous encounters with men who try to court her. Hurston presents these, like the romantic appeals from Joe and Tea Cake, as inextricably linked to an understanding of Janie as a particular type of woman: "Janie found out very soon that her widowhood and property was a great challenge in South Florida" (90). Thus, she begins to hear familiar lines from her suitors: "Uh woman by herself is uh pitiful thing . . . Dey needs aid and assistance. God never meant 'em tuh try tuh stand by theirselves . . . you needs uh man" (90). The portrait of Janie as a woman who needs and well deserves the care that only a man can give is based on the position of Joe Starks more than of Janie herself: "They were all so respectful and stiff with her, that she might have been the Empress of Japan. They felt that it was not fitting to mention desire to the widow of Joseph Starks. You spoke of honor and respect" (92–93). Meanwhile, desire—or the lack thereof—is exactly what concerns Janie. She again runs into the problem that Nanny chastises her for when she is married to Logan Killicks—she is seen as an "empress" and is not grateful. Further, formality is mixed with exoticism here, keeping Janie at a distance for others to stand back and look at, even if in the name of "honor and respect." In his speech to the town introducing Joe and Janie Starks, Tony Taylor echoes this perception of Janie's nobility by using the rhetoric of royalty:

> Ladies and gent'men, we'se come tuhgether and gathered heah tuh welcome tuh our midst one who has seen fit tuh cast in his lot amongst us. He didn't just come hisself neither. He have seen fit tuh bring his, er, er, de light uh his home, dat is his wife amongst us also. She couldn't look no mo' better and no nobler if she wuz de queen uh England. It's uh pledger fuh her tuh be heah amongst us. Brother Starks, we welcomes you and all dat you have seen fit tuh bring amongst us—yo' belov-ed wife, yo' store, yo' land—. (42)

Here, Janie's gendered status is conflated with Joe's wealth, as Taylor references his wife, possessions, and property in one contained series. This depiction of Janie as "de queen uh England" is, largely, shared by the rest of the community for whom she serves as something of a local first lady while married to Joe. However, for the townspeople of Eatonville, it is shared by a strong set of expectations about the way Janie is to conduct herself.

As the wife of a new mayor in a growing town, Janie is held to a different standard of behavior, and she works under a different set of expectations than those imposed while she was married to Logan Killicks. With a change of place comes a change of social context and consequence. Migration, thus, disrupts the possibility for a stable self that scholarly readings of the novel too often expect and, therefore, identify. Throughout the text, Janie's travels confuse the signs of gender and labor. In the particular move to Eatonville, she is immediately expected to gain a new understanding of what work should mean for her. She moves from working a plow to working the counter at the general store, but her work remains delegated by her husband.[14] Thus, her own gaze is effectively blurred by Joe and the townspeople, who understand being a "lady" as being quietly deferential. An important way that Hurston addresses ideals of femininity and work is through the gossip and judgments of an all-black community that is "shaped," as Leigh Anne Duck notes, "by a bourgeois, class-conscious ethos" (279). The migration away from her grandmother, who had worked for whites her whole life, and from Logan Killicks, who had a very insulated work ethic of self sustenance, to Eatonville, where she encounters a collective social consciousness, frame the shifting understandings of work and womanhood. At work specifically in constructing such ideals are the townspeople as a general collective and Joe Starks as a representative of patriarchal gaze, both of which impose a vision onto Janie as a lady of a particular class.

As long as Janie stays within the confines of these societal expectations, her community appreciates her role. However, even as they expect this "lady" to maintain a certain affect and demeanor, they form and maintain an undercurrent of class resentment. Strangely, Janie accepts, if not clings to, notions of power that Joe touts and, often, exploits. As the couple talks about the life they will live in Eatonville, Joe explains his plans in terms of power: "Ah aimed tuh be uh big voice. You oughta be glad, 'cause dat makes uh big woman outa you" (46). Soon, Janie internalizes the very ideas on power and status that she ultimately begins to disrupt. In this way, Hurston does not present her as a rebellious feminist icon. Rather, she echoes the idea of being made "big." When Joe buys the old mule to save it from harassment, Janie speaks to his power:

> Jody, dat wuz uh mighty fine thing fuh you tuh do. 'Tain't everybody would have thought of it, 'cause it ain't no everyday thought. Freein' dat mule makes uh mighty big man outa you. Something like George Washington and Lincoln. Abraham Lincoln, he had de whole United States tuh rule so he freed de Negroes. You got uh town so you freed uh mule. You have tuh have power tuh free things and dat makes you lak uh king uh something. (58)

This same event that makes "uh mighty big man outa" Joe is, contrarily, what he calls a "mess uh commonness" that Janie needs to avoid (60). When the mule dies and she asks to go with him to the "dragging-out," Joe responds, "Dat's right, but Ah'm uh man even if Ah is de Mayor. But de mayor's wife is somethin' different again . . . *you* ain't goin' off in all dat mess uh commonness" (60). Once again, her status as his wife serves to set her apart from and above the rest of the community, and it distances her from what she wants and where she wants to go.

Joe's perception of Janie as a "somethin' different" translates to the gaze of the townspeople themselves, and Janie notes this transition: "[She] soon began to feel the impact of awe and envy against her sensibilities. The wife of the Mayor was not just another woman as she had supposed. She slept with authority and so she was part of it in the town mind" (46). Here, sexuality engenders power. Nonetheless, there remains an undercurrent in which the townsfolk critique the capitalist ethos of the mayor and, by association and extension, his wife. Hurston explains with the adage "any man who walks in the way of power and property is bound to meet hate" (48). In this way, a conversation between some of the men in town turns into a critique of a capitalist ethos: "Joe Starks is too exact wid folks. All he got he done made it offa de rest of us. He didn't have all dat when he come here" (49). The critique extends to Janie as well as the town raises concern with her flowered spittoon. Hurston describes their problem with her in both economic and racial terms:

> Maybe more things in the world besides spitting pots had been hid from them, when they wasn't told no better than to spit in tomato cans. It was bad enough for white people, but when one of your own color could be so different it put you on a wonder. It was like seeing your sister turn into a 'gator. A familiar strangeness . . . (48)

Here, the lofty status that separates Janie from the rest of the town economically shifts to a racial separation, one that stacks up her alterity even as it notes her high status.

Even as Janie maintains a gendered power dichotomy between the "mighty big man" and herself, she reworks womanhood in important ways, unsettling the very rules she simultaneously follows. In this way, Hurston resists static understandings of gender and work. One way Hurston does so is to show Joe's thought process that reduces Janie's position. On one such occasion, Hurston compares Joe's frustration with Janie to a mind-set born out of the context of slavery: "She wasn't even appreciative of his efforts and she had plenty cause to be. Here he was just pouring honor all over her; building a high chair for her to sit in and overlook the world and she here pouting over it! Not that he wanted anybody else, but just too many women would be glad to be in her place. He ought to box her jaws!" (62). Janie uses similar terms to describe her "Grandma's way" to Pheoby. She says of her grandmother, "She was borned in slavery time when folks, dat is black folks, didn't sit down anytime dey felt lak it. So sittin' on porches lak de white madam looked lak uh mighty fine thing tuh her. Dat's whut she wanted for me . . . Git up on uh high chair and sit dere" (114). She goes on to suggest the problem with such a position: "She didn't have time tuh think whut tuh do after you got up on de stool uh do nothin' . . . So Ah got up on de high stool lak she told me, but Pheoby, Ah done nearly languished tuh death up dere. Ah felt like de world wuz cryin' extry and Ah ain't read de common news yet" (114). Of note here is not only Janie's impulse to be dynamic and not just "sit dere" but also her desire to have a better sense of what she calls "de common news." She thus rejects the very status that she touts upon her initial arrival in Eatonville.

Hurston provides other, more overt, indications of Janie's shifting notions of her gender status outside the ruminations of Joe Starks. When Joe hits her, for example, Hurston describes her reaction as an understanding of an inside/outside split: "She found that she had a host of thoughts she had never expressed to him . . . Things packed up and put away in parts of her heart . . . She was saving up feelings for some man she had never seen. She had an inside and an outside now and suddenly she knew how not to mix them" (72). Strangely, this pivotal moment is not repeated when Tea Cake hits Janie on the muck "to show he was boss" (147). Likewise, Tea Cake is able to remain for many critics Janie's "equal partner" (Meisenhelder 1441). Barbara Johnson calls their relationship "a joyous liberation from the rigidities of status, image, and property—one of the most beautiful and convincing love stories in any literature" (46). What is present in this latter instance, however, is Hurston's reiteration of Janie's ambivalence when it comes to gender expression. His hitting her "aroused a sort of envy in both men and women," as it is paired with his "pett[ing] and pamper[ing] her" and her "helpless[ly]" clinging to him (147). This is, oddly, the progress that comes after making such liberating strides earlier in the text, "thrust[ing] herself into the conversation" and speaking back to Joe, for example (75). Here, Janie's position, while not given much attention in the criticism of the text, is fodder for the community's speculation. In discussing Hurston's ambivalence about *Their Eyes* (which she admits to having hastily written in Haiti), Michael Awkward notes in his introduction to *New Essays on "Their Eyes Were Watching God"* the contrast between her analysis and that which seems so ubiquitous in the text through the community porch-sitters of Eatonville. He distinguishes between Hurston's necessary acquiescence to a published text (and its subsequent reception) and the storytellers in the novel, who "were able to retell, modify, and perfect the tales with which they entertained and enlightened other members of the community" (1). The relationship here between discourse and subject formation is key.

Hurston addresses migration, ideals of femininity, and work, through the judgmental gossip of this all-black community. Presented very early in the novel, the perceptions of others establish a nexus of gender and labor that Hurston casts within the context of a series of migrations. When Pheoby tries to defend Janie to some of the disapproving townspeople in Eatonville, they use travel as a trump card, telling her, "Maybe us don't know into things lak you do, but we all know how she went 'way from here and us sho seen her come back" (3). During Janie's time in the community, the townsfolk have much to say about her womanhood, not only in the instances outlined above in which she is revered as nobility but also in the ways she is subjugated on account of it. Of particular concern is Joe's strict insistence that she tie up her hair while working in the store: "Whut make her keep her head tied up lak some ole 'oman round de store? Nobody couldn't *git* me tuh tie no rag on mah head if Ah had hair lak dat" (49).[15] They resign the mystery to power relations, with no one daring to question Joe Starks: "The town had a basketful of feelings good and bad about Joe's positions and possessions, but none had the temerity to challenge him. They bowed down to him rather, because he was all these things, and then again he was all of these things because the town bowed down" (50). Gender and power constructions are, thus, part of the same conversation.

The gazes and perceptions of others establish a nexus of gender and labor that Hurston frames within their own economic situations. Guttman rightly suggests that the novel—inasmuch as it presents Janie as a participant in a particular class dynamic—is "both a historically sound portrayal of exploitative labor conditions for working-class black Americans and a protest against them" (93). Such ambivalence productively disrupts a stable sphere of status and economy. Hurston places the gossip upon Janie's return from the Everglades to Eatonville in a context of labor, the conversations occurring only after a long workday: "It was the time for sitting on porches beside the road. These sitters had been tongueless, earless, eyeless conveniences all day long . . . But now, the sun and the bossman was gone, so [they] felt powerful and human . . . They passed nations through their mouths. They sat in judgment" (1). There is an important irony here, in that the relief from an oppressive work structure is what allows the townspeople enough voice to then antagonize the novel's heroine. Power structures are certainly not isolated monoliths in themselves—power, like work or gender expectations and performances, shifts depending on context. Philip Joseph notes the role that the community plays in this sense: "No longer simply a static cultural object to be translated or a reward to be recovered, Eatonville, in the hands of those [folk] characters whom [Hurston] admires most, becomes a focal point of judgment itself" (458). Joseph goes on to note the irony of this role in terms of race: "While white Southerners systematically embrace judgments that are beyond reconsideration, Hurston's black characters are fully capable of this arrogance of certainty" (466). Eatonville thus internalizes some of the very mind-sets that would ostracize them in white society. This comes back to the power of place, as context—not essence or authenticity—dictates the ways in which race, and certainly gender and work, are manifested.

The town's impressions of Janie translate ambivalence to gender as well, specifically their ideals of femininity. The men and women take note of Janie's body with strikingly different responses:

> The men noticed her firm buttocks like she had grape fruits in her hip pockets; the great rope of black hair swinging to her waist and unraveling in the wind like a plume; then her pugnacious breasts trying to bore holes in her shirt . . . The women took the faded shirt and muddy overalls and laid them away for remembrance. It was a weapon against her strength and if it turned out of no significance, still it was a hope that she might fall to their level some day. (2)

The difference between the men's and women's responses to Janie's appearance marks an important incongruity that unsettles an otherwise facile gender dichotomy. While the gendered responses maintain a stereotype with one part lustful men and one part jealous women, Hurston places this veneer before a backdrop of the gender and labor expectations that Janie must confront from both. This reaction to Janie is evident, too, in the vitriolic questions that the townspeople use to critique her femininity:

> What she doin coming back here in dem overhalls? Can's she find no dress to put on?—Where's dat blue satin dress she left here in?—Where all dat money her husband took and died and left her?—What dat ole

forty year ole 'oman doin' wid her hair swingin' down her back like some
young gal? . . . why she don't stay in her class? (2)

Their criticisms specifically address her gender and station, as a forty-year-old woman needs to "stay in her class," but these are cast in a larger framework of place. The opening question is why she is "coming back here" in overalls, and the townsfolk bookend this quandary with a desire to see her remain still—to *stay* in her class. Hurston thus presents her protagonist in the midst of narrow gendered dialogue that would seem to offer separate communities of men and women, each with its formulaic reception of Janie's homecoming.[16] However, also at work in these introductory pages is the offering of another option that comes in the form of Janie, specifically her relationship with Pheoby. Janie uses Pheoby as a mediating voice between her and the community. In this sense, Janie's story, like the others in this book, is relayed but simultaneously filtered by another. The authenticity of her voice, then, is something not to identify but rather to interrogate.

As a lady, Janie has an obligation to associate with a certain "kind" of people. Like the townspeople who wonder "why she don't stay in her class" when she comes back to Eatonville, Joe Starks tells Janie when they first move there that he does not want her to talk to what he calls "trashy people" (54). He tells her, "You'se Mrs. Mayor Starks, Janie. I god, Ah can't see what uh woman uh yo' stability would want to be treasurin' all dat gum-grease from folks dat don't even own de house dey sleep in" (54). Once again, Janie is a "woman of stability," and a key factor in what makes the townspeople "trashy" to her husband is their economic lack. This sort of rebuke from Starks is what moves Guttman to make a comparison between Joe Starks and a plantation master, as he "use[s] the power of voice to explain his domination over those institutions and technologies that signal Eatonville's transition into the twentieth century" (Guttman 98). Not surprisingly, this kind of domination happens just as much on a gendered level as it does on an economic one:

> The intimate relation between ownership of voice and body epitomized in slavery is manifest in Joe's demand that Janie keep her hair tied up in public. Little more than another of Joe's possessions, Janie's position as "Mrs. Mayor" resembles both that of a bourgeois wife and a female house slave. While she takes on a privileged place in Eatonville, like a concubine, her relative privilege denies her both voice and control of her sexuality. (Guttman 98)

Guttman rightly points out the seeming duality of Janie's place, playing both the high-society lady and the domestic laborer. However, Janie's "privileged place in Eatonville" is more complex than Guttman allows. She is neither fully privileged nor fully denied. Rather than focus on the liberation or denial of her voice, a more productive approach is to examine the ways in which such liberation *becomes* denial and vice versa. It does so through a series of migrations and displacements.

The town retains their vision of Janie as Mrs. Mayor Starks when she begins spending time with Tea Cake.[17] Of particular concern are her decidedly unladylike behaviors that he encourages. Pheoby cautions Janie about the image that comes across to everyone else: "Janie, everybody's talkin' 'bout how dat Tea Cake is draggin' you round tuh places you ain't used tuh. Baseball games and huntin' and fishin'. He don't know you'se useter uh more high time crowd than dat. You always did class off" (112). The notion of Janie as a "high time" woman here speaks directly to gender expectations. Baseball, hunting, and fishing are considered not only representative of male behavior but also indicative of a lower class status. Janie responds with a so far uncharacteristic statement of her own desires:

> Jody classed me off. Ah didn't . . . Tea Cake ain't draggin me off nowhere Ah don't want tuh go. Ah always did want to git round uh whole heap, but Jody wouldn't 'low me tuh. When Ah wasn't in de store he wanted me tuh jes sit wid folded hands and sit dere . . . Pheoby, dese educated women got uh heap of things to consider. Somebody done tole 'em what to set down for. Nobody ain't told poor me, so sittin' still worries me. Ah wants tuh utilize mahself all over. (112)

Significantly, her emphasis remains cast in the familiar terms of utilization employed by Nanny, Joe, and the townspeople. As she rebels, she remains positioned in the vocabulary of a woman's work and of what she is to do with herself. When she travels with Tea Cake to the Everglades, her work remains in conflict with a certain notion of femininity—she learns to shoot and works outside with the other laborers—but this new community rejoices in these abilities that bring her scathing critique in Eatonville.

MIGRATION AND "A WOMAN'S WORK"

Because the expectations that follow Janie regarding her gender roles are consistently freighted with ones concerning her work, there is a more productive conversation to be had than in previous readings in terms of the ways in which the novel construes labor. Janie's travels allow for a dynamic representation of work, her own definitions and perceptions evolving with each new place and community she encounters. Her decision to leave Killicks is marked by her throwing off her apron, and her work at the store in Eatonville is described as "such a waste of life and time" (54). Specifically important to her final transition of labor are the brief textual passages that depict the Caribbean workers in the Everglades. Their presence in the text, though brief, provides a way to examine the coalescence of work and gender that rejects Western patriarchal constructs that would otherwise confine Janie with strict understandings of what a lady is to do. They are an example of how this "high time" woman, as Pheoby and Tea Cake describe Janie, attempts to rearticulate the parameters of a woman's work.

In Eatonville, Janie's work "kept her with a sick headache" (54). Significantly, the monotony—the professional equivalent of the kind of sitting still on the "high chair" glorified by Nanny and Joe—is what makes it intolerable. Hurston describes her work as "waste," even as Janie worries about the difficulty of certain requests:

> The labor of getting things down off of a shelf or out of a barrel was nothing. And so long as people wanted only a can of tomatoes or a pound of rice it was all right. But supposing they went on and said a pound and a half of bacon and a half pound of lard? The whole thing changed from a little walking and stretching to a mathematical dilemma . . . She went through many silent rebellions over things like that. Such a waste of life and time. (54)

The store serves as an instance to reinforce gender stereotypes as well: "This business of managing stores and women store-owners was trying on a man's nerves" (92). When Janie travels to the Everglades with Tea Cake, because of the work available there, the notion of "a woman's work" changes, and the former construction does not hold.

Because the judgment and expectations of Janie in Eatonville concern her work and duty as much as they concern her femininity or womanhood, an easy reading of her relationship with Tea Cake and her migration to the Everglades suggests that this transition is a necessarily liberating space. After all, she works alongside Tea Cake on the muck in a seeming partnership. However, whatever productivity is seen in this new space has less to do with her doing work alongside Tea Cake or doing a man's work (after all, she does "a man's work" on Logan Killicks's land), and more to do with the attempt at reconfiguring or redefining such a space. To discuss this transition, I stack her work in Eatonville in contradistinction to her work on the muck. However, a consideration of the Caribbean workers present in the Everglades is vital to situating Hurston's work in a transnational—what has been called an "extended"—South.

In the Everglades, Janie not only learns to shoot and hunt but also embraces domesticity. In this way, she engages but never fully inhabits either traditionally gendered sphere. At home, she "boiled big pots of blackeyed peas and rice. Sometimes baked big pans of navy beans with plenty of sugar and hunks of bacon laying on top . . . She didn't leave [Tea Cake] itching and scratching in his work clothes, either. The kettle of hot water was already waiting when he got in" (132). This new space is not free from its own community's expectations of her, however. In fact, Tea Cake echoes Logan Killicks's call for Janie to get out of the kitchen and do "real" work. In this case, though, Tea Cake wants her to join him on the muck and "git uh job uh work out dere *lak de rest uh de women*" (133, emphasis mine).[18] Here, she is still expected to do "lak de rest uh de women—so [he] won't be losin' time comin' home"—but the definition of "a woman's work" has changed (133). Again, Janie is initially exposed to the criticism of the people around her when she begins to do work in public:

> So the very next morning Janie got ready to pick beans along with Tea Cake. There was a suppressed murmur when she picked up a basket and went to work. She was already getting to be a special case on the muck. It was generally assumed that she thought herself too good to work like the rest of the women and that Tea Cake "pomped her up tuh dat." But all day long the romping and playing they carried on behind the boss's back made her popular right away. (133)

Again, Janie is a prize in the community but for different reasons. No longer is she a "noble"; rather, she receives privilege because of her rebellious opposition to authority.

Throughout the novel, Janie must negotiate different, distinctly gendered, work spheres. She endures tedious domestic work with Killicks. With Starks, she plays compliant wife as her husband renders her sexually invisible by forcing her to tie back and cover her hair as she works in the general store. Once she meets Tea Cake, her work extends to a broader collective of laborers in the Everglades. As noted above, however, this seemingly egalitarian experience Tea Cake offers is not unproblematic, as he still shows "all those signs of possession" present in Killicks and Starks (105). Such instability, present both in relationships and in real estate, is what unsettles otherwise fixed categories of Janie's place not only geographically and culturally but also relationally. Judie Newman notes another interesting irony, that "Janie only 'goes folk' once she has made her money, rather as a modern-day millionaire may choose to collect art objects from the oppressed past of his ancestors" (825). However, as Newman is quick to follow, "her story is framed and structured in such a way as to prevent the reader functioning in any naïve fashion as a mere consumer of another culture" (825). Janie is not reducible to pedestrian assumptions of material gain and subsequent social privilege. The instability of place referred to above prevents an easy reading of intent or desire.

Hurston describes the scene in the Everglades as one presenting these sorts of complex disparities. Furthermore, she introduces workers by where they travel from:

> Day by day now, the hordes of workers poured in. Some came limping in with their shoes and sore feet from walking . . . They came in wagons from way up in Georgia and they came in truck loads from east, west, north and south. Permanent transients with no attachments . . . All night, all day, hurrying in to pick beans. Skillets, beds, patched up spare inner tubes all hanging and dangling from the ancient cars on the outside and hopeful humanity, herded and hovered on the inside, chugging on to the muck. People ugly from ignorance and broken from being poor. (131)

Migration is inextricable from the description of the workers who arrive. Specifically revealing in this regard is the group of Bahamians, whose presence marks a significant link between the South and the Caribbean. As Bone suggests, their inclusion "further destabilizes neo-Agrarian ideas of 'southern places' and 'community' by extending Hurston's representation of migrant labor in the rural South from the intraregional to the transnational" (765). While Hurston does not spend much time discussing this group, their presence in the text provides a way to examine the coalescence of work and gender in the locus of a complex relationship between the West and the Caribbean. Specifically, they offer to Janie a vision of cultural and personal flux, one that she employs with her rejection of fixed ideas of how she should perform her identity as a woman or a worker. These Caribbean laborers also signal an important consideration of place and migration within the South: "Hurston constructs a detailed narrative cartography of migrant labor patterns around the rural South—patterns more localized but no less 'monumental' than those involving the more familiar Great Migration to the urban North" (Bone 760–61). These patterns suggest a way to read a more diverse set of experiences of the diaspora in the South that allow for more options within dialogues about migration beyond a North/South dichotomy.

The first mention of the Bahamian workers is a description of cultural expression and performance, something Janie was finally allowed the time to appreciate at the close of her first season: "For instance during the summer when she heard the subtle but compelling rhythms of the Bahaman drummers, she'd walk over and watch the dances. She did not laugh the 'Saws' to scorn as she had heard the people doing in the season. She got to like it a lot and she and Tea Cake were on hand every night till the others teased them about it" (139). Important here is that, even as Hurston introduces Caribbean expressivity as a positive force for Janie and Tea Cake, she nonetheless marks it as subject to the ridicule of Western sensibilities.[19] This is what allows Janie to disrupt her own gaze as a "proper lady." The Western ethos represented in the adopted bourgeois rhetoric of Eatonville porch-sitters that positions Janie as a woman of power and prestige is what she rejects in her embrace of the Bahamian workers. Bone notes, referring to the work of Robert Mykle, "the Bahamian and other Caribbean workers in the Everglades were generally 'unseen, uncounted, unwanted, except at planting and harvest time'. . . No one thought very much about them, though" (768). Thus, Janie unsettles a presumed notion of status by making an "uncounted, unwanted" group a key part of her social growth and overall experience. In this way, the very concept of the American nation-state—so often linked to ideals of individual agency and self-governance—receives aspersion in Janie's journey, which instead receives more direct construction from the immigrants who do not fit the national model for welcome subjectivities.

Hurston uses Janie and Tea Cake as an avenue of entry for the Bahamians into the broader community of workers in the Everglades:

> Since Tea Cake and Janie had friended with the Bahaman workers in the 'Glades, they, the "Saws," had been gradually drawn into the American crowd. They quit hiding out to hold their dances when they found that their American friends didn't laugh at them as they feared. Many of the

Americans learned to jump and liked it as much as the "Saws." So they began to hold dances night after night in the quarters, usually behind Tea Cake's house. Often now, Tea Cake and Janie stayed up so late at the fire dances that Tea Cake would not let her go with him to the field. He wanted her to get her rest. (154)

Guttman offers what she understands to be the importance of Tea Cake's and Janie's time in the Everglades with the Caribbean workers: "By portraying a marginal migrant community whose members choose to be separate from white society, Hurston locates Tea Cake and Janie in a place of implicit (though hardly revolutionary) resistance to the economics underlying white supremacy" (107). She goes on: "Rather than conflate slavery and sharecropping, Hurston uses slavery as a metaphor for migrant labor. This use of metaphor functions as a protest against worker exploitation" (95).

THE PROBLEM WITH "CLASSING OFF": UNSETTLING STATUS AND STASIS

In the Everglades, Janie is still not able to escape the sort of preconceptions of her status that she confronted in Eatonville. This time, such notions come in the form of Mrs. Turner, who conflates class status with skin color.[20] Turner's own features, a "slightly pointed" nose and "thin lips," "set her aside from Negroes" (140). Seeing an ally and equal in "Janie's coffee-and-cream complexion," Mrs. Turner befriends her and "forgive[s] her for wearing overalls like the other women who worked in the fields" (140). Like the townspeople for whom Janie is Mrs. Mayor Starks, Mrs. Turner sees Janie as a class above. She attempts to appeal to Janie on this level, suggesting that the people Janie associates with are "beneath" her. When she tells her, "Mis' Woods, Ah have often said to mah husband, Ah don't see how uh lady like Mis' Woods can stand all them common niggers round her place all de time" (140), Janie answers with an interesting ambivalence. In a sweep of simultaneous defense and patronization, she replies, "They don't worry me atall, Mis' Turner. Fact about de thing is, they tickles me wid they talk" (140). Mrs. Turner expresses her solution to what she sees as irreconcilable race difference in terms of class, telling Janie, "Us oughta class off" (141). Even as Janie offers a condescending explanation, she rejects Turner's proposal that would form a fixed space of class identification for her.

Certainly, race and economic status conflate throughout the text, triangulating then with gender constructions and variations. Bone suggests that a reading of the Everglades must take into account "the more pervasive power of white Southern racism, both on and beyond the muck" (765). The racism apparent in the Everglades—the segregated graves, the figures like Mrs. Turner—are what, Bone rightly notes, should keep us from "romanticiz[ing] Janie's time on the muck as living in [what Jan Cooper calls the] 'harmony with the luxuriant natural world surrounding them'" (Bone 765). Bone makes an important point here. To take just the example of the role of race in the post-hurricane work of burying the dead, we witness a scene with issues similar to those present in the politics of marking the burial sites of Jack Rudolph and Boysey Brown at the University of Alabama, as described in my introduction. Tea Cake and "the small army that had been pressed into service to clear the wreckage in public places" find bodies strewn "under houses, tangled in shrubbery, floating in water, hanging in trees, drifting under wreckage" (170). The storm destroyed not only property but also corporeal racial signifiers, causing confusion for the workers who are told to identify and separate the black and white bodies, as "They makin' coffins fuh all de white folks. 'Tain't nothin' but cheap pine, but dat's better'n nothin'" (171). While black and white men work together in unified directive of labor, the graves remain distinguished: "Miserable, sullen men, black and white under guard had to keep on searching for bodies and digging graves. A huge ditch was dug across the white cemetery and a big ditch was opened across the black graveyard" (170). The confusion in identifying white and black corpses results in the guards telling the workers to "Look at they hair, when you cain't tell no other way" (171). The interest in "good" and "bad" hair—first seen in Joe Starks's insistence that Janie wrap and render invisible her alluring hair—reappears here in the use of hair to designate race and, by extension, privilege.

Contra Bone's reading, other critics like Gordon Thompson would reduce the workings of race in the novel to a platitude of empowerment: "Hurston's privileging of black folkloric materials represents the key to her championing of black and black female 'self-determination'" (738). Thompson concludes, then, that "Racial conflict in Hurston, hence, remains muted and indirect and her handling of gender concerns somewhat problematic, especially in light of contemporary feminist ideology" (738). While I certainly agree that there is much to be done in the vein of complicating what Thompson calls "gender concerns," I would hardly deem the racial conflicts in the text "muted and indirect." Rather, they serve to underscore the shifting understandings of other facets of identification—namely gender and work—as Janie moves throughout the South. Racialized conceptions and conflicts are, at the very least, key facets of Mrs. Turner's call for Janie to "class off."

The idea of "classing off" follows Janie throughout the text, with her community consistently identifying her as a "high time woman." Hurston presents this construct as a dubious one, however, subject to those defining her at any given time and the contexts of such definitions. While the notion of Janie's voice is certainly important to consider, her voice is always necessarily determined by the sociocultural nomenclature of what kind of work a real woman is expected or forbidden to do. Meanwhile, she embodies ambivalence through the text as a "high time woman" who works on the muck, simultaneously caught in the troubling contradictions that define her relationship with Tea Cake. As Miller notes, such contradictions imply a multilayered importance: "The scope of power Janie achieves through submission to Tea Cake is far-reaching" (85). And as Joseph points out, the end of the novel gives a "lingering sense of an unbalanced and unknowable world" (458). Thus, even as she comes to represent a powerful feminist heroine, Janie is, in Joseph's words, "hitched to the tedious rig of economic progress, consigned to an impoverished identity by the closed texts and calcified dreams of her grandmother" (470). Within such a framework of ambiguity, Janie rejects an authentic narrative, even as she tells her story to Pheoby. This rejection, rather than taking away her voice, creates a space in which authenticity—as sought in racialized power relations of gender and labor—is reduction rather than redemption. Work and womanhood, as well as the American South and the Caribbean, converge again in a novel published fifty years after *Their Eyes:* Gloria Naylor's *Mama Day.* Once again, a woman traveling from place to place tells her story, and once again, the quest for a true or real history proves to be a false endeavor.

3

Familiar Ground

The Rhetoric of "Realness" in *Mama Day*

> A lot can happen between your leaving and getting back to a place.
> —*Mama Day* (52)

> I drew strength from moving in the midst of familiar ground.
> —*Mama Day* (308)

GLORIA NAYLOR'S *Mama Day* (1988) centers around an island community off the coasts of Georgia and South Carolina, where an old woman named Miranda Day serves as communal caretaker and medicinal conjure woman. The story of her familial ancestry is also the story of the island's history. That legend is one of a nineteenth-century slave woman who, in 1819, was sold to one Bascombe Wade and who somehow convinced him to deed to all his slaves the land in Willow Springs. Her tale is told many different ways, but she is rumored throughout the island to have married and then killed Wade, giving birth to seven sons somewhere along the way. Her lineage is the Day family, and Miranda (also known as "Mama Day") is the mysterious slave woman's great-granddaughter. *Mama Day* tells the story of Willow Springs and the slave Sapphira with three narrative strands. Specifically, we hear in first person from Miranda's great-niece Cocoa (whose birth name is Ophelia) and Cocoa's husband, George, a native New Yorker. Then there is an omniscient "voice of the island" that tells us about events in Willow Springs, about Miranda and her sister Abigail (Cocoa's grandmother) in particular.

Like in Mary Prince's *History* and Zora Neale Hurston's *Their Eyes Were Watching God*, migration and displacement prove key, as Cocoa moves to New York for work opportunities and comes back to Willow Springs to introduce her new husband to Abigail and Miranda. While back home on the island, Cocoa suffers under a jealous woman's spell, and George must try to save her. Cultural ideologies conflict as he fights with Miranda over what he sees to be Cocoa's obvious need for Western medicine. In the meantime, Abigail comforts her ailing granddaughter by singing the James Cleveland spiritual that, significantly, suggests the importance of journeys and place: "Oh, I don't feel no ways tired. / I've come too far from where I started from. / Nobody told me that the road would be easy / I don't believe He brought me this far— / I can't believe He brought me this far to leave me" (288). Meanwhile, Miranda travels back and forth to "the other place," migrations that, while local, prove sweeping in their traversals of memory and history. Throughout the novel, these displacements frame constructions and disruptions of gender and work, signs that appear simultaneously maintained and unsettled.

Like *Their Eyes Were Watching God*, *Mama Day* presents the South as a space in which ideologies and identities are both constructed and destabilized. While this concurrent construction and destabilization can be said to be true of all places, such ambivalence is particularly key to a study of the transnational South, where multiple and diverse histories of power and oppression converge. In this sense, *Mama Day* is a "southern" text, offering a small island community off the coast of South Carolina as a microcosm of a transatlantic story, as Bascombe Wade is "Norway-born or something" and "Sapphira was African-born" (5). Meanwhile, the present-day Willow Springs also holds on to both southern and Caribbean rituals and cultural identifications. Thus, as Paula Gallant Eckard suggests in "The Prismatic Past in *Oral History* and *Mama Day*," "While Gloria Naylor can't be labeled a southern writer, *Mama Day* is richly southern in its setting and treatment of the past" (129). Meanwhile, Margaret Earley Whitt in *Understanding Gloria Naylor* suggests that "Down deep, there is something inherently southern in Gloria Naylor" (4). This appeal to an essential "Southernness" that Naylor possesses is not what I see working in the novel. On the contrary, Naylor's contextual positioning of a transnational, extended South resists such appeals to the "inherently southern," thought to be held somewhere "down deep."

Thus, as stated above, especially important to my reading is Naylor's initially strange rhetoric of an authentic "realness," a rhetoric likewise employed—though less productively—by the criticism surrounding the novel. The text is packed with references to the "real" South, "real" men and women, "real" experience, and so forth. However, the appeal to what is "real," or "true" in some cases, is undermined by a persistent indeterminacy of reference. This notion of the "real" and the text's sustained critique of the concept is an important way in which place figures into what Miranda says is the problem with young people—that "everyone wants to be right in a world where there ain't no right or wrong to be found" (230). This question of what is "real" or "true" is at the heart of the struggles of women throughout *Mama Day,* as dislocation resituates the meanings of such notions with new social conditions.

Significantly, in Naylor, the presentation and disruption of realness come into play through the displacement of women in the text. I focus specifically on Cocoa's geographical displacement and Miranda's imaginative displacement (i.e., separation in terms of ancestry and memory) to show Naylor's manipulation of concepts of realness. Through Cocoa's and Miranda's displacements in turn, Naylor uses migration and the importance of place to unsettle the seeming realness or truth of all categories. By simultaneously employing and destabilizing the very rhetorical and categorical formations that she proceeds to interrogate, Naylor offers a heuristic value to categories as tools of engagement. Like Hurston, she relies on the convenience of classifications like "woman" and "work," all the while maintaining these notions as merely that: conveniences. Naylor, thus, shows how these formations are deployed by societal strictures and how they might begin to be seen as more malleable. Particularly of interest are the ways in which Naylor addresses Southern views and expectations of womanhood and accompanying definitions of "lady" or "femininity." The "Southern" is also interrogated in relation to women and conjure and an assumption of female trickery. Naylor also brings revealing attention to the rhetoric of work and socioeconomic status in relation to race. Grounding theory with more specific discussions of the work women do in *Mama Day* is one way to more productively approach the novel. Ann Folwell Stanford, for instance, reads *Mama Day* through the lens of medicinal politics. Lindsey Tucker discusses Miranda Day's work, focusing specifically on how Naylor recuperates conjure work in the novel. I want to analyze the rhetoric of "realness" in the novel in order to dismantle reductive constructions of womanhood and labor.

"CROSSED OVER":
MIGRATION AND IDENTITY FORMATION

Most of *Mama Day*'s narrative takes place in Willow Springs. The island is connected to the mainland by a rickety bridge. As a "state" that is not identified as such, Willow Springs is a distinct signifier of space and community, resisting stable definitions of place. The inhabitants describe the island as a borderland: "all forty-nine square miles curves like a bow, stretching toward Georgia on the U.S. end and South Carolina on the north, and right smack in the middle where each foot of our bridge sits is the dividing line between them two states. So who it belong to? It belongs to us—clean and simple" (5).[1] As a separated non-state, Willow Springs represents what George calls "another world." George and Cocoa are two of the three voices that braid the narrative. Their journey to Willow Springs carries with it the primary plot elements of the novel. Cocoa foreshadows the complications that arise from their travels, casting Willow Springs as a place in which the traditional Western paradigms of logic and pragmatism do not apply:

> And as we crossed over the bridge . . . was that the time to turn everything around? . . . At what point could we have avoided that summer? At the beginning of that bridge? . . . And . . . George, when I try to pick a point at which we could have stopped, there is none. I don't think it would have mattered if we had come a year before or a year after. You and I would have been basically the same, and time definitely stands still in Willow Springs. No, any summer we crossed over that bridge would be the summer we crossed over. (165)

The bridge here serves as a deciding point, while Willow Springs is a whole other world to which one "crosses over." The passage cited above serves as a textual bridge between Parts I and II of the novel. Naylor presents Willow Springs and its bridge as places not of destination but of flux.[2]

The island is marked by deep historical roots that are entangled by racial conflict and the legend of a woman who convinces her owner to deed his land to his slaves:

> Bascombe Wade was not American ("Was Norway-born or something"): So thanks to the conjuring of Sapphira Wade we got it from Norway or

theres about, and if taxes owed, it's owed to them. But ain't no Vikings or anybody else from over in Europe come to us with the foolishness that them folks out of Columbia and Atlanta come with—we was being un-American. And the way we saw it, America ain't entered the question at all when it come to our land: Sapphira was African-born, Bascombe Wade was from Norway, and it was the 18 & 23'ing that went down between them two put deeds in our hands. And we wasn't even Americans when we got it—was slaves. And the laws about slaves not owning nothing in Georgia and South Carolina don't apply, 'cause the land wasn't then—and isn't now—in either of them places. (5)

The two descendants of the Day family, Miranda (Mama Day) and Abigail, are left to handle developers who still approach them with offers to buy the land. They refuse every proposition, citing places like St. John's and Hilton Head:

Got them folks' land, built fences around it first thing, and then brought in all the builders and high-paid managers from mainside—ain't nobody on them islands benefited. And the only dark faces you see now in them "vacation paradises" is the ones cleaning the toilets and cutting the grass. On their own land, mind you, their own land. Weren't gonna happen in Willow Springs. (6)

The residents of Willow Springs, then, cultivate in-between spaces of geography and societal norms. A discussion of Cocoa's time in New York in contradistinction to her time in Willow Springs reveals Naylor's simultaneous appeal to and critique of fixed notions of womanhood and work. While her travels are arguably her choice, they still serve to displace her sense of Southern and gendered identification. She is effectively removed from the place she identifies as "home." Removed from Willow Springs, she is separated from what Edward Casey calls "a certain place of origin as . . . an exemplar against which all subsequent places are implicitly to be measured . . . an ur-place" (xv). Accordingly, Cocoa engages in an unwitting project of changing preconceived definitions, making new meanings for concepts like "home." George—the man she meets and marries in New York—plays a role as representative of Western ideologies of pragmatism, a role that provides a useful parallel to Cocoa's shifts and movements.

Cocoa initially harbors an extreme aversion to New York, and she stacks herself squarely in opposition to her newfound urban space. She senses that people in New York are not "real." She remembers, "God, I wanted to go home—and I meant, home home. With all of Willow Springs' problems, you knew when you saw a catfish, you called it a catfish" (22). In an important later comparison of New York and Willow Springs, Cocoa calls New York "A whole kaleidoscope of people," saying that "nothing's just black and white [there] like in Willow Springs. Nothing stays put" (63). There is a hint of irony here, as Willow Springs is anything but absolute. She thus destabilizes the very binaries she constructs with regard to place and identity. Simultaneously, she critiques what she perceives to be the pseudo-reality of people in New York and, with the words "home home," ties herself to a "real" home in Willow Springs. Thus, her longing for authenticity is one that is fostered by the text's steady but multiple definitions of home, even though the "real" in Willow Springs is an extremely tenuous construct that relies strongly on belief and alternate understandings of reality. Notions of "home" thus use the rhetoric of, though never arrive at, a singular definition. Naylor provides three descriptions, all of which speak to Willow Springs's power of paradox:

> Home. Folks call it different things, think of it in different ways. For Cocoa it's being around living mirrors with the power to show a woman that she's still carrying scarred knees, a runny nose, and socks that get walked down into the heels of her shoes . . . Home. It's being new and old all rolled into one. Measuring your new against old friends, old ways, old places. Knowing that as long as the old survives, you can keep changing as much as you want without the nightmare of waking up to a total stranger . . . Home. You can move away from it, but you never leave it. Not as long as it holds something to be missed. (48–50)

Thus, inhabiting the space of moving away while not leaving, Cocoa wraps her travels back home in their own sense of ritual and tradition. Even in her interview at George's company, she tells her would-be boss, "I have to go home every August" (30).[3] In this sense, Cocoa simultaneously occupies spheres of home and occupational ambition.

George shares Cocoa's desire for economic movement and growth, but his drive is born out of a more pragmatic necessity. Working as an engineer for the production and design company Andrews & Stein, he lives the practicality he learned to appreciate and cling to since boyhood. He remembers growing up in the Wallace P. Andrews Shelter for Boys, where "There were only rules and facts" (24). There, he constantly heard and repeated the mantras "Keep it in the now, fellas" and "Only the present has potential, *sir*" (22–23). Mrs. Jackson, the tough but caring woman who ran the shelter, presented a mind-set of fierce independence for the boys, which transferred even to the ways she administered discipline. George remembers, "And the discipline she tailor-made for all of us said, like it or not, the present is *you*. And what else did we have but ourselves? We had a more than forgettable past and no future that was guaranteed" (26). There is a conflict between not only the West and Third World but also the sensibilities of individualism and communalism. Women like Miranda and Cocoa are fiercely independent, but they retain a hold on rituals, traditions, and practices that maintain their roles—if not their very identities—within a larger community.

George understands the potential problems of a place like Wallace P. Andrews and its all-consuming pedagogy of self-reliance and pragmatism. He explains, "No, it wasn't the kind of place that tuned out many poets or artists—those who could draw became draftsmen, and the musicians were taught to tune pianos. If [Mrs. Jackson] erred in directing our careers, she erred on the side of caution. Sure, the arts were waiting for poor black kids who were encouraged to dream big, and so was death row" (26–27). George, thus, cultivates and maintains a strong understanding of the societal implications for him and the other children growing up as black orphans in a place like the Andrews shelter. He has little time for luxuries like luck or superstition, as he explains to Cocoa:

> When I left Wallace P. Andrews I had what I could see: my head and my two hands, and I had each day to do something with them. Each day, that's how I took it—each moment, sometimes, when the going got really rough. I may have knocked my head against walls, figuring out how to buy food, supplies, and books, but I never knocked on wood. No rabbit's foot, no crucifixes—not even a lottery ticket . . . So until you walked into my office, everything I was—all the odds I had beat—was owed to my living fully in the now. (27)

For George, realness is a very tangible, empirically available construct, and one lives authentically by resisting illusory notions of the supernatural and keeping oneself "in the now."

It is his introduction to Cocoa that makes him admit that there may be, with her and certainly with his trip to Willow Springs, other powers beyond his own at work. George's sense of owing everything to "living fully in the now" contrasts itself against the strong presence of the past as a dynamic, living thing in Willow Springs. Suddenly, he experiences a community whose sense of self comes from its history and heritage. Miranda, for instance, must live within the ancestry of the Day family, remembering back in order to see ahead. She does so in order to save Cocoa when she becomes so ill, in fact. Protecting one's lineage in this sense necessitates communing with one's ancestors. George, on the other hand, identifies his struggle as one between facts and feelings, asking Cocoa, "How was I to reconcile the *fact* of seeing you the second time that day with the *feeling* I had had the first time?" (27). The challenge of determining what is "real" or "true" in the midst of what "seems" becomes a difficult prospect the more George and Cocoa travel together around New York.

Cocoa's strained relationship with the big city is what starts her relationship with George. Place, thus, gives them a reason for their initial incompatibility. George's self-reliance extends to his calling New York "my city," and, significantly, his conversations with Cocoa about the city also involve economic and racial politics. He critiques Cocoa and the way she and others live in New York: "You often arrived young and sometimes grew old, making your own small town among us . . . So you'd rarely meet a native New Yorker: we gave you, the tourists, and our riffraff the streets at night . . . And there you were, offering me your projections about the future of my city" (62). Organizing his claim with semantic categories, he distinguishes between "ghetto" and "permanent" residents in New York:

> No, you're not a vacationing tourist. You live and play in the ghettos for our permanent tourists. And like any ghetto resident, you pay more for cramped, shoddy housing and the local support services than the rest of us . . . you've bought the illusion that this is where you *have* to live—midtown is New York, and you try to stay as close to it as possible. And if they stick you in Brooklyn or Queens, it's downtown Brooklyn or Long Island City—the closer to a bridge, the better, right? . . . Most people are confined in ghettos by economic circumstances, so there's no chance for them to grow and explore, to be enriched by the life of a city. And I just think it's a little sad that here, of all places, the young and talented confine themselves by choice. (65)

Particularly of note alongside George's descriptions of the economic implications associated with travel and migration is his reference to bridges, as that will become the very symbol of civilization that he clings to and attempts to fix when a hurricane threatens Willow Springs. George is also irritated with Cocoa's seeming racism, telling her, "Your opinions of our political system were only a bit less horrifying than your attitude on race relations. You were one of the youngest—and most evenhanded—bigots I had ever met" (62). A stereotype of Southern racism is manifested in Cocoa, as George associates her social myopia with her regional home.

Thus, for a man of categories and convenient orderings of life experiences, Willow Springs presents an initially pleasant, albeit puzzling, anomaly. However, when the stakes are raised and Cocoa becomes very sick, his Western sensibilities can no longer see the island as a charming and provincial caricature of "small town" folk life. Kindly condescension becomes a total, vitriolic disconnect as he turns against Willow Springs, casting his frustration with Cocoa's illness in terms of place. He repeatedly muses that things would be okay if only they could leave. It is the reason he emphasizes equal parts pragmatism and place as he obsesses about rebuilding the bridge that a hurricane destroys.[4] The bridge speaks to both his need to work hard and consistently on a tangible project and his desire to leave Willow Springs. Indeed, he expresses his fear for Cocoa by showing his anger at a place, saying, "I wanted nothing more than to get the hell off of that island" (286).

Not only the experiences but also the expectations that change with each place play key roles in characters' ideas of how they relate to or dwell within certain spaces. After Cocoa moves to New York from Willow Springs, her great-aunt looks to big-city stereotypes in order to "understand" the kind of place and people Cocoa is encountering. Conflating large Northern cities, Miranda becomes a steady viewer of Phil Donahue's talk show to get a sense of Cocoa's social surroundings in New York: "[The show] gave her an idea of the kind of people Cocoa was living around since she'd moved north. Even the folks in Atlanta were different from the folks in Willow Springs, and when you started talking Chicago, Philadelphia, New York, they were way different again" (38).[5] Even though Donahue's show is broadcast from Chicago, the nuanced differences between large metropolises are lost on Miranda. Chicago might as well be New York, as far as she is concerned. The majority of Willow Springs share Miranda's distrusting view of the North. As they speculate about Cocoa's husband when they hear she has married, they simultaneously invoke stereotypes of New York and perpetuate a geographical sense of self-loathing. Misunderstanding George's work as an engineer, the townspeople gossip accordingly: "New York City is full of con artists. Muggers, pickpockets, and God knows what else. Why didn't Cocoa come home and get herself a husband, somebody she could trust? . . . Who was she gonna marry here? This sorry lot in Willow Springs can't even *spell* train, no less run one" (132). Certainly Cocoa shares this double-sided perception at first, originally viewing New York as too dirty and busy, meanwhile believing that Willow Springs holds no opportunities for professional or economic gain.

For George, the tiny island is initially both utterly confusing and appealing. George's narration that describes his first encounter with Willow Springs is telling: "It's hard to know what to expect from a place when you can't find it on the map" (174). Used to maps and atlases that helped him prepare for a trip, George feels completely helpless when confronted with a place that is not an "actual" place. He is dissatisfied, then, with Cocoa's description of the island as being positioned exactly between South Carolina and Georgia. His anxiety is wrapped up within the idea of preparation, of being ready for a place. He goes on: "But where was Willow Springs? Nowhere. At least not on any map I had found. I had even gone out and bought road maps just for South Carolina and Georgia and it was missing from among all those islands dotting the coastline. What country claimed it? Where was the nearest interstate highway, the nearest byroad?" (174). George understands place in terms of its markers and boundaries. If it exceeds or traverses border identifications, or is, in the case of Willow Springs, not able to be identified with markers like state affiliation, George is unable to appreciate its existence at all. His cursory description of Willow Springs admits as much:

> I had to be there and see—no, feel—that I was entering another world. Where even the word *paradise* failed once I crossed over The Sound. Sure I can describe what I saw: a sleepy little section of wooden storefronts, then sporadic houses of stucco, brick, and clapboard all framed by palmettos, live oaks, and flowering bushes; every now and then a span of marshland, a patch of woods. But how do I describe air that thickens so that it seems solid as the water, causing colors and sounds and textures to actually float in it? . . . And if someone had asked me about the fragrance from the whisperings of the palmettos, or the distant rush of the surf, I would have said that it all smelled like forever. (175)

George's description perpetuates the both/and sense of place at work in Willow Springs. His convoluted understandings of "solid" air and surf that smells like "forever" are the only ways for him to absorb such an otherworldly place. The way in which Willow Springs enacts its own sense of place thus speaks to the impossibility on the island of thinking of one's own "place" in terms of fixed categories.

While Cocoa's movements back and forth between Willow Springs and New York show traceable shifts in "real" social norms and definitions, Miranda takes a less literal journey and experiences what I call *imaginative displacement*. I use the term "imaginative" to suggest the ways in which memory and ancestry (and the separation from each) construct and destabilize subject position. Much of Willow Springs's social and ritualistic makeup comes from the legend of the slave Sapphira,[6] who is said to have killed her master, Bascombe Wade, after she gave birth to seven of his sons and after she convinced him to deed to his slaves his land. For Miranda, then, as a direct descendant of Sapphira, the island's history is also her family's history. Place is not, to borrow from Casey, "a matter of arbitrary position" (xiii). In order to avoid focusing on "what happens in a place rather than . . . the place itself," I see the context of Willow Springs—Deep South, island community, former slave plantation—as a necessary and distinct positioning for Miranda's gendered work (Casey xiii).

Willow Springs, and certainly Miranda herself, is the lineage of the thus far unnamed but omnipresent slave-turned-murderess Sapphira. At the beginning of the book, before even the text itself begins, Naylor places a map of Willow Springs, followed by a Day family tree and then the conditions of sale for Sapphira. The pairing of a map with genealogy and slave ancestry/history is a key move in literally placing lineage and memory. Textually, the beginning of the novel follows much the same order set up in the prefacing materials of place, family, and slave ancestry. The first two words in the text are "Willow Springs," and are immediately followed by a note on a slave ancestor: "Everybody knows but nobody talks about the legend of Sapphira Wade. A true conjure woman: satin black, biscuit cream, red as Georgia clay: depending upon which of us takes a mind to her" (3). An important juxtaposition lies within the sentences following the initial specificity of place. The ambiguity of Sapphira's coloring describes a "true" conjure woman. Immediately following Sapphira's introduction comes a description of what she was able to do, striking chords resoundingly similar to Tituba's description of a "witch":

> She could walk through a lightning storm without being touched; grab a bolt of lightning in the palm of her hand; use the heat of lightning to start the kindling going under her medicine pot: depending upon which

of us takes a mind to her. She turned the moon into salve, the stars into a swaddling cloth, and healed the wounds of every creature walking up on two or down on four. (3)

This passage, like Tituba's idea of what it is to be a witch, maintains important strains of "benevolent labor," even as it resituates them. Such strains are articulated within a context of geographical connectivity and displacement. Thus, following this description of Sapphira's abilities is the idea I cited earlier of how meaning is made and remade: "It ain't about right or wrong, truth or lies; it's about a slave woman who brought a whole new meaning to both them words, soon as you cross over here from beyond the bridge" (3). The ambiguity in *Mama Day* is, thus, articulated through tropes of migration, specifically the bridge that serves as a connective tissue for meaning and notions of truth and reality.

Significantly, there is no one true story of Sapphira. Her legend is as ambiguous as the place to which she acquired the deed, with people offering different versions of her story:

Somehow, some way it happened in 1823: she smothered Bascombe Wade in his very bed and lived to tell the story for a thousand days. 1823: married Bascombe Wade, bore him seven sons in just a thousand days, to put a dagger through his kidney . . . 1823: persuaded Bascombe Wade in a thousand days to deed all his slaves every inch of land in Willow Springs. (3)

Introducing Sapphira with her bill of sale is an important move in situating the island's history and the Day family's ancestry. Very early on, Naylor establishes Sapphira as a key figure in Willow Springs's system of meaning-making. The community refers to "18 & 23" as a colloquial expression that comes from the date surrounding Sapphira's legend. Further, Naylor presses the fact that, for the people of Willow Springs, "Sapphira Wade don't live in the part of our memory we can use to form words" (4). Her role is a visceral, ineffable one—at once a vital part of the island's cosmogony and a myth with unknown origins. Important pieces of the island's identity and history dwell in shapeless spaces that do not allow for a structured or identifiable formation.

As Sapphira's great-granddaughter, Miranda has an added layer of self-identification surrounding the legend of 1823. Sapphira's story has a direct relationship to Miranda's self-knowledge. Indeed, Sapphira holds deep significance both for the Day family and for the island itself. However, rather than searching for a clear and identifiable truth to Sapphira's legend—the real story—Miranda finds meaning in memories of and relationships between ancestors. Thus, she navigates her authenticity by exploring her family's history and ancestry, both of which are informed by their salient relationships to place. When wondering how she should respond to Bernice's pleas for help in conceiving a child, Miranda thinks of her family:

> Lord, she ain't never tried to get *over* nature. Hadn't she seen enough in this very house to know that that couldn't be? John-Paul woulda moved the earth for his wife, but . . . he couldn't give her Peace. And Abigail, trying to form with her flesh what Daddy couldn't form from wood, still didn't get Peace to live again. (262)

Appealing to an idea of what is or is not natural, Miranda lays claim to the very rhetoric that would reject the abilities that allow her to both work outside Western constructs and "find" Sapphira. She sees familial stories as their own oral history to pass down through generations. When Ambush gives Miranda and Abigail a rocking chair for Candle Walk, they remember their mother's anguish after their sister Peace died—how she would sit in her rocking chair endlessly (115). Miranda assures Abigail that Ambush cannot possibly know the story: "Mother died before his *grandfather* was out of diapers" (116). However, she goes on to chastise their keeping such stories from Cocoa: "And we ain't even told Baby Girl about . . . And we should, you know, Abigail. It ain't nothing to be ashamed of, it's her family and her history. And she'll have children one day" (116).[7] Here again is a simultaneous assumption of the value of self-knowledge and recognition of the complexities inherent in such a quest.

Significantly, remembering the Day family's stories and reliving their pain are necessary in order to heal Cocoa when she falls ill from Ruby's hex. Miranda stays at "the other place," where her memories serve as fundamental extensions of her knowledge and abilities. There is thus an intricate connection between her family's history and her work. When she discovers that Cocoa is sick, a telling passage describes her thinking about what must be done by thinking about the past:

> So Miranda is staring past her dried herbs, past the birth of Hope and Grace, past the mother who ended her life in The Sound, on to the Mother who began the Days. She sees one woman leave by wind.

Another leave by water. She smells the blood from the broken hearts of men who they cursed for not letting them go . . . She finally turns to face her sister, the weight on her soul reflected in the eyes that meet hers. "It's gonna take a man to bring her peace"—and all they had was that boy. (262–63)

As my earlier discussions may have suggested, Naylor ironically makes a man the answer to the women's trouble. At once, they both need and are too powerful for George. The person who can help them is also the one who does not believe in the powers that helping them requires.

Naylor abandons any form of quick feminist plot development here—Cocoa's healing is not solely a matter of a community of independent and like-minded women coming together to intervene for her, as is the case in other texts like *Beloved, The Salt Eaters,* and *Parable of the Sower*. There is a seeming departure from the positive castings of women as able to "heal" themselves in their own right, whether from physical or psychological impediments. However, what would otherwise be a problematic need for a man's help in the face of a woman's turmoil is actually a subversive, but nonetheless present, venture away from patriarchal power structures. George must fix the situation on Miranda's terms and, what's more, on her turf. He has to go to her henhouse and take whatever he finds from an unruly hen's nest.[8] Meanwhile, Miranda maintains her own power in a significantly ancestral sphere. She explains to George their individual roles in trying to save Cocoa:

> I had to stay in this place and reach back to the beginning for us to find the chains to pull her out of this here trouble. Now, I got all that in this hand but it ain't gonna be unless I can reach out with the other hand and take yours. You see, [Cocoa] done bound more than her flesh up with you. And since she's suffering from something more than the flesh, I can't do a thing without you. (294)

Miranda is thus able to "reach back to the beginning" but nonetheless understands the power of the community in working toward a common goal.

Having grown up in a place that privileged Western notions of individualism and self-reliance, George is unable to understand the problem or solution in terms of community. Cocoa foreshadows George's inability to understand Willow Springs's structures of power and belief when she reminds him of her own place in her family and on the island. She tells

George that she belongs to her grandmother and great-aunt, that she is "theirs." Appropriately, this is something George realizes as they travel into Willow Springs, "the moment [they] crossed over the bridge" (177). Cocoa describes George's experience back to him: "you were entering a part of my existence that you were powerless in. Your maps were no good here, but you still came, willing to share this with me" (177). Nodding to the very same point of Miranda's, that now her life depends on George even if she still "belonged" to her family, Cocoa immediately follows her statement regarding the inadequacy of George's worldview with one on the new importance he adds to her familial space: "And from another perspective, that room was now a place my family couldn't touch" (177). Her room in Abigail's house, her specific domestic space that signifies her place in the Day family, becomes one that George shares. The prior system of who is able to do what work is thus complicated.

George, however, is unable to situate Cocoa's illness without absolute understandings of a problem and tangible solutions. He recalls to Cocoa, "You were sick and I was totally helpless. It was a feeling that I hated even though your grandmother said that it seemed as if you'd only caught a virus. *Seemed as if* wasn't good enough for me" (260). George maintains an appeal to and privileging of the real. Significantly, Miranda references place in order to explain George's inability to think between absolutes: "The Days were all rooted to the other place, but that boy had his own place within him" (285). Working as a conduit for George as he attempts to navigate the space between "his own place" and that at work in Willow Springs, Miranda understands her necessary role as guide: "No, she'd think on some way to get him to trust her, by holding her hand she could guide him safely through that extra mile where the others had stumbled. But a mile was a lot to travel when even one step becomes too much on a road you ain't ready to take" (285).[9] The goal, then, is for both George and Miranda together to signify a new, healing place for Cocoa—specifically, a bridge: "A single moment was all she asked, even a fingertip to touch hers here at the other place. So together they could be the bridge for Baby Girl to walk over" (285). Bridges take on a different value here apart from that which George gives them as a symbol of certainty and industry. They are at once markers of human ingenuity and of human interconnectivity.

Miranda begins her work by wading through memories of her family and stories of her ancestors. To help Cocoa, she must find Sapphira. In finding Sapphira, accordingly, she learns more about herself and her own familial place. As soon as she begins staying at the old family home in the other place, she puts her memory to work, retelling herself the story of Bascombe Wade and Sapphira.[10] When she stumbles over memories of family tragedy and loss, she remembers the work left to do and stops, thinking, "No, these ain't the memories she needs. Think of others. But, Lord, it's so hard 'cause she was so young when Peace died" (278). She ultimately comes across an old ledger in the house and later taps her memory to find the heretofore unnamed Sapphira (280). She sees the record of Sapphira's sale and resituates within this ancestral context both her own positionality and the work she has left to do. As Miranda exhaustedly opens doors in the family house and tries to discover more about the Days, she finds a new understanding of her own place within the family:

> And when she feels that even her will done run out, that she just can't turn another knob to reach out and do it—she finds herself in a vast space of glowing light. Daughter. Word comes to cradle what has gone past weariness. She can't really hear it 'cause she's got no ears, or call out 'cause she's got no mouth. There's only the sense of being. Daughter . . . Miranda. Sister. Little Mama. Mama Day. Melting, melting away under the sweet flood waters pouring down to lay bare a place she ain't known existed: Daughter. (283)[11]

This vague "sense of being" speaks to how place becomes expanded in the text to include not only geographical space but also subject positions. Such connotative latitude is particularly important for the ways in which notions of authenticity get displayed and collapsed throughout the text. Naylor presents the institutions of Southern womanhood and work (both raced and gendered) as fluid spaces in which there is room to play with and even reconstitute traditional meanings that would otherwise impose labels of authentic experience driven by these very institutions.

The Day family house in the other place is thus representative of the transient but vital roles of place in constructing and understanding subject positions. George provides a useful description of the family home, noting the irony of its beauty when weighed against all the pain it held within its walls:

> That house had known a lot of pain. And more than what you talked about: your great-grandmother, Ophelia, losing her baby daughter at the bottom of a well; closing herself off from her husband and her children. Your grandmother hating the place so much she hadn't set foot

there in over fifty years. No, there was something more, and something deeper than the old historical line about slave women and their white masters. A slave hadn't lived in this house. And without a slave, there could be no master. What had Miss Miranda said—he had claim to her body, but not her mind? Yes, that house resonated *loss*. A lack of peace. And both had begged for peace. What caused those two people to tear each other apart in this old house with a big garden? But, God, it was a lovely place. (225)

When Cocoa and George approach the family home after a walk in the woods, there is a striking moment that speaks to issues of both ancestral history and the significance of place. As Cocoa hears voices in the woods recalling other women in her family and telling her "you'll break his heart," she and George come across the old Day home (224). In the middle of Cocoa's narrative description, the South becomes a performative space. She recalls to George, "You wanted to sit in the rocking chair and *play* southern gentleman with me on your lap. I wanted us to get out of there; I couldn't stand it anymore" (224, emphasis mine).[12] Here is another important instance of Naylor deploying stereotypes while simultaneously undermining them. The seeming glamour of the antebellum plantation, the Southern lady and gentleman, and the elegant plantation are heavily racialized as constructions of whiteness and assertions of white supremacy.[13]

Naylor uses such constructions to shape her characters while also offering them as problematic units of measure that others impose on these same characters. In so doing, she interrogates the power of whiteness as a rhetorical and imaginative tool, and she rejects claims to or labels of racial authenticity. Examining how the social construction of race constructed formations of gender in contexts of slavery, Evelyn Brooks Higginbotham suggests that "gender itself was both constructed and fragmented by race. Gender, so colored by race, remained from birth until death inextricably linked to one's personal identity and social status" (258). As George would play "southern gentlemen," Cocoa, by extension, would have to play "southern lady," a role that she resists. Higginbotham rightly notes that "segregation's meaning for gender was exemplified in the trope of 'lady.' Ladies were not merely women; they represented a class" (261). The whiteness attendant with such a trope is part of what complicates the role for Cocoa. As Susan V. Donaldson and Anne Goodwyn Jones suggest, "The stories of southern bodies have been structured in large part by the interlocking logics of dichotomy—

masculine and feminine, white and black, master and slave, planter and 'white trash,' Cavalier and Yankee" (2). Indeed, these binaries come into sharper focus as George and Cocoa leave New York and enter Willow Springs. The ambivalence to which Donaldson and Jones refer is one that Naylor exploits in a move that emphasizes and likewise questions such categories.

Miranda expresses similar ambivalence about the house, questioning the degrees to which place and the people within place matter. Significantly, she feels her ambivalence in terms not only of place and subjectivity but also of her work:

> Maybe my sister was right, this old place needs to burn down. But something deep inside of her won't let her truly believe that. A house is a house, ain't it? Wood and plaster and brick. It's the people that brings the sorrow. Or the hope. That same man told her that she had a little more than others to give. You have a gift, Little Mama. But who asked her for it? Who made her God? . . . Most folks just don't know what can be done with a little will and their own hands. But she ain't never, Lord, she ain't never tried to get *over* nature. (262)

The Day family home is thus a tangible paradigm of the construction and demolition of social and societal structures that would be otherwise singular in their depictions of gender and work.

Fittingly, the text presents place as having not only a substantive but also a transformational role for Miranda. Maintaining her understanding of how important place can be, she meanwhile takes on the very attributes of place itself. The text offers Miranda as both manipulator and constituent of place. Thus, "She can still stand so quiet, she becomes part of a tree" (81). Familial history, again, becomes part of the mix here, as it is her father, John-Paul, who teaches Miranda to revere place and make it part of herself. She remembers his telling her, "*Little Mama, these woods been here before you and me, so why should they get out your way—learn to move around 'em*" (79). The text goes on: "But younger, the whole island was her playground: she'd walk through in a dry winter without snapping a single twig, disappear into the shadow of a summer cottonwood, flatten herself so close to the ground under a moss-covered rock shelf, folks started believing John-Paul's little girl became a spirit in the woods" (79). Miranda's intimate relationship with the natural world around her is a key factor in what allows her reconsiderations of what is or is not real.

DISPLACING THE "REAL"

Throughout *Mama Day*, there are numerous references to the notion of "realness" bandied about by various characters. The stacking up of ideas of what is or is not real is paired with a simultaneous tearing down of these same imaginative impulses. Naylor thus examines and critiques the substance of such categories. Particularly significant are the ways that place manifests itself as a meaningful part of the creations and dismantlings of constructs like Southern definitions of womanhood. Specifically, place dominates configurations and disintegrations of gender (especially womanhood and femininity), belief, and the relationship between race and socioeconomic status. Before discussing each of these in turn, one should consider how general notions of realness are maintained.

In New York and looking for work, Cocoa comments on how little she cares for the "phony" job applicants who share a lobby to wait for interviews: "I out-and-out resented the phonies, and when I could pick one out I felt a little better about myself. *At least I was being real*: I didn't have a job, and I wanted one—badly" (15, emphasis added). George appeals to a "real" Cocoa when he talks about how she changed upon traveling around New York with him: "And it had been loads of fun, watching you change. You weren't becoming different, you were going back to the way you were" (100). A very literal and strict understanding of what is or is not real is made manifest in the figure of George, the one-time tenant at a home for boys, where the mantra "Only the present has potential" was repeated. He represents a linear, Western worldview that celebrates pragmatism and hard work. Thus, George uses a fixed, no-nonsense approach to realness to understand the world and people around him. He employs this in his reception of Cocoa's stories about Willow Springs:

> New Orleans. Tampa. Miami. None of these cities seemed like the *real* South. Nothing like the place you came from. I was always in awe of the stories you told so easily about Willow Springs. To be born in a grandmother's house, to be able to walk and see where a great-grandfather and even great-great-grandfather was born. You had more than a family, you had a history. And I didn't even have a *real* last name. (129, emphasis added)

Significantly, George sees an easy correlation between place and familial history. The stories that he hears about Willow Springs are stories about

Cocoa's ancestry. George's identification and pursuit of the so-called real become even more intense as he negotiates new relational territory with Cocoa. Thus, the supernatural elements that operate in Willow Springs are extremely frustrating for him. When Cocoa falls ill and the two converge—his sense of realness in relation to Cocoa and Willow Springs's disruption of the same—Naylor offers realness, and thus the categories that it would construct and maintain, as a fluid and unsettled prospect. As George narrates his story, he tells Cocoa, "There were times when I tried too hard, pushing myself with the knowledge that I was all I had. And now you were all I had, and with you needing me, I had to hold on to what was real" (291). He identifies part of his problem as the fact that his "real" knowledge as an engineer does little for him in his efforts to make Cocoa better: "Why hadn't I studied medicine instead of a subject as useless as engineering science? What good was all that math and logic now?" (263). As George begins to understand more fully the extent to which his pragmatism and knowledge are ineffective in Willow Springs, he feels more and more thwarted by a society with which he is essentially at odds. He reflects on the death of Bernice's and Ambush's son, Little Caesar, during which the elements of place, realness, and sanity (or the lack thereof) intertwine for him: "It was frustrating sitting behind that steering wheel, trying to reconcile the sanity that would slip car keys over a visor to the insanity of carrying dead children into the woods without so much as a word from anyone, and not being able to throw you into the back and just drive us the hell away from there" (260). His instant reaction to the seemingly unreal circumstances and people surrounding him is to remove himself from that *place.*

With its reliance on thinking otherwise and trusting powers beyond the individual, Willow Springs disturbs—or at least recontextualizes—the concept of realness. People on the island still employ it as an idea, but its connotation is a much less specific one. Cocoa, for example, tries like George to work through her illness by tightening her grip on reality. This requires her attempt to reason through her hallucinations that show her a distortion of her "real" face in the mirror, confusing her sense of what is "really" there or not (275–77). She describes this need for a confirmed reality when she describes the hallucinations that did not allow her to see any of the welts on her body: "Where were the welts? Right there on my arms, shoulders, and chest when I looked down my body, but nowhere to be found when I took in my mirrored reflection. So the mirror was never to be trusted. Trust only your natural eyesight. Only what you literally see is real" (281).

Miranda is another unlikely figure to use the rhetoric of the real. Naylor uses this very irony to show the slippery nature of such tropes. When George attempts suspending disbelief and travels to the other place to receive instructions from Miranda, she wonders at his insistence that her words present only impossibilities. After Miranda tells George about the importance of family history to Cocoa's fate, he frowns and answers with a call for practicality: "I still don't see what you want me to do" (294). He says he can't understand what she's saying so far because of what he perceives to be her figurative worldview: "Well, you're talking in a lot of metaphor. But what it boils down to is that I can be of some use to you, and I came here for that. So, please, what is it, Miss Miranda?" (294). She thinks in response, "Metaphors. Like what they used in poetry and stuff. The stuff folks dreamed up when they was making a fantasy, while what she was talking about was *real*. As real as them young hands in front of her" (294). However, Miranda simultaneously questions George's insistence that there be a real or right way to save Cocoa. As she thinks about what is real, she understands that such a concept is a necessarily faulty one. She tells George that helping Cocoa is not a matter of finding the right way to go about doing so: "There are two ways anybody can go when they come to certain roads in life—ain't about a right way or a wrong way—just two ways. And here we getting down to my way or yours" (295). Finding one's "way," and the issue of "believing in oneself" rather than sustaining a belief in what is beyond the self, that which is not considered to be real, is at the heart of George's struggle. This problem with so-called realness, then, is how Naylor finds new ways to present an otherwise singular, categorical notion of belief.

Naylor uses Dr. Buzzard, who endures Miranda's consistent accusations against his "real" abilities to help people, to introduce the problems and potential of belief to George. When he tries to convince George to go to the other place and listen to Miranda's directions for how to help Cocoa, Dr. Buzzard begins, significantly, by admitting to Miranda's longtime critique and revealing himself as not a "real" conjuror and root worker: "Ya see, I've always been an old fraud" (292). He proceeds to critique the value George places in the notion of belief in oneself:

> That's where folks start, boy—not where they finish up. Yes, I said *boy*. 'Cause a man would have grown enough to know that really believing in himself means that he gotta be afraid to admit there's some things he just can't do alone. Ain't nobody asking you to believe in what Ruby done to Cocoa—but can you, at least, believe that you ain't the only one who'd

give their life to help her? . . . 'Cause if you can bring yourself to believe just that little bit, the walk you'll take to the other place won't be near as long as the walk back over to that vat of tar. (292)

Dr. Buzzard's emphasis here is one of rejecting absolutes—one sure way to cure Cocoa, one clear explanation of what happened to her, and so forth. His emphasis is further couched in a concern with place, as he tells George that going to the other place will not be as difficult a journey as the steps back to the tar he uses to rebuild the bridge. Cocoa presents a problematized notion of reality as well, referring George to the complicated narrative of their relationship: "Because what really happened to us, George? You see, that's what I mean—there are just too many sides to the whole story" (311).[14] This same interruption of the idea of one absolute or real story is what Naylor uses to disrupt the very categories that remain too singularly discussed in critical conversations of gender and race theory.

"REAL" WOMEN AND FAKE GENDER

The simultaneous construction and interrogation of realness translate to the reification and disruption of several societal categories. Naylor casts a notion of being a "real woman" or "real lady" in terms defined by a narrow stereotype of traditional Southern social conventions and gender roles. As she does this, however, she also critiques such a limited understanding. One way this happens is a consideration of the voices that project a vision of real womanhood and femininity. The first description of a woman in the text occurs in the form of Sapphira's bill of sale that prefaces the actual text. The details used to portray the woman for sale are telling, as they set up several stereotypes that repeat themselves centuries later in twentieth-century notions of blackness and womanhood. The allegations against Sapphira are as follows:

> All warranty against the vices and maladies prescribed by law do not hold forth; purchaser being in full knowledge—and affixing signature in witness thereof—that said Sapphira is half prime, inflicted with sullenness and entertains a bilious nature, having resisted reasonable chastisement the performance of field or domestic labour. Has served on occasion in the capacity of midwife and nurse, not without extreme mischief and suspicions of delving in witchcraft. (1)

The accusations leveled against Sapphira sound extremely similar to the critiques against Mary Prince that come to light in Pringle's supplementary material. In both cases, the men offering such descriptions appeal to a concern with character, especially as it takes the shape of obedience and deference. Thus, there is the emphasis on Sapphira's "sullenness and ... bilious nature" which keeps her from responding "appropriately" to "reasonable chastisement" and which makes her impervious to dictated tasks.

Miranda is a later example of Naylor's maintenance of gender stereotypes alongside progressiveness. She is one of the quickest to tell Cocoa how her gender should dictate certain behaviors, even though she is also a representation of a woman who "breaks the rules" in the ways that she exhibits her own gender identity (gives life without being a mother, pushes definitions of "power," etc.). For every word in the text that gives deference to the system of fixed gender roles, there are two about how to manipulate that very system. At one point, Cocoa "hear[s] [her] grandmother's gentle voice: Cocoa, a real lady never has to get mad—if she knows how to get even" (103). When Cocoa brings George to Willow Springs, she again muses on what she perceives to be the manipulative power of Southern women. She explains Miranda's and Abigail's view of how George should be handled:

> There was a soul ... to be saved with hard work. They were going to demand practically every minute of [his] day while [he] would think [he was] volunteering [his] butt off. When she puts her mind to it, no one can beat a southern woman at manipulating a man. And these women had been around long enough to take it to the level of art. (216)

Important here is that manipulation as a gendered behavior is cast as a characteristic particular or exclusive to Southern women. Also worthy of note is the sort of separatist rhetoric that would tout manipulation as a desirable gender trait. Naylor plays with this same essentialist form of heteronormative gendered contests through Miranda. When Cocoa and George fight in Willow Springs, Miranda tells Cocoa that reconciliation is the woman's responsibility: "And you oughta make the first move ... 'Cause we got more going for us than them. A good woman is worth two good men any day when she puts her mind to it. So the little bit we gotta give up, we don't miss half as much" (240). The faux condescension that would patronize or pander to men in order to mitigate power dichotomies is one that Naylor uses in order to interrogate the very gender dichotomy that would set up such an "us versus them" strategy in the first place.

Not unlike—as I discuss in the next chapter—the ways that Condé uses second-wave feminist rhetoric in *I, Tituba* to play on stereotypes of female empowerment, Naylor employs traditionally limiting notions of gender roles in order to show how those roles, especially as they are exhibited in the South, are not fixed ideas. She places these ideas into the mouths of women who defy them. Miranda, with no children or husband of her own, expects Cocoa to "find a man" and have children who "would be there for their old auntie" (203). Early in the novel, Miranda presents marriage as a simple matter of business to Cocoa, chastising her for seeming unable to find a husband in a place like New York: "Ain't no kinda sense, you living in a place with more men than the whole of Georgia and South Carolina combined, and can't take care of business" (35). Key here are Miranda's appeals to the "work" of marriage and the points of access available in different regions.

As she worries about Cocoa's relationships, Miranda presents a useful paradox that strays away from reductive gender roles even as it relies on them. When Cocoa fights with George in Willow Springs, Miranda mitigates her thoughts on Cocoa's strength with nods to a gendered vulnerability: "And not that any man—even if he tried—coulda ever soaked up the best in [Cocoa]. But who needed to wake up each morning cussing the day just to be sure you still had your voice? A woman shouldn't have to fight her man to be what she was; he should be fighting that battle for her" (203). She praises the notion of retaining voice but believes that a battle for voice is essentially a man's to fight. And, while she believes in Cocoa's strength, she still carries a general fear that women might "just fold up and melt away" (203). Women, here, are characterized as slight, frail things, subject to utter disappearance.

Cocoa, meanwhile, responds to such notions with sarcasm and frustration, often commingling gendered and geographical place. When she and George visit Willow Springs, they begin to fight over George's pseudo-serious idea of moving there. When Cocoa refuses outright and George feels betrayed, she responds, "Okay, George. This is what you want to hear: anywhere in the world you go and anything you want to do, I'm game. I'll freeze myself, starve myself, wear Salvation Army clothes to be by your side. I'll steal for you, lie for you, crawl on my hands and knees beside you. Because a good woman always follows her man" (221). She further rebels against a traditional rule of femininity by claiming, "Anything that gave me pleasure wasn't a waste of time" (58). With parallel moves, Cocoa sarcastically offers what she sees as the pedestrian female script of unthinking obedience to men and maintains a transparent claim to the value of her own pleasure.

George complicates a dichotomized configuration of gender roles as well, both repeating misogynistic epithets and sharing a seemingly liberating relational space with Cocoa. Like Tea Cake in *Their Eyes Were Watching God* and John Indian from *I, Tituba*, George is an ambivalent relational force—a devoted and loving partner who nonetheless reduces the woman he loves with rhetoric that universalizes women and stereotypes gender roles. After a fight with Cocoa, he resents how "complicated" women had made his life: "There I go, thinking about women again, and there was a time when I didn't have my whole world complicated with them. A wonderful time. Just dozens of boys. Clean fights. Straight talk. Order. You did what you were supposed to and left it at that. No tantrums. No nonsense" (247). He goes on to cast his frustration in terms of work, defending even the slave owner Bascombe Wade and finding camaraderie with him on a gendered level: "And your hard work was appreciated. Just look at that poor slob [Bascombe Wade] buried there—he gave [Sapphira] a whole island, and she still cut out on him" (247). George conflates linear systems of logic and maleness, and he even goes as far as to privilege his "male bond" with a slave owner, once again giving odd favor to whiteness as he does with his vision of playing "southern gentleman." Naylor, thus, employs a rhetoric of antebellum nostalgia even as she undercuts it with an emphasis on performativity. It is not a true or real paradigm; rather, it is something one *plays* at.

Meanwhile, George expresses his desire to know and understand the real Cocoa by speaking to the important relationship between place and personality. He tells her, "All I wanted was for you to be yourself. And I wondered if it was too late, if seven years in New York had been just enough for you to lose that, like you were trying to lose your southern accent" (33). He asks her to call him George because "There isn't a southerner alive who could bring that name in under two syllables. And for those brief seconds it allowed me to imagine you as you must have been: softer, slower—open" (33). George's idea of Cocoa's real self presents images of a stereotype of the antebellum South. In the moments when he glimpses Cocoa's "realness," "It conjured up images of jasmine-scented nights, warm biscuits and honey being brought to me on flowered china plates as you sat at my feet and rubbed your cheek against my knee" (33).

These visions are racialized in specific ways, of course. Again, Naylor mobilizes these stereotypes of (white) southern gender roles, including a wife actually sitting at his feet, in order to undermine them. Here we see a black man from the North imagining himself as a Southern plantation master, enjoying "jasmine-scented nights" and a loving, submissive wife—ideals that are inherently and problematically racialized.

Understanding that this portrait of the South is a contrivance, he explains, "I had never been south, and you couldn't count the times I had spent in Miami at the Super Bowl—that city was a humid and pastel New York. So I had the same myths about southern women that you did about northern men. But it was a fact that when you said my name, you became yourself" (33). George thus associates a sense of the real Cocoa with where she comes from. The stereotypes that he admits to having about the South receive, at least imaginatively, humored scorn from Cocoa, as he doesn't have a grasp on the "real" South. There are two notions of realness going back and forth here, both of which underscore the relationship between place and subject formation.

Gender stereotypes are further maintained and undercut through the figure of woman as trickster or conjuror. As discussed earlier in this chapter, this construct begins with Sapphira, whose bill of sale refers to her "bilious nature" and to "suspicions of [her] delving in witchcraft" (1). Her powers of persuasion allow her to convince a cruel slave owner to deed all the land in Willow Springs to the slaves, a feat achieved largely, it is implied, through her cunning. George's distrusting reductions of women modernize this characterization, translating it into his notions of the manipulative "tricks" women play on men.[15] He holds fast to the idea pervasive throughout the text that whatever one cannot "figure out" is a threat. As he remembers thinking soon after meeting Cocoa, "Don't get near a woman who has the power to turn your existence upside-down by simply running a hand up the back of her neck" (33). Accordingly, he responds in kind, with attempts at manipulating the perceived manipulator and generalizations along the way: "When women run around screaming that men lie to them, it's because we've learned that they want—or even need—to be lied to. They aren't programmed to accept the fact that in the beginning, sex is sex" (105).[16] Imposing ideas of trickery onto female sexuality is the tactic Junior Lee uses as well to explain his flirtations with Cocoa to the jealous Ruby. When Ruby sees the two talking at the party that Abigail and Miranda throw for Cocoa and George, Junior Lee says preemptively, "Baby . . . she tricked me out here" (241).

Significantly, Cocoa's perceived "tricks" are the impetus for Ruby's reciprocal hex that threatens Cocoa's life. Thus, trickery is a process, eliciting other magic as a response.

The obvious conjure woman in the text is Miranda, who maintains otherworldly powers despite her insistence that she will not work outside of "nature." Her position on the matter of how and when to use her abilities is another way that Naylor makes use of contradictory forces to undercut a would-be reductive characterization. As a conjure woman with little time for the charlatanism of Dr. Buzzard or for trying to work outside of natural courses, Miranda inhabits an otherwise difficult space in which there exist both Christian rhetoric and Afro-Caribbean spirit work. This space is an obviously difficult one for George's sensibilities to understand. George describes Miranda's cryptic response to his question of why she cuts off all of Cocoa's hair: "I was answered with a riddle. You have a choice, she said to me. I can tell you the truth, which you won't believe, or I can invent a lie, which you would. Which would you rather have? What a crazy old woman" (266). He associates the knowledge systems that he cannot adopt with the place that he cannot understand: "All of these people, with their convoluted reasoning, were starting to wear on me. As sick as you were, how dare she play these types of games? What I want, I said, getting up from that table, is some way to get my wife out of this godforsaken place as soon as I can" (266). He thus casts his priority of Cocoa's wellness in terms of geography. As Naylor shows George to be well-meaning but undeniably outside the norms and systems at work in Willow Springs, she contrasts his outsider status with strong communities of women.

Despite the seeming manipulations that accompany Naylor's presentation of her female characters, there are sustained threads of strong relationships between and among women. Naylor both reinforces and allays the otherwise facile and essentializing battle-of-the-sexes types of gender relationships with intimate communities of women. Even these are complicated, however, when these safe spaces of gendered familiarity become dangerous. When Ruby braids Cocoa's hair, an act of closeness grounded in ritual and comfort is also an act of harm, as Ruby uses Cocoa's hair to perform her hex.[17] In this moment, a seemingly "natural" response to what Ruby identifies as her competition is contextualized with a ritual that emphasizes community. Even when, in most instances, Naylor presents relationships between and among women as nurturing, ritual is still a key part of these collectives. When Cocoa is sick from Ruby's curse, she becomes a child again and rests in the comfort of a familiar domestic space as she lies in bed: "I was a little girl again and it was so nice . . . Are you feeling better, baby? Yes, call me baby again. You'll be the one to make the gray light disappear. To protect me from that strange man peering over your shoulder. He reached out to touch me and I shrank away. I begged her to make him leave me alone" (261). She rejects George here, preferring instead to maintain a space in which only the women in her life are allowed to come and go.[18] Domestic rituals turn familial in the more specific context of Miranda and Abigail. The bond between sisters relies on a call-and-response ritual, with Miranda leading, "You there, Sister?" and Abigail responding, "Uh, huh" (35).[19] Then, when the three women are together toward the end of the novel, Naylor gives them the context of the very ritualistic Candle Walk. Significantly, traveling together is what casts their bodies as unidentifiable, one from another: "It's the three of them under two umbrellas with Cocoa in the middle as they take the stretch toward the bridge junction. Bunched together, so it's hard to say who's holding who up when one stumbles in the fog" (307).[20] In this way, race and gender identity—especially as identified and negotiated by place—are signs that converge and that, just like the bodies of the three women, cannot be teased apart or distinguished.

SOUTHERN SPACES, WOMEN'S WORK

I have explained above several ways that Naylor complicates dialogues on gender roles, especially those linked to Southern constructions of femininity. The other level on which the text generates and then challenges traditional labels is that of work. Naylor casts labor in race- and gender-specific terms, simultaneously playing into and undercutting problematic assumptions. When Cocoa looks for a job in New York, she thinks of how easy the search must have been when job and housing listings were clearly marked "colored" or "white":

> You were spared a lot of legwork and headwork . . . I said as much at one of those parties . . . One of [the] certain people was so upset his voice shook: "You mean, you want to bring back segregation?" I looked at him like he was a fool—Where had it gone? I just wanted to bring the clarity about it back—it would save me a whole lot of subway tokens. (19)

In examples like this, Naylor chides pedantic ideals of progress that do not take into account material realities of raced and gendered subject positions. Reading women's work alongside George's concept of practical material economy reveals Naylor's ironic—and productive—use of limiting notions like "a woman's work" to complicate and make more productive dialogues of gendered labor.

There is a striking difference between the work done by women who stay in Willow Springs and those who do not. Sapphira's work is certainly that of a slave, but she nonetheless engages in the kind of duties that would constitute "benevolent labor." Her legend describes her as a healer, one who could bend the natural elements to her will in order to help others. Miranda, like her ancestor, works to heal and remedy with means that are distinctly outside the Western knowledge or comfort zone.[21] However, her talents earn the respect of the mainland doctor the people in Willow Springs call when they require "real" medicine: "Being an outsider, he couldn't be expected to believe the other things Miranda could do. But being a good doctor, he knew another one when he saw her" (84). Sapphira and Miranda both thus do "women's work," but they do so in a context that is removed from, albeit occasionally respected by, Western patriarchal power systems. Miranda, for instance, is a nurturing midwife even as she plays the roles of inseminator and creator—traditionally deeply masculinized abilities—when helping Bernice conceive her child.

Cocoa, however, once she leaves the island and crosses the bridge into the industrial giant of New York, takes a different approach to earning a living. She works nine-to-five office jobs, and it is her interview at George's firm that allows her to meet him. Once the two decide to get married, Cocoa both sets up and dispels stereotypes of women's work in relation to their new lives as wives: "And yes, I was quitting work. No, he wasn't forcing me. I was hardly the type to be chained to a stove barefoot and pregnant. I'd be starting school in the fall" (147–48). At one and the same time, Cocoa reduces women to a type and refuses to be likewise reduced. Similarly, she invokes traditional understandings of a wife's duties when she and George receive the quilt that Abigail and Miranda sew for them as a wedding gift: "After I unfolded the quilt . . . You wanted to clear a wall in the living room and hang it up. But it had been made to be used, and I also knew they hadn't gone through that kind of labor just for me. I ran my hands along the multicolored rings. They had sewed for *my* grandchildren to be conceived under this quilt" (147). Female domestic duties, particularly sewing and maternity, are at work here, paired with an emphasis on the need to put such forces to practical use. Naylor, then, puts into play notions of "a woman's work," a trope that is used over and over again in *Their Eyes* and *I, Tituba* and that is a key point of both validation and critique in the views surrounding Mary Prince's slave experience.

George's work is consumed by an obsession with performing well and being efficient. When people in Willow Springs talk about Cocoa's new husband, they misread his work as an engineer: "Hooked up with a city boy—a big-time railroad man . . . An engineer and all—owns his own train. Some argue back that an engineer only *runs* a train. But Miss Abigail says—and she should know—that the boy has his own business. What other kinda business would an engineer be into?" (132). Earlier, George explains to Cocoa what a mechanical engineer does when he tells her that his job is "to redesign the structures that take care of our basic needs: water supply, heating, air conditioning, transportation" (60). Cocoa's response rejects the Western ideal of professional stability: "Oh, and they make you go to college for that?" (60). Once he is in Willow Springs, work becomes his link back to the world of identifiable problems and fixed solutions that he understands.

When the hurricane destroys the tangible representation to his other, more rational life, he makes fixing the bridge a key priority. Prioritization quickly becomes obsession, and George expresses his need to fix the bridge in terms of frustration with place: "I was thinking that since my one hope for deliverance from the acute madness of this place . . . was in front of me, going up in smoke, I would do the only thing left for me to do: help work on that bridge" (286–87). Cocoa remembers his preoccupation with the bridge, noting, "Finishing the bridge. Finishing the bridge. A constant obsession when you left in the morning, coming back for lunch, and returned again in the evening. No one was working fast enough, no one was working long enough" (273). As George continues to think in terms of solution, he does so by considering place. He distinguishes Willow Springs from "the real world," and he is convinced that if only the bridge could be built just so far, he could "take a running jump over the gap, and . . . make it back to the real world and charter a boat, or demand that the Coast Guard come over and get [them]" (274). The bridge construction makes George also consider place in the sense of his own life: "watching them as my hands moved by rote, stroking the sides, stroking the bottom of the boiling vat, I thought of how I had lived beyond the bridge. I mean, all my life" (291). His problem with the project reveals his need for clear practicality: "The needless complications were driving me up a wall. When you have a job to do, you do it. You don't stand around, discoursing on the obvious" (274). As discussed earlier, the appeals to pragmatism and linearity are tied to a strong identification of masculinity for George. To his qualitative assessment of what needs done when a task presents itself—"you do [the job at hand]. You don't stand around," he might easily add, "you be a man."

When George wakes up early and goes for a walk around Willow Springs, his thoughts keep hold of this same sort of pragmatism, this time straying to a significant relationship between time and place. First remembering that, as a boy, he liked to study in the morning and breathe "unused air" so that he could keep his "brain cells from being dirtied up by everybody else's carbon dioxide," he noticed that whatever the type of air in Willow Springs, neither he nor his childhood friends "could even imagine an atmosphere like this" (185). As he walks, his narration emphasizes a primordial sense of place: "More than pure, [the atmosphere] was primal. Some of these trees had to have been here for almost two hundred years, and the saltwater feeding into the marshes dated back to eternity" (185). The importance placed on familial ancestry and pasts is paralleled within the place itself. The South is represented in terms of age and history—how the past helps to inform the present and predict the future. Importantly, his thoughts on space then immediately begin to include speculations as to what sorts of industry might help pump income into the island:

> A lot of this land and open space could be put to good use: nothing parasitic like resorts or vacation condominiums, but experimental stations for solar energy, marine conservation. I could even see small test sites for hydraulic power. It would bring much-needed income to the island, new people. A beating of wings and a high screech as a snow-tipped heron flew up from the marsh grass I stopped and shook my head—beautiful. But what kind of people? (185)

Interesting here is that distinctly Southern natural elements interrupt his intellectual practicality. Place takes precedence over his system of thought, but not for long. His immediate return to this train of thought, "But what kind of people," brings his focus back to what to *do* with a place rather than what to think about a place or how to experience a place. Here again we see the overarching functionalism that presides in his approach to work. Still, he registers a moment of desire to "straddle both worlds": "And they'd never give up this land to anyone but. They know that even well-meaning progress and paradise don't go hand in hand . . . If I'd followed Mrs. Jackson's philosophy, I could have straddled both worlds: Don't redesign water systems, she would have said, become a plumber"

(185). This kind of ambivalence is key to the way in which Naylor presents gender and work as ideas that are not at all "real" systems of identification.

"ANY CITY IS THE PEOPLE": PLACE AND IDENTITY

Mama Day is a text full of a productive ambiguity surrounding discourses of gender and work as framed within the context of racial identity and slavery. Naylor presents such ambiguity by way of the travels that take place throughout the text. Oddly, the final journey described in the novel is back to urban space, with Miranda and Cocoa traveling by train to New York to move Cocoa out of her apartment. It is the first time we see Miranda leaving Willow Springs, and she immediately tries to find out about the city by listening to the stories of the people who live there. She explains to Cocoa, "Any city is the people, ain't it?" (305). She also makes sure to explore the city while she's there. Cocoa tells George, "With all I had to worry about, there she was, wandering through the streets alone, dragging in shopping bags full of junk souvenirs from Woolworth's" (304). Miranda's approach to travel makes her feel an immediate affinity to New York, as she tells Cocoa, "New York [is] full of right nice folks" (305). Meanwhile, Cocoa maintains a vision of New York that is inextricable from her memories of George, making it "a relief to leave for good" (305).

Naylor closes *Mama Day* with a final Candle Walk—significantly, one in which tradition is tempered with improvisation when Cocoa wants to head back home from the walk down the main road. As Miranda suggests, "Tradition is fine, but you gotta know when to stop being a fool" (307). Even, or especially, here at the end of the text, Miranda rejects a "real" or "authentic" way to perform even the oldest and most traditional of rituals. Cocoa echoes this rejection when she thinks in overarching ways about her time with George in Willow Springs and about how to talk about George to her youngest son, who bears his namesake: "Mama Day was right—give him the simple truth. And it's the one truth about you that I hold on to. Because what really happened to us, George? You see, that's what I mean—there are just too many sides to the whole story" (311). Even as she speaks in terms of a "one [simple] truth," she cannot rest comfortably on an idea of "what *really* happened."

Their Eyes Were Watching God and *Mama Day* show Caribbean themes and images at work in an extended, transatlantic South. In the next chapter, I discuss Maryse Condé's *I, Tituba, Black Witch of Salem*, the English translation of which was published in the United States only four years after *Mama Day*.[22] With *I, Tituba*, my study travels back to the Caribbean, where Condé sets the story even as she frames it with an American historical context. In Mary Prince's *History*, we see British editorial interventions, and in *Their Eyes* Janie is shaped by Nanny's slavery ethos that sees gendered success as highly racialized—hence Nanny's desire for her granddaughter to be able to sit still on a porch and do nothing (her vision of white plantation mistresses). The presence of slavery in *Mama Day* comes in the legend of Sapphira Wade, which the community forms and reshapes according to its purposes. There remain traces of rhetorical and ideological privileging of whiteness, as evidenced by the conversation between George and Cocoa that goes back and forth with visions of him as a plantation master, and of her as his devoted mistress. While it is a productive shift that would place the slave history and narrative in the hands of the people rather than those in power, a real or authentic story of Sapphira's experience is rejected as a goal in the novel. *I, Tituba* attempts to put such a story squarely back in the hands of the slave to whom it belongs. Once again, there is a critical search for an authentic voice, and once again, this agenda is subverted by the very figure to whom this singular voice is said to belong. In every case, the seeming monolithic voice of a strong feminist worker that critics are quick to praise is a false construct, as evidenced by the displacements these women undergo that destabilize fixed notions of gender and labor.

4

"Recuperating" the Subject in *I, Tituba, Black Witch of Salem*

MARYSE CONDÉ'S *I, Tituba, Black Witch of Salem* brings the textual framework back to the Caribbean and back to a genre of slave narrative with a revision of the story surrounding Tituba, the slave who was the third person to be accused of witchcraft during the 1692–93 Salem witch trials. Like Mary Prince's narrative, which was subjected to ideological and editorial revision depending on who was characterizing Prince, the details of Tituba's story are fodder for historical and anthropological debate. She thus quite literally represents the rejection of sociohistorical and literary authenticity that I have traced throughout this book. Even her race remains in question. Condé sets her squarely within Barbados, even as the self-identifying title allows Salem to lay at least a contextual claim to her. Casting her home in the Caribbean, Condé locates Tituba in a nexus of creolization, inviting readings of racial ambiguity and ethnic hybridity. In this way, location "races" Tituba in significant ways, disallowing a singular or stable identification. Nonetheless, Tituba is classified as "Indian," with scholars like Elaine Breslaw specifically suggesting that she was an Arawak Indian. Other historical accounts refer to her as a "Spanish Indian," which then would have set her place of origin in the very contexts of *Their Eyes* and *Mama Day:* Florida, Georgia, and the Carolinas.[1] In the face of details about her life that are less than specific, these critical speculations make static claims to an authentic Tituba through a troublesome preoccupation with the character's racial classification. *I, Tituba* situates a narrative that was never able to be written and, in so doing, exemplifies the notion of history as inventions or fictions.[2] Accordingly, the many critical appeals to the authentic voice that Tituba exercises within the text are at best misplaced.

First published as *Moi, Tituba, sorcière . . . Noire de Salem* in 1986, the book was published in English translation in the United States in 1992. Combining fiction and first-person slave account, Condé offers Tituba's story as something of a mock slave narrative. As such, it resonates with the major strands of slavery, migration, labor, and oppression found in Mary Prince's narrative. It also presents Tituba's story through an authorial lens that plays a role not so dissimilar to that of Mary Prince's amanuensis, Susanna Strickland. Once again, we are able to see authorial agendas and emphases subtly manipulating the narrative that aims to recuperate a woman's experience. While Mary Prince's narrative is a traditional example of the slave narrative genre, written as a contemporary text of Afro-Caribbean slave experiences, Condé's is a fictionalized exercise in telling a similar story. In *Something Akin to Freedom,* Stephanie Li sustains a focus on "postbellum forms of bondage" and discusses the ways in which recent narratives render the repercussions of that trauma on women. In reference to the projects of writers like Gayl Jones and Toni Morrison, Li mentions Bernard W. Bell's term "neoslave narratives," which he applied in the 1980s to novels by African American writers dealing with contexts of slavery. She challenges the terminology, suggesting, "Although the neoslave narrative is now understood as a distinct literary form, I prefer Angelyn Mitchell's term 'liberatory narrative' to refer to 'a contemporary novel that engages the historical period of chattel slavery in order to provide new models of liberation by problematizing the concept of freedom'" (87–88). Li favors the term because, among other things, it emphasizes the ways that the narratives analyze freedom rather than merely describing the journey from enslavement to freedom. In a similar fashion, I find productive an analysis of how the migrations and displacements in Prince's *History* and Condé's *I, Tituba* shape the constructions of gender and labor identity. In the case of Tituba, migration frames her thoughts on womanhood, desire, and her work as a witch. Her choices and removals throughout the text, for example her decision to become a slave in order to marry John Indian, thus result in a certain emotional, as well as geographical, fluidity and flux.

As in the critical literature surrounding the books in my project, the issue of voice has maintained a significant place in scholarship dealing with Condé's text—Tituba's acquisition of voice, Tituba's voice in relation to Condé's, and/or Tituba's voice as representative of a larger collective of Caribbean women. Indeed, before even the foreword, Condé invites this by offering the following by way of explanation: "Tituba and I lived for a year on the closest of terms. During our endless conversations she told me things she had confided to nobody else" (v). As a pseudo slave narrative, made of such conversation rather than dictation, *I, Tituba* is thus not only Condé's critique ultimately of Puritan—that is, Anglo-American colonial—intolerance but also her attempt to resurrect awareness of the woman who allegedly confessed to practicing witchcraft in order to save her life. However, while some believe Condé to be fully yielding her own authority over the text and bestowing Tituba with a powerful sense of voice, Tituba's first-person subject position (as well as the agency literary critics typically associate with it) is consistently challenged, if not undercut, throughout the narrative by the very author inviting her to speak. Thus, even as the title itself is a definitive, what Angela Davis calls a "strong, self-affirming," assertion of her personhood—*I, Tituba*—Tituba's story does not hover in isolation as a simple, unfettered, or unstructured truth. That is, it is still very much "author-ized." And while this fact does not escape critics who have written on this text (certainly they understand the various strands of genre and authorship at work in the novel), their frequent appeals to the monolithic importance of the unique and authoritative voice that Tituba is thought to possess or inhabit suggest otherwise.

In the context of *I, Tituba*, I do not believe the challenge to Tituba's autonomy to be accidental, as if Condé wanted to rescue an authentic narrative for Tituba as a historical figure but could not help but to intersperse her own strands of contemporary social critique, intertextuality, and revisionism. On the contrary, I see *I, Tituba* as a possible way to reimagine the genre of the slave narrative and to rethink conventions of witchcraft and captivity. While the text purports to be a first-person account of the travails Tituba endures as a slave, relayed by a translator interested in presenting the narrative as a social critique, Condé interrogates categories even as she constructs them. Specifically, she simultaneously establishes and undermines a specific understanding of gender performativity with the second-wave feminist rhetoric that comes from the anachronistic Hester Prynne, with whom Tituba shares a prison cell. Furthermore, Condé uses conflicting definitions of "witch" to complicate notions of "a woman's work." Along with the obvious ways in which the term gets leveled against her, there is an internal sense of pride that Tituba enjoys in relation to her status as witch. When she passes Salem's residents attempting to divine the best uses for this or that herb, Tituba laughs to herself:

> Once or twice while wandering through the forest I met some of the villagers bending awkwardly over herbs and plants, their deceitful faces revealing the schemes in their hearts. I got great amusement from this. The art of doing evil is a complex one. If it is based on the knowledge of plants, this must be combined with the power to act on the unseen forces, which are rebellious by nature, transient as air, and need to be invoked. Not just anyone can set herself up as a witch! (67)

In this way, *I, Tituba* resonates with *Their Eyes Were Watching God* and *Mama Day*, making similar productive misuse of formations of gender roles and "a woman's work" that appear in those texts.[3]

I, Tituba also lends itself to comparative analyses—at least in the vein of interrogating categories of witchcraft and the supernatural in relation to performative spaces of race, gender, and work—with readings of the novel alongside those like Toni Morrison's *Sula* and *Song of Solomon*. In the former, one might look to Ajax's mother—a conjure woman of whom Sula reminds the elusive Ajax. In the latter, Pilate is worth noting as the goddesslike sister of Macon Dead Jr., born without a navel and read as a representation of the so-called mystical or divine. In the arena of critical analysis, Karen Fields and Barbara Fields provide a useful look at how inequality and ideology intersect to forge what they call "racecraft"—a term "highlight[ing] the ability of pre- or non-scientific modes of thought to hijack the minds of the scientifically literate" (5–6). In doing so, they offer a comparative study at one point in their book of racecraft and witchcraft, both relying on, to their way of seeing, a particular "invisible ontology." They effectively invert a common way of thinking such that, rather than seeing race giving rise to racism, we might think of racism as providing the cause for the subsequent effect of manufactured and illusory notions of race. In the course of Condé's novel, this is certainly the case. The actions surrounding Tituba's being interpreted as witch provide a foundation on which reflections on her race and gender are built.

In the sequence of the novel, after being tried for witchcraft, being imprisoned, and finally returning home to her island, Tituba thinks about her legacy and how her story will be remembered by history if it is at all. She asks about rather than affirms what will become her memory: "And what about me, is there a song for me? A song for Tituba?" (153). My examination of the conditions and limitations that Condé imposes on Tituba's "voice" follows the basic direction taken in my readings of Prince, Hurston, and Naylor. Specifically, Tituba's attachment to and removal from place serve to frame the novel in which Condé casts certain contextual formations of gender and labor. In this chapter, I look at the presentations of "home" as related to history and nation, relationships among women, sexuality, maternity, and the work of witchcraft in order to offer a more critical answer to the question of whether there is, as Condé puts it, a "song for Tituba." The appeals to home echo the way in which this trope appears in Naylor's *Mama Day* as a shifting, fluid entity with different definitions depending on one's considerations. With this in mind, while Condé ensures that there is a song *for* her, the proverbial tune should not be perceived as or conflated with a song *by* her, as some scholars would suggest. Indeed, regardless of the preposition, the "her" in relation to song is contingent, constructed only in and through discourse *about* her. After discussing what I perceive to be, consequently, generally narrow critical interpretations of Tituba's voice, I offer a brief analysis of Tituba's own imagined desire for more complicated tools to articulate meaning for what are otherwise inhibiting categories of identification. This desire is evident when one examines the geographical migrations through the novel. They show how Condé manipulates Tituba's voice in order to effect broader understandings of tropes like "home," "sexuality," "maternity," and "work"—understandings which ultimately critique the very meanings of freedom and autonomy.

Like much of the criticism surrounding the texts I have so far discussed in this book, critical readings of Condé's *I, Tituba* make appeals to voice and tout, occasionally cavalierly, what they see to be the broad implications of reading Tituba as a powerful, speaking subject. In her article "Giving a Voice to Tituba: The Death of the Author?" Elisabeth Mudimbé-Boyi investigates Tituba's voice in relation to Condé's and argues that Condé uses Tituba's narrative to tell the story of Caribbean women as a whole. She suggests that Condé willfully abdicates authorial authority: "In withdrawing to the unauthorial position of an interpreter and mediator, Condé ensures the *authenticity* of the character's voice" (753, emphasis mine). She later puts it another way: "In textualizing Tituba as an 'I,' a subject, the writer withdraws her own authority from the narrative" (753). The notion of authenticity, I suggest, is more complicated than what Mudimbé-Boyi allows.[4] She argues, "The authenticity of her voice is preserved thanks to specific narrative strategies implemented by Condé: self-effacement and subversion, interplay with the subject pronouns, and the creation of an autobiographical narrative" (754). Of course, Tituba is unable to access any sort of authenticity if doing so requires a commitment to realness or truth. Whether imagined or real, like Mary Prince, she has multiple degrees of separation from the voice that would tell her story.

In *Autobiographical Voices: Race, Gender, Self-Portraiture,* Françoise Lionnet offers a discussion of Hurston's *Dust Tracks on a Road* and Condé's *Heremakhonon*. Read alongside one another, the texts receive a useful rendering through Lionnet's lens of autobiography theory. She suggests that "Hurston and Condé are consumed by the need to find their past, to trace lineages that will empower them to live in the present, to rediscover the histories occluded by History" (25–26). That Hurston and Condé may have an expressed interest in projects of reclamation or rediscovery is not in itself the analytical *sine qua non* for discussions of diasporic women writers. More productive would be for scholars to ask what kind of work such rhetoric does for the authors and texts reproducing it. There is the tempting presumption to "allow" the texts—especially those written in first-person narrative voice—to "speak for themselves," to give one's analysis over to the presumed intentionality of the author. To that end, Lionnet says the following:

> I try to derive my interpretive strategies from the texts themselves rather than to adopt a single theoretical lens from the vast array of critical approaches available to the contemporary critic. This approach enables me to analyze the ways in which rhetorical structures produce meaning and to elucidate the process whereby text and context can ultimately be derived from the linguistic structures interacting on different levels of textual productions . . . I try never to impose a theoretical grid on the text; instead, I draw from it the means of theorizing its own process of production. (27–28)[5]

As enticing as it is to think of first-person narrative as allowing access to the memories and memoirs of a marginalized subject, Houston Baker in *The Journey Back* calls to our attention the simple but piercing question "How reliable are such [autobiographical] acts?" (27).[6] Citing some notable voices critical of autobiographical veracity,[7] Baker proceeds to launch an incisive examination of just how precarious the particularities of first-person narration proved for slave voices. Using Frederick Douglass's *Narrative* as an example, Baker notes, "the nature of the autobiographer's situation seemed to force him to move to a public version of the self—one molded by the values of white America" (39). The appeal to a close consideration of text *as* context (rather than "and" context, as if they exist as separate entities) here is key.

The contextual framework at work in the novel—namely Tituba's migrations to and from her homeland—is what challenges appeals to authenticity at every turn. While much of the criticism on Condé's work pays a great deal of attention to the symbolism and importance of the Caribbean as a cultural context, relatively little time is spent on the geographical specificity and uniqueness of migrations in her novels. One notable exception is Mildred Mortimer's "A Sense of Place and Space in Maryse Condé's *Les derniers rois mages*." In her essay, Mortimer uses Condé's 1992 novel *Les derniers rois mages* (*The Last Magi*) to examine what she suggests is a key element of Caribbean literature, namely "a tension between place and space, rootedness and freedom" (758).[8] Mortimer rightly distinguishes between the two terms "place" and "space," which, she notes, are "often used interchangeably" (758). Interesting in relation to *I, Tituba* is the tension to which Mortimer refers, although the text does not offer so easy a binary as place/space. "Rootedness and freedom," to use Mortimer's terms, are not so isolated as they might seem. She is right to caution against quick conflation of "place" and "space"; however, these do not so easily or predictably transfer to power relations and differentiations such that "place" equals stability or "rootedness" and "space" equals liberation. The Caribbean presents complex layers of history and memory, of slavery and postcolonial imagination. As Françoise Lionnet contends in *Postcolonial Representations: Women, Literature, Identity,* Caribbean narratives by women often obscure the boundary between "self" and "other" through a serious handling of *métissage,* or cultural interchange and mixing. It is these layers, especially as they manipulate constructs of gender and labor—Tituba's womanhood and sexuality alongside her work as a witch—that offer opportunities to rethink the role of displacement that leaves Tituba, as well as the women in the other narratives discussed in this project, neither rooted nor free.

Interesting to the specific production and reception of *I, Tituba,* the travels in the text mirror the travels *of* the text. Like the societal influences and cultural context that shaped Prince's narrative, various editions of *I, Tituba* were published in different places with their own cultural agendas. Starting out in France within the genre of *histoire Romanesque* and its attendant white female readership, it landed in the hands of American readers as a narrative of feminist and racial redemption—a recuperated story of an oppressed woman reclaiming her voice.[9] Thus, Tituba's story, like Prince's (and, indeed, like any literary work), is not immune to the publication and production concerns of her editors. Lillian Manzor-Coats, in "Of Witches and Other Things: Maryse Condé's Challenges to Feminist Discourse," rightly parallels Tituba's travels with those of the text:

> If Tituba's travels from Barbados to New England are part of the history of slavery and colonialism in the Americas, the travels of Condé's Tituba from the author's native Guadeloupe to France . . . and now to the United States with the English translation are also symptomatic of a colonial and neocolonial history in the twentieth century. (738)

Such comparisons and implications are more productive to feminist and postcolonial inquiries than are analyses that would simply perpetuate an insistence on the importance of voice in its own right.

Mudimbé-Boyi argues that Condé grants Tituba a voice merely by allowing her to "tell her story in her own words" (751). This definition of an independent voice that identifies it solely on the basis of the ability to tell a story seems problematic. So, too, does the notion that "Tituba unfolds a long monologic 'conversation' in which the writer becomes the simple listener of a narrating subject telling her own life story" (Mudimbé-Boyi 752). Mudimbé-Boyi argues that Condé "has completely disappeared," but I see her presence, especially as she frames the story ideologically, as remaining prominent throughout the text (752). This seems especially the case when considering Condé's own words. Manzor-Coats cites one of Condé's interviews in which she explains that she did not set out to write a "historical novel." Condé says of the persona she creates, "I was not interested at all in what her real life could have been . . . I really invented Tituba. I gave her a childhood, an adolescence, an old age. At the same time I wanted to turn Tituba into a sort of female hero, an epic heroine, like the legendary 'Nanny of the maroons'" (qtd. in Manzor-Coats 738). Condé thus presents herself as a creator with an agenda and Tituba as a creation of this agenda.[10] Any notion of Tituba's voice, therefore, needs to take this authorial presentation and inevitably laden readership into account. This is not to say, of course, that the constructed Tituba is inconsequential. I am not suggesting that the artifice of Tituba's presence as a self renders a sense of voice entirely absent. In fact, I agree with Manzor-Coats, who says that Tituba's first-person narration "destabiliz[es] Condé's own authorial position" (737). Condé, then, is simultaneously present and destabilized, just as Tituba is both a speaking subject and a speaker subjected to decisive agendas and ideologies outside her narrative. Thus, the conversation between Tituba and Condé is more a dialogic experience than the monologic kind that Mudimbé-Boyi presents.

On the further extreme of a "sole" narrator, criticism of *I, Tituba* also often speaks to what scholars see as the broader cultural implications of the text. Mudimbé-Boyi argues that Condé's protagonist "is certainly speaking of herself, but her narrative also tells the story of many other black women who, like her, have been relegated to the margins of history, if not erased from it, reduced to invisibility and silence" (753). According to such an analysis, "Tituba, in reconstructing one individual's story, also allegorizes the collective history of the Caribbean" (755). However, I read Tituba's story as a much more intricate quest of individualized meaning-making. Throughout the novel, she dwells in paradox and contradiction as she searches for ways to interpret subjective experiences outside categorical fixity. My reading departs from a postmodern analysis that would focus solely and simply on the blurring of historical narrative and fiction or on the hybrid constitution of the character Tituba inasmuch as my discussion attempts to cast doubt on an approach that would suggest a knowable "Tituba" in the first place. Any effort to place "her"—geographically, ethnically, or otherwise—is an immediately flawed and even impossible endeavor.

Tituba herself makes her desire for a complex assessment of her own story most apparent on her trip back to Barbados after leaving America and the events in Salem. On the ship returning to Barbados, the sailor Deodatus approaches Tituba and at once confronts and conflates her with her familial history: "They tell me your name is Tituba. Aren't you the daughter of Abena, who killed a white man?" (136). While she worries that histories of the witch trials will recall her merely as "a slave originating from the West Indies and probably practicing 'hoodoo,'" she casts in contradistinction Western historical apparatuses and what seems to her the Caribbean people's ironic penchant for remembering (110). She intimates, "Having someone recognize me after ten years of absence brought tears to my eyes. I had forgotten this ability our people have of remembering. Nothing escapes them! Everything is engraved in their memory!" (136). Upon affirming her name, the sailor sympathetically tells her, "I hear they gave you a difficult time over there" (137). His strange knowledge causes Tituba to "burst into tears," and he tries to soothe her by saying, "You're alive, Tituba. That's all that matters" (137). This is an echo of the sentiments of John Indian, that "the duty of a slave is to survive" (22) and that "the important thing is to survive" (92). It also reiterates what Tituba recalls from Mama Yaya, that "what matters is to survive" (136). She reacts strongly to Deodatus: "I shook my head violently. No, it wasn't all that mattered. Life, life had to be given a new meaning. But how?" (137). Rejecting the philosophy of staying alive at any cost, Tituba looks to reinterpret and reconfigure the systems surrounding her rather than merely dwelling within them.

As Deodatus comforts Tituba with folklore, telling her "why the sky moved away from the land" and "why the palm tree is the king of trees," Tituba feels that "exile, suffering, and sickness had combined in such a way as to make me almost forget these simple stories" (137). Thus, the inherent complexity of Tituba's circumstance is one that disallows a chance for her to apply easy interpretations to narratives. The "new meaning," then, that must be given to life is, for her, one that necessitates questioning and revising systems that would impose specificity or linearity. Thus, the presumed voice throughout the text, whether it belongs more to Tituba or, more likely the case, to Condé, recurrently focuses on reconstituting new definitions for signs in light of the old—often narrow—interpretations. It is a voice that goes about the business of finding new meanings, attempting to impose ambiguity onto fixed spaces and allow for more options in considering ideas like "witch," "work," "home," "sexuality," and "woman." Thus Condé embarks on a critical and revisionist project in her novel by complicating Tituba's relationship to Barbados, by giving meaning—through a sustained inquiry into sexuality and a series of strong ties to other women—to an otherwise abject body, and by attempting to redefine witchcraft in terms of distinctive (and distinctively gendered) labor.

The work that Condé does with signs of gender and labor is situated in Tituba's travels away from and back to her home in Barbados. Perhaps it is not surprising, then, that Condé plays with the pedestrian uses of complex notions related to place—notions like "history" and "diaspora"—and infuses productive ambiguity into each. There are several kinds of history operating in Condé's project as the author and in Tituba's own journey. First, there is the literal, documented sort of history that Condé uses as an impetus for writing the novel in the first place and for recuperating a story lost to the holes left in historical accounts, whether these holes are the result of deliberate intent or of more systemic privilege and power. Second, there is the hypothetical (or future tense of one's) history, of how one *will* be remembered once one's own story becomes a part of history. This is the type to which Tituba refers in her skepticism surrounding the question of what part, if any, she will play in the history that is yet to be written. Alongside this anxiety is a third presentation of history that Condé uses to deal in broader terms with the notion of a history of a people. While I am not convinced that Tituba's story is somehow representative of an entire collective of Caribbean women (and why should it be?), Condé does impart a particular interest in what it means to explore the personal and individual narrative of someone whose history is necessarily freighted with a shared experience of oppression and forced migration. By adding layers of complexity to a term like "witch," Condé demonstrates how words like "history" and "diaspora" should also be rethought in order to give a fuller account of those whom these ideas marginalize.

In an interview published in the afterword of *I, Tituba,* Condé tells Ann Armstrong Scarboro that "history" for people of the African diaspora is a difficult term in its traditional Anglo-European singularity. The focus of black history, she argues, is not only myopic but also troublingly and inextricably linked to colonialism and slavery (to maintain contextual solidarity, I include her full statement):

> As I said, for a black person, history is a challenge because a black person is supposed not to have any history except the colonial one. We hardly know what happened to our people before the time when they met the Europeans who decided to give them what they call civilization. For a black person from the West or from Africa, whatever, for somebody from the diaspora, I repeat it is a kind of challenge to find out exactly what was there before. It is not history for the sake of history. It is searching for one's self, searching for one's identity, searching for one's origin in order to better understand oneself. (203–4)

Condé is rightly critical of the dominant ideology that traces black history to slavery and colonization. However, this critique is easily problematic in itself. If we take Condé's version to its logical end, we are still left with the question of what part colonization indeed should play in thinking about black history. There cannot merely be a quick and quiet erasure of the power structures put in place that subsequently shaped generations. While this does not seem entirely to be what Condé is suggesting, the problem of diasporic history she presents here is an important point to consider. This is why—far from merely a clever comparative analysis—it is productive on the level of theory to include discussions of figures like Mary Prince and Tituba alongside Janie Crawford and other "troublesome" characters. These women engage in discursive alternatives to the problem that Condé presents. The traversal of eras and genres, the commingling of history and fiction, and the negotiations of different geographical spaces allow for a way to both engage and move beyond the theoretical singularity inherent in reducing discussions of black history and diaspora to colonization and slavery. Thus, colonial terms prove too narrow. More layers need to be engaged in an attempt to approach and understand a "history."

As Tituba mulls over her complex relationship to both her personal and contextual histories, she constructs an understanding of herself through a sustained consideration of her national identity, at least inasmuch as such an identity would be constructed during the seventeenth century. "History" thus begins to converge with an understanding of "home," offering place and movement as key reference points in a reading of her narrative. Her own persona is transmogrified into the characteristics of Barbados, manifesting itself as the island of its origin. In this way, she is like Miranda Day, who, as mentioned in the last chapter, becomes a very tangible part of the woods in Willow Springs.[11] This interrelation between Tituba and her home is ultimately what allows her to believe that there is in fact a song for her, a positive remembrance of who she was and a legacy that she can appreciate. In the epilogue, she celebrates this inversion of island and identity through her daughter:

> For this child of mine has learned to recognize my presence in the twitching of an animal's coat, the crackling of a fire between four stones, the rainbow-hued babbling of the river, and the sound of the wind as it whistles through the great trees on the hills. (179)

Before she is able to actualize her legacy as a living presence in and through the island, Tituba ponders the meanings of the very notions of country and home. First, she contemplates the way in which one's country makes itself part of one's sense of self. She thinks of this idea especially in relation to migration and removal: "How strange it is, this love of our own country. We carry it in us like our blood and vital organs. We only need to be separated from our native land to feel a pain that never loses its grip welling up inside us" (48). Here, one's country is not only a place of departure and return but also an anthropomorphized physical presence. Comparing it to "blood and vital organs," Tituba, furthermore, understands it as the necessary inner workings of the body that carries it. Upon arrival back in "her country," however, Tituba encounters a more particular concern of "home." As soon as Tituba returns to Barbados, she finds herself mourning the loss of her relationship with John Indian. The spirit of Abena reprimands her daughter's preoccupation with "that wretch" and tells her to "go home" (142). Tituba immediately launches into yet another linguistic quandary: "Home! There was a cruel irony in this word. Apart from a handful of dead people, nobody was waiting for me on this island and I didn't even know whether the cabin I had squatted in ten years earlier was still standing" (142). At work here is what she calls an "irony" that results from the dissonance between the definition of "home" she maintains imaginatively—one that offers close relationships and a sense of origins—and the home she actually encounters. A fixed definition does not stand in the text.

Thus, Tituba's first day back in Barbados is full of the multiple ambiguities that Condé presents in order to unhinge singular constructions of nation and homeland. Present are both this ambiguity and a conflation of terms. As tropes become more slippery, "nature" and "man" become directly proportional in their benevolence and wrath. And Tituba positions this realization against the backdrop of her travels—in this instance, her being back home again. She thinks, "Yes, nature changes her language according to the land, and curiously, her language harmonizes with that of man. Savage nature, savage men! Protecting, well-meaning nature, openhearted and generous men! My first night on my island!" (147). Tituba accordingly juxtaposes the seeming duplicity of men with the return to the island, onto which she imposes a possessive pronoun. Thus, on the first night back on what she considers to be *her* island, she muses about the ambiguity swirling within the midst of both nature and men. Here again we see, through Tituba's supposed voice, Condé's commingling of place and gender foregrounded by Tituba's migration.

Tituba's migrations have much to say and show about her relationships with others. Lawrence R. Rodgers asks in *Canaan Bound,* "How have migrants forged and retained human relations?" (4). This question is key in my own study of migration literature; however, my focus lies more specifically on the relationships between (or among communities of) women to show a particularly gendered expression of relational solidarity in the midst of regional flux. In the context of Condé's novel, although Tituba is "too fond of love" with men, she nonetheless remains emotionally linked to Mama Yaya, Abena, and Hester Prynne (101). She even forms short-lived but strong relationships with the wives of her masters, Elizabeth Parris and, on an arguably more tenuous level, Benjamin's wife, Abigail.

On the boat to America, Tituba and Elizabeth Parris fashion an unlikely bond. Significantly, much of their affinity for one another is a result of their conversation on gender and sexuality. However, alongside these intimations of the pains suffered by women is Elizabeth's initial appreciation of Tituba's journey: "So you're Tituba? How cruel it must be to be separated from your own family. From your father, your mother, and your people" (38). The narrative fusion of geographical and gendered flux is one that complicates the otherwise simple relationship between mistress and slave. While there is an impassable distance between them racially and economically, there is a closeness that they appreciate on the level of being women. Seeing that Elizabeth is not well, Tituba asks her from what ailment she suffers. Elizabeth explains with a litany of profoundly gendered hardships: "All I know is that my life is a martyrdom . . . I am taken with nausea as if I were pregnant, whereas Heaven has seen fit to grace me with only one child. Sometimes unbearable pains stab my stomach. My menstruation is a torture and my feet are constantly like two blocks of ice" (38). Then, motioning for Tituba to sit, Elizabeth tells her, "How lovely you are, Tituba" (38). The idea of not understanding one's condition, as Mary Prince iterates, is important here. She "unbelievingly" mutters "Lovely?" and as soon as a physicality is assigned to her, as a condition is spoken into existence, loyalty is prompted out of Tituba (39). She entreats, "Mistress, let me take care of you!" (39). Interestingly, Elizabeth's trust is cast in terms of Tituba's physicality, specifically (and notably), her skin. She answers Tituba's request by saying, "So many others have tried before you and have failed. But your hands are so soft. As soft as cut flowers" (39). Tituba's reaction is of racialized hesitation: "Have you ever seen black flowers?" (39). It is this seeming contradiction in terms that Elizabeth believes Tituba to inhabit: "No, but if they existed they would be like your hands" (39). Thus Tituba's physicality, like her national/familial history and labor, is just as indeterminate as it is important. It is a piece of her subjectivity that is describable only when using a paradox. In this way, studying migration helps us think about women who occupy multiple spheres of identity.

In startling fictive counterpart, Condé introduces the unlikely presence of Hester Prynne in Tituba's New England prison cell. This moment of cross-textual communication, while seemingly a clever opportunity to play with historical and literary figures of the era in a bit of authorial indulgence, offers important considerations of the dynamic created between the two. Upon meeting Hester, Tituba again confronts issues of race and status through a gendered camaraderie.[12] Hester's first observation that she notes aloud when she sees Tituba is "What a magnificent color she's got for her skin" (95). Tituba replies as Hester cares for her wounds with an appeal to her supposed station, as she is expected to do with Elizabeth: "Mistress . . ." (95). Hester immediately chastises her for such a distinction and appeals instead to their gendered connection. When she learns that Tituba's father named her, she launches into an essentialist feminist critique: "Her lip curled up in irritation . . . 'You accepted the name a man gave you?'" (96). Condé is present again here in her play on this anachronistic brand of politicized feminist rhetoric. Hester aligns herself with Tituba not only as a woman but also as a societal pariah, denouncing her community and asking, "Aren't I an outcast like yourself?" (96). Conversations on gender traverse conversations of sociopolitical place here, and they invite more space for other category expansions.

Just as quickly as Condé establishes allegiances between the two women, she presents another relationship to complicate meaning—that between physicality and goodness. Like Elizabeth Parris's sentiment that Tituba may be successful in taking care of her by virtue of her soft skin, Hester holds Tituba's face and exclaims, "You cannot have done evil, Tituba! I am sure of that, you're too lovely!" (96). Tituba, again moved like she was at Elizabeth's expression of her loveliness, is "bold enough to caress her face" and call her "lovely" too (96). Hester later serves as an impetus for Tituba to consider a more complex meaning of sexuality, one that does not restrict itself to receiving pleasure solely from men. When Hester lies down next to her one night, Tituba holds her and is surprised as "a feeling of pleasure slowly flooded over [her]" (122). She wonders, "Can you feel pleasure from hugging a body similar to your own? For me, pleasure had always been in the shape of another body whose hollows fitted my curves and whose swellings nestled in the tender flatlands of my flesh. Was Hester showing me another kind of bodily pleasure?" (122). Especially in her physical self-awareness, referencing "the tender flatlands of my flesh" feeling a "flood[ing]" pleasure, her description of this same-sex intimacy sounds much like her encounters with John Indian. However, the self-reflection comes in this case from thinking of how Hester's body matched her own, how her "hollows fitted my curves." The rest of her relationships depict, in albeit different ways, Tituba as a desiring subject but also a necessarily exoticized sexual object. Indeed, her body is the very condition of trade later in the text with a maroon leader in Barbados. Further, when she has a nightmare about being raped, her husband and master have the same identification as sexual assailant. While her encounters with several partners throughout the text can be read as a privilege of her sexual liberation, they do not escape a problematic conflation of race and sexual prowess. In prison with Hester, in a moment of desire and pleasure between two women, Condé introduces a more intricate way to think about corporeal pleasure, a way that disrupts what is otherwise a stereotype of exoticized hyperactive sexuality in heteronormative contexts.[13]

As a fictional literary text, *I, Tituba* offers similar questions of truth and difference by navigating the relationship between corporeality and identity. In "A Narrative of Violated Maternity," Mara L. Dukats states that the novel "is much more than the life of an individual": "Like any autobiographical account, it is indicative of ways in which identity is socially constructed; but it also illustrates ways in which the historically marginalized might articulate a vision of self . . . Tituba's story is imbued with ambiguity" (747). Tituba's so-called voice, then, is spoken out of contradictions and ambiguities that resist a clear understanding of truth.[14] This is quickly apparent when one looks at the ways in which Condé presents sexuality in the text. Like in Prince's *History*, migrations serve to inform and interrogate the meanings and contexts of sexuality in Tituba's narrative. Her story begins with her mother's rape at the hands of a white man, thus introducing sexuality as an immediate and volatile component of her identity formation. However, as Manzor-Coats points out, such an introduction cannot be glossed over in broad feminist or racialized terms. She argues that the rape should be read neither as a "foundational act in women's lives" nor as "a metaphor for the rape of Africa under colonialism" (739). For Manzor-Coats, the beginning of the narrative comes back to the issue of voice: "What we have in the first lines of *Moi, Tituba* is Tituba's voice speaking to us, telling us about her mother's rape. This telling aspect forces us to see this act of rape as a question of language and subjectivity" (739).

This reading of voice, unlike those that would relegate the notion to a limited definition of authenticity or tout it as a representative of all Caribbean women, is productive in what it offers as the disruptive possibilities of voice. Manzor-Coats suggests, "When rape is seen in this fashion, there is the liberating possibility that women will not play their role right, will actually refuse to play the role of subjects of fear and thus thwart the rape attempt" (740). By "not playing their role right," women reject "the grammar of violence" that would tether gender and sexuality to violence (740). Condé thus presents Tituba outside an identifiable or categorical set of gender roles. Perpetual travels provide a fitting context for such a presentation, as Tituba never remains in a fixed subject position that would allow her, again remembering Mary Prince, to "understand rightly her condition."[15]

Tituba's quest to understand and fully experience her own sexuality is maintained throughout the novel in her tempestuous relationships with men. John Indian sparks her initial interest in her own body when he tells her "You could be lovely if you wanted to" (13). When she considers his words, Tituba begins questioning the condition of her physicality: "Up until now I had never thought about my body. Was I beautiful? Was I ugly? I had no idea. What had he said? 'You know, you could be lovely'" (15). On a corporeal level, Tituba again expresses the same sentiment as Mary Prince—that she did not "understand rightly [her] condition." The question of her physical ontology—"Was I beautiful? Was I ugly?"—results in a brief but telling masturbation scene:

> I took off my clothes, lay down, and let my hand stray over my body. It seemed to me that these curves and protuberances were harmonious. As I neared my pudenda, it seemed it was no longer me but John Indian who was caressing me. Out of the depths of my body gushed a pungent tidal wave that flooded my thighs. (15)

This moment offers a couple of interesting considerations. First, Tituba at once considers her body to be "harmonious," and her specific physical contours are immediately celebrated.

Second, however, the imagined presence of John Indian is a significant abdication of personalized physical pleasure.[16] In other words, he plays the role of a sort of benefactor of her sexual excitement that does not exist in its own right apart from his bestowing it. It is ultimately, in the sequence of the text, John Indian who causes her to climax. She is, thus, able to explore her own body in new and valuable ways at the same time that she becomes further tied to John Indian. She is at once belonging to herself and not her own. It becomes, after all, no longer herself but John Indian who caresses her body. Manzor-Coats rightly shows ambivalence working, too, in the conflict between freedom and sexual desire: "Tituba is fully aware of the contradictions her choices entail. That is, she knows that her desire to be a free woman and her desire to be in control of her sexuality are incompatible" (742). Tituba, thus, *chooses* to leave her freedom and become a slave again in order to be with him. This paradox travels with Tituba throughout the text, later manifesting itself in her telling

Benjamin Cohen she "does not want [his] freedom" when he tells her she can go home (134). Later, she states it another way, this time with another bit of irony but in terms that she knows would anger Hester: "some men who have the virtue of being weak instill in us the desire to be a slave!" (140).

The nod that Tituba makes above to how Hester might react to her missing her master and lover points to the general role that women play as sources of advice and critique in the text. The women in Tituba's life chastise her for being ruled by her desires, which they find especially dangerous in relation to men. For Hester Prynne, Tituba's romantic impulses threaten her politics. She tells her, "You're too fond of love, Tituba! I'll never make a feminist out of you!" (101). "Feminism" here is obviously a narrowly defined term with its own essentialist rejection of emotionalism—what it would identify as women's internalized oppression. Abena similarly links female empowerment to the erasure of men. Thus she appears, unsolicited, to offer a joint concern of sexuality and migration: "Why can't women do without men? . . . Now you're going to be dragged off to the other side of the water" (15). Tituba stops her there: "To the other side of the water?" but Abena merely replies, "in a distressed voice": "Why can't women do without men?" (16). The voices of Hester and Abena resonate with Tituba when she later asks, in the servitude of Benjamin Cohen d'Azevedo, "Why must any relationship with the slightest hint of affection between a man and a woman necessarily end up in bed?" (126). As she finds herself in the position of "being both mistress and servant," though, she is still able to complicate even this "odd situation" with feelings of sexual pleasure (127). While she cannot help but compare Benjamin's "crooked, pasty body" with John Indian's "dark-brown muscles," she is still able to "pitc[h] and heav[e] just as well on the sea of delight with [her] misshapen lover" (127). Condé actively pursues here the tension between corporeal pleasure and hierarchical gender dynamics. Tituba is aware of the problematics of serving both as slave and mistress, yet she nonetheless celebrates the physical pleasure the relationship affords.

Tituba again inhabits a similar contradiction back in Barbados, where she becomes the lover of Christopher, the maroon leader.[17] She understands that he is manipulating her, trading sex for the invincibility he believes her magic will provide him. However, she explains her willing flirtations in ironically antifeminist terms: "I had not lost that deep instinct that makes me a woman" (145). Condé mitigates the incongruities of Tituba's sexual desires and roles with Christopher's myopia. When

Tituba attempts to break out of what is, in Christopher's view, a singular sexual utility and to be productive on a political level, she suggests that she be allowed to join the maroon's struggle and fight alongside him. He laughs at her and responds, "Fight? You're going too fast. A woman's duty, Tituba, is not to fight or make war, but to make love!" (151). This attempt to tether women to a particular notion of sexuality and feminine duty is what Tituba must struggle to challenge and rearticulate for herself, often by occupying several gendered roles at once.

This is the case when Tituba is again confronted with her own contradictions as she embarks on a relationship with Iphigene. After Tituba makes her home again in Barbados and joins the maroons, Iphigene is brought to her by other slaves after being whipped and left for dead. As she continues to care for him, she believes herself to be performing the symbolic role of a maternal figure. She tells him, "I was once pregnant and I had to do away with the baby. It seems to me you have come back in its place" (166). Thus, when Iphigene presents himself as a sexual partner, the functions of mother and lover become conflated, so much so that Tituba is initially horrified: "I was ashamed of offering up my old age to his caresses and I almost pushed him away for I had the absurd feeling of committing incest" (169). As with her initial hesitation with Benjamin, however, she stifles her protest as "his desire became contagious" (169). Much of her interest and focus, however, remains allied with the maternal role that she still hopes to fill even as she complicates it.

Condé offers motherhood as a particularly difficult prospect for Tituba throughout the text in terms of the relationship between sexuality and gender. When she realizes she is pregnant in Boston, Tituba notes, "There is no happiness in motherhood for a slave. It is little more than the expulsion of an innocent baby, who will have no chance to change its fate, into a world of slavery and abjection" (50). Her sentiment is reminiscent of the anxiety surrounding maternity in Harriett Jacobs's narrative. In her essay "A Narrative of Violated Maternity: *Moi, Tituba, sorcière . . . Noire de Salem*," Mara L. Dukats examines the ways in which slavery violently manipulated maternity to its own pragmatic ends of property. She uses Morrison's *Beloved* as an example of attempted reclamation of "the intersubjective bonds between mother and child," suggesting that "the only way that Sethe can preserve all this is to become the agent of the death of her child" (746). She goes on to argue, "Infanticide thus becomes a sacrificial act, the expression of Sethe's maternal responsibility" (746).[18] This is not the experience for Tituba, however. The ambivalence of both her feelings on maternity and her feminist strands is again present as she states, "I had trouble getting over the murder of my child" (Condé 52). In an act of attempted maternal redemption, Tituba gives the very ill Betsey a "magic bath," "plung[ing] her up to her neck in a liquid to which [Tituba] had given all the properties of amniotic fluid" (63). Replicating a birth moment, she recuperates a lost sense of positive maternity: "Plunging Betsey into this scalding hot bath, it seemed to me that these same hands, that not long ago had dealt death were now giving life, and I was purifying myself of the murder of my child" (63). Significantly, this mock birthing scene is what instigates the questions/craze over Tituba's witchcraft, escorting her into social critique and condemnation. Maternity, again, turns dangerous in the context of slavery.

There is a second incident in which Tituba attempts to recreate the life that she takes. Living with the maroons, Tituba saves a baby who "was hardly out of her mother's womb" (152). As the moments of birth and death begin to converge, Tituba "h[olds] the little thing back" from "stepp[ing] through death's door" (152). When she returns the infant to the mother, she thinks about the experience of maternity and wonders about her own would-be child as she invokes the decisive Hester Prynne: "How mysterious motherhood is! For the first time I asked myself whether my child, whose life I had taken, would not after all have given my existence a meaning and a purpose. Hester, did we make a mistake and shouldn't you have lived for your child instead of dying with her?" (152). Here, the feminist rhetoric she hears from Hester gets flipped as she wonders whether her child would have "given [her] existence a meaning and a purpose." Meaning and purpose are externalized, and she does not look solely to herself to find them in this case. Tituba again finds herself caught in the middle of dueling strands of the same experience. Maternity, then, is forced into flux alongside matters of race, labor, nation, and sexuality. When Tituba considers her own maternity during her second pregnancy, motherhood is again a concept with multiple meanings. She wonders about the consequences of raising a child who will be marginalized on the levels of gender, labor, and societal mores: "My child made me combative. I was sure it was a girl! What sort of life was in store for her? That of my brothers and sisters, the slaves, ruined by their conditions and their labor? Or a life like mine, which forced me to live in hiding as an outcast and a recluse on the edge of a secluded valley?" (158). Having experienced society's restrictions as a slave, a witch, and a woman, she sees no good options for her daughter.

Alongside such obvious and numerous problems associated with maternity as a product of the slave economy generally and of Tituba's particular experience, Condé positions the very trope of mother as a dubious one. Thus "mother" itself is a term for which Condé acknowledges multiple meanings. It is equal parts sanctity and setback. To this paradox, Condé adds the realm of what the term means socially. The day Tituba returns to Barbados, she is approached by a group of young female maroons, one of whom says, "Honor us, mother, with your presence" (142). Tituba recoils at this, explaining, "Mother? The word made me jump and boil with rage, since it was a term of respect reserved for old women" (142). Troubled by the thought of her being perceived as an old woman, Tituba is again ambivalent when she later discovers she is pregnant with Christopher's child. This causes her to ponder the apparent capriciousness of pregnancy: "Christopher's brutal embraces had conceived what the love of my Jew had not been able to do. You've got to face up to it. A child in fact is not the fruit of love but of chance" (158). Thus a child is potentially and paradoxically one's arbitrary purpose. Despite this, in the epilogue, Tituba is able to "choose a descendent" after dying without giving birth (176). It is through this child, Samantha, that Tituba inhabits and perpetuates a legacy of her own. She is thus able to be generative *after* death.

The idea of "a woman's work" that attends reactions on all sides to the prospect of motherhood is one that Tituba must also confront when considering and answering to charges of being a witch. Condé presents "witch" as a slippery trope, one that productively troubles singular understandings of labor that would see it as a category unto itself. Throughout the text Tituba, especially as a figure of Salem Village who does not fit within the bounds of New England sensibilities, is consistently presented and frustrated with others' pejorative notions of witchcraft. Often, her witchery is vaguely tied by her persecutors to her imagined history, a relationship that confronts her with a simultaneous problem of what she is and where she came from. One day after Tituba dutifully recites the Apostles' Creed, her new mistress Susanna Endicott asks her, "Weren't you brought up by a certain Nago witch called Mama Yaya?" (26). Tituba hesitates, with a troubled, "Witch . . . Witch? She took care of people and cured them" (26). She thus explains Mama Yaya's "witchery" by attempting to clarify what it was Mama Yaya *did*. Later, when Tituba tells John Indian about the exchange, he casts the problem in racialized terms: "Governor Dutton had two slaves who had been accused of dealing with Satan burned in the square at Bridgetown. For the whites, that's what being a witch means . . . !" (27). Tituba's response is telling: "Dealing with Satan! . . . Before setting foot inside this house I didn't know who Satan was!" (27). Essentialist definitions become key here. Without ever having heard of good and evil in Westernized Christian terms, she has no vocabulary or system of meaning for what actions would be considered righteous or evil through that lens. As a racial and cultural outsider, she has no "real" or "pure" conception of "good-ness," as it is conceived by Anglo-Christian society, for example. This conversation with John Indian sets in motion Tituba's search throughout the text for a broader understanding of what it is to be a witch.

John Indian is the first to call her a witch, in this case as an ironic flirtation, after she scratches his finger while stealing his handkerchief: "Ow! What are you doing, little witch?" (17).[19] She takes note of the negative connotation of the term, as she does from Susanna Endicott and characters throughout the text. This leads her to a series of questions that create a discrepancy between how she and her society alternately perceive witchcraft and, thus, to two readings of the term:

> What is a witch? I noticed that when he said the word, it was marked with disapproval. Why should that be? Why? Isn't the ability to communicate with the invisible world, to keep constant links with the dead, to care for others and heal, a superior gift of nature that inspires respect, admiration, and gratitude? Consequently, shouldn't the witch (if that's what the person who has this gift is to be called) be cherished and revered rather than feared? (17)

Immediately after her musing on the terminology, she remembers her mother's question about the problems of desire: "Why can't women do without men?" reiterating with her own "Yes why?" (17). She considers this as the environment around her echoes her desperation: "Outside, the black cord of night was strangling the island. Not a breath of air. The trees were motionless, like stakes" (17). At once, the island's naturalistic torment of being strangled is her own early sentiment of suffocation at the hands of men. Thus her gendered position is commingled with her nationalistic one.

Once living with the Parrises in America, Tituba is again confronted with the idea of witchcraft as a distinctly "evil" practice. Encircled by Abigail and her friends, Tituba is taunted by the little girls. Mary Walcott asks her, "Tituba, is it true you know everything, you see everything and can do everything? You're a witch then?" (61). Tituba responds with "Don't use words whose meaning you don't know. Do you know what a witch really is?" (61). "'Of course we do,' intervened Anne Putnam.

'It's someone who has made a pact with the devil. Mary's right. Are you a witch, Tituba? I think you must be'" (62). The idea of "what a witch *really* is" here interests me. Even as Tituba makes an appeal to an essential witch-ness, she attempts to trouble the children's definition, one fraught with racial and cultural otherness. Here again Condé inserts a tether to the rhetoric of essence to confront the very notions of singularity.

For Tituba, one's witchery is inseparable from one's work. In her musings about the meaning of witchcraft, she casts it in terms of the work done *as* a witch. In so doing, she aligns it with the kind of acts that Cheryl Fish identifies as "benevolent labor." Fish's *Black and White Women's Travel Narratives* in part examines the work done by women who travel with missions of humanitarian good will. Fish uses the term "benevolent labor" to "include work related to helping the poor, the fallen, the oppressed, and the injured and linked to mobile subjectivity away from the traveler's home" (137 n. 2). This is in relation to the studies done on what Lori D. Ginzberg calls "benevolent femininity." Tituba, as well as the Puritan community surrounding her, significantly feminizes the work of witchcraft, the latter identifying it in terms of and in distinction from Anglo-European conventions of "benevolent" women's work. Tituba thus reinterprets "benevolent femininity" subversively in order to take it out of this narrow space. Further, Tituba uses her voice vis-à-vis her witchcraft and takes revenge as she speaks in the trials: "Whose names did they want me to give? Because I wasn't just going to give the names of the poor wretches who were being dragged along with me in the mud. I was going to strike hard. And at the top" (93). Her status as a witch here affords her to strike back at the very powers who would condemn her for it. Thus Condé presents witchcraft as a slippery category in terms of both labor and gender, rejecting the fixity that those around Tituba try to assign to her on either front.

Back in Barbados after her miserable experience in Salem, Tituba is troubled to find that even the people from her homeland look for logical explanations of her powers. Christopher, the leader of the maroons whom Tituba encounters, demands of her, "Are you a witch? . . . Yes or no!" She sighs with frustration at the call for fixed answers to be attached to such a vague trope like "witch" and responds in kind: "Everyone gives that word a different meaning. Everyone believes he can fashion a witch to his way of thinking so that she will satisfy his ambitions, dreams, and desires" (146). Here, her frustration with a clear categorization of the term is evident. Ignored, Tituba's words are immediately followed by Christopher's deal: "Listen . . . I'm not going to stay here listening to you philosophize!

I'm offering you a deal. You make me invincible and in exchange . . . I'll give you everything a woman desires" (146). Christopher's "deal," freighted with highly sexualized inferences, does two things at once. First, even back in Barbados, it reinforces the stereotype of black female sexuality as hyperactive, as if the terms of transaction would obviously and immediately appeal to Tituba's womanhood (since his phallocentric logic extends to a broader category of what a "woman" desires). At the same time, however, Tituba's reaction is one of desperation and longing.

She immediately appeals to Mama Yaya and Abena, "Can't I try to help him?" attempting to justify her supplication with "He's fighting for a noble cause" (146). After their deaths, Mama Yaya and Abena maintain strong presences, often of advice and even chastisement, throughout the novel. Like the ancestral manifestations of the Day family, especially Sapphira Wade, in *Mama Day*, Tituba's mother Abena continues to speak to her daughter and offer analysis and judgment. In this instance, Abena laughs with a caustic reply: "Hypocrite! Is it the cause he's fighting for that interests you? Come now!" (146). Because of Tituba's reaction, we can interpret Christopher's deal as another example that reveals Tituba's strong tether to her own sexuality. In this sense, it serves as an opportunity for her to maintain an expression of desire. Of course, whether Tituba achieves any sort of sexual *independence* or not is an entirely different matter. Christopher alone spells out the conditions of the trade and, in so doing, renders Tituba simultaneously desirous lover and chattel in a very particular kind of labor arrangement.

Tituba's putative relationship to her powers also manifests itself in her concern over the retention of her personal history. After giving her deposition in the Salem court, as she is taken to the prison at Ipswich, she panics at the thought of how she will be remembered, if at all:

> I was racked by a violent feeling of pain and terror. It seemed that I was gradually being forgotten. I felt that I would only be mentioned in passing in these Salem witchcraft trials that would arouse the curiosity and pity of generations to come as the greatest testimony of a superstitious and barbaric age. There would be mention here and there of a "slave originating from the West Indies and probably practicing 'hoodoo'" . . . Tituba would be condemned forever! There would never, ever, be a careful, sensitive biography recreating my life and its suffering. (110)

The idea of how society will continue to define witchcraft and consequently define her by her dubious connection to it is a worry that accompanies Tituba throughout the text.

Navigating fluid spheres of gender and work, Condé uses Tituba's journeys to challenge ultimately any consistent reading of a would-be univocal, overarching voice that proves her authenticity. After returning to her homeland, Tituba notes, "Ah yes, life had pushed me around! From Salem to Ipswich. From Barbados to America and back. But now I could sit down and rest and say: 'You won't manhandle me anymore!'" (145). Her migrations from place to place are what, she implies, allow such strong resolve. These same migrations are what erase any resolve, however, from social conventions that would put too fine a point on Tituba's own experience. Early on, Condé complicates ideas like "enslavement" and "freedom," throwing each into flux as Tituba *chooses* to place herself back within the bonds of slavery in order to marry John Indian. Early on, she appears to understand the problem that arises upon her deciding to take on the life of slavery, and she is harshly critical of the system that she is about to enter. When John Indian makes his ultimatum to Tituba about her living with him in his home if they are to be together at all, she asks ironically, "Your home? . . . Since when does a slave have a 'home'? Don't you belong to Susanna Endicott?" (18). He tries to explain, "Yes, I belong to Susanna Endicott, but she's a good mistress . . . ," but she interrupts: "How can a mistress be 'good'? Can a slave cherish his master?" (18). While Mary Prince concludes her narrative condemning the corrupting influence of the *institution* of slavery, Tituba directs her antagonism squarely at the slaveholder with her own question of moral character. Tituba complicates and contradicts her argument as she decides to marry John Indian despite the implications for her free status. And again with Benjamin, as stated earlier, Tituba romanticizes him and their relationship such that, when she thinks of him after they part, she reminds his memory that "I begged you to leave me my chains" (140).

Upon Benjamin's emancipating her after her period of enslavement, Tituba discovers as soon as she boards the ship to sail back home to Barbados that "emancipation," "manumission," and "freedom" are themselves complicated words that do not at all have the same meaning. Boarding *Bless the Lord* for her passage, she is confronted by a sailor with the irony of her condemnation. When he warns the captain, "Be careful, she's one of the witches of Salem!" and she responds that the governor issued a general pardon, the sailor tells her, "But you confessed your crime so there's no pardon for you" (135). Trapped in the impossible ambivalence of her status as a witch, Tituba once again finds herself manipulated into a service role. The captain stipulates that he will take her to Barbados in exchange for her maintaining good weather and the health of his crew. When Tituba tries to explain the limits of her powers, he spits and says,

"Negress, when you speak to me, say 'Master' and lower your eyes; otherwise I'll smash those stumps out of your mouth" (135). Even as she exits the system of slavery, phantom shackles still impede her journey.

Toward the end of the novel, Tituba's understanding of freedom is again questioned by Mama Yaya, a consistent voice of wisdom and advice. When she hears from Iphigene that he and others are going to burn the houses of landholding whites, Tituba mutters half to him, half to herself, "Do we have to become like them?" (162). Once he leaves, she calls upon Mama Yaya to remind her of what she had once told Tituba: "Don't pervert your heart! Don't become like them!" and to ask Mama Yaya "Is this the price to pay for freedom?" (162). In reply, Mama Yaya again turns Tituba's attention to the meaning and importance of words. She says to her, "You talk about freedom. Have you any idea what it means?" (162). Leaving the question as a rhetorical one, Mama Yaya disappears.

Despite her dubious understandings of what it is to be a free agent, Tituba affirmatively answers the question of whether she has a "song" in the epilogue. She is able to hear the song all over the island, and it lives on through her "daughter," Samantha. Importantly, however, this song is experienced and created in the section of the novel that takes place after any and all historical records. The story of Tituba after her death is what she calls her "real story" (175). However, this nominal authenticity is created solely by Condé. She thus retains total control over Tituba's "voice" as it ostensibly lives on. On a broader level, the entirety of the text, while superficially a reinforcement of stereotypes like the exoticized black woman and essentialist forms of feminism, Condé effectively challenges these images by presenting these forces and tropes as inherently unstable. Such is the larger destabilizing potential of her diasporic text.

As the narratives in this book have shown, looking back (as long as we do not nostalgically imagine history as a stable or *sui generis* space) can indeed be a productive enterprise, as it often aids in the practice of looking ahead. As Laura Alexandra Harris suggests, "Only in looking back can I interpret my race and class as inextricable from my sexuality and feminist consciousness, and only in looking forward can I predict what a schizophrenic narrative it constructs" (13). The productive implications of Mary Prince's *History* for women's fiction need not remain in a fixed position themselves.

CONCLUSION

Writing Women across the African Diaspora

> All articulation is partial and precarious.
> —Ernesto Laclau, *Reflections on the Revolution of Our Time*

GENDER—and certainly "women" specifically—is a category born out of its being written and performed. And depending on who's writing or performing, where and for whom and with what interests, the category will bear in its signification a certain set of ideas governed by a certain set of rules. The same is true for classifications of work, race, and region. These signifiers are contingent and constitutive in relation to other markers of identity. As I hope to have shown in my discussions of Mary Prince's *History* alongside twentieth-century diasporic texts, gender takes a particular shape as it comes into contact with various contexts of racial and geosocial space. What appears likewise clear is that, as authors and readers write women into the texts, there is also present an interest in "righting" women—providing a proper account of their stories, indeed in getting the story "right"—and thus tendering an authentic subject whose voice and experience readers can access. As scholars write women across the African Diaspora, then, we are also attempting to right them—to offer a clear subject for analysis. These analytical projects are often cast in the progressive language of recovery and reclamation. In this manner, we scholars who are interested in recovering women's voices (thought to lie in a specific and identifiable space all its own called "the margin") see ourselves doing important work on the academic first responders' team—"righting" the ship that would render women's identities invisible to mainstream discourses in literary criticism.

In the January 2011 issue of the *Chronicle of Higher Education*, Glenda R. Carpio and Werner Sollors published "The Newly Complicated Zora Neale Hurston"—a piece that showcased what they gleaned from three of Hurston's short stories that had not been reprinted before and that they deem "important because they provide fuller insight into Hurston's engagement with urban black life" (3). Gaining new access to as yet unseen literature is undoubtedly a fortuitous result of archival research, and adding new pieces of data to the corpus of works by Hurston is a productive enterprise. Carpio and Sollors describe some of the ways in which Hurston complicates many readings of who she was:

> She was also more complicated than the anti-establishment thinker some 1970s feminists wanted her to be. Focusing on *Their Eyes Were Watching God,* they traced a black woman's resistance to male domination; the heroine Janie Crawford's search for a voice and for fulfillment became the touchstone for viewing Hurston as a progressive foremother. Yet Hurston's rural folk orientation seemed to go along with her conservative leanings and made some of her views compatible with those of the Southern Agrarians like Robert Penn Warren and Allen Tate. She thought Reconstruction was a deplorable period, favored Booker T. Washington over W. E. B. Du Bois even decades after Washington's death, and opposed the New Deal; in 1954 she also opposed the U.S. Supreme Court's decision in *Brown v. Board of Education.* (5)

Carpio and Sollors are right to complicate the reductive critical moves that would call Hurston one *kind* of author or another and that would suggest her writing was doing a single, definable work when she was a Harlem Renaissance standout. As I emphasized in my earlier discussion of *Their Eyes,* critiques of the text are misguided indeed if reading the book purely as a protofeminist *bildungsroman*. However, Carpio and Sollors do not go far enough. Implicit in their discussion is a vision of Zora Neale Hurston *the person,* and "she" (or her biography), in the process of being newly complicated, is still presented as a self-evident and clearly identifiable subject for scholarly discussion.

The language I find noteworthy here is that of a "newly complicated Zora Neale Hurston" *qua* Zora Neale Hurston. Carpio and Sollors's ultimate assessment is that "New discoveries will require us all to expand our understanding of who Hurston was and what she produced. If we think of her within only one of the categories of protofeminist, political conservative, Southern folk writer—or even a combination of those—we will miss the 'cosmic Zora' that existed betwixt and between, and even fully outside, such categories" (7). What we are left with, then, at the end of an introduction to three heretofore unknown stories, is "the cosmic Zora" that transcends categorization, existing completely outside of the boxes into which scholars would place her. The problem, however, is not that scholars categorize Hurston. After all, what else are we to do? How do we offer critical discussion about literature and the authors who produce it—about anything at all, for that matter—without bounding the discourse within certain limits? To pretend that we can do otherwise is disingenuous at best. The aim, then, as I see it, is for scholars to be more cognizant and straightforward about what interests are brought to bear in their particular categories and classifications. If the scholarly caricatures of Hurston that Carpio and Sollors admonish constitute a reduction, the impulse to suggest Hurston can hover outside all categories or discourse is a delusion.

Ironically, it would seem to be the insistence on the *person* "Zora"—in all "her" humanness and ordinariness (we might point out that her conservative stances on the *Brown v. Board of Education* decision or the New Deal frustrate her fans but also make her "real")—that suggests an exceptional or transcendent status for the author. In claiming her as this or that kind of person, we are choosing the "Zora" that we want her to be—the Zora who fits our particular purposes, the one who showcases our own proximity to her life and work. Like the various agents at work in Mary Prince's text who fashion a specific Mary Prince who fits their needs—as an unruly detriment to polite society, a doting wife, or an earnest spokesperson for the anti-slavery movement—literary critics create various Zora Neale Hurstons. Depending on one's scholarly interests, she is the apologist for disenfranchised black working communities who constitute "the folk" of her Southern settings; she is the self-assured contrarian who stood up to male literary counterparts; she is the anthropologist interested in Caribbean culture and folklore; she is the unlikely political conservative; she is an innovator within the canon of Harlem Renaissance writers. Even when the scholarly point is to complicate a single portrait, as is the case for Carpio and Sollors, there is an imagined "real" Zora Neale Hurston lurking behind the description of her multidimensionality.

Michael Awkward's introductory essay for *New Essays on "Their Eyes Were Watching God"* addresses the thorny issue of readership in relation to Zora Neale Hurston. The antagonistic response to her work by her contemporaries, followed by years of critical obscurity, provides a complex space in which scholars now talk about her writing. In describing the harshly negative reception of the novel by writers like Alain Locke and Richard Wright, Awkward suggests, "Such negative reactions were to become quite common, and made an unbiased evaluation of Hurston's work nearly impossible during her lifetime" (3). Of note here is the issue of an "unbiased evaluation" that would have presumably been more fair or accurate but that was sadly unattainable during her life. Awkward cites Barbara Johnson's assessment that Hurston's personality-based "successful strategy for survival" in her adoption of a "'happy darkie' stance" "does not by any means exhaust the representational strategies of her writing" (qtd. in Awkward 3). In Awkward's view, "Johnson's statement suggests the fruitfulness for contemporary readers of looking past the numerous attacks on Hurston's character and closely examining the works of this prolific and provocative Afro-American woman writer" (4). The Awkward and Johnson image of Hurston as a calculating thinker who responds strategically to the biased claims leveled against her by other writers is as problematic as a singularity as Carpio and Sollors's "Cosmic Zora." To Awkward's reading, I would suggest that "Hurston" is *always necessarily* a product of discourse surrounding her. Putatively newer, positive responses to her work that have followed in the wake of Alice Walker's heralded recuperation efforts are no more neutral or unbiased than those of Alain Locke and Richard Wright. They merely arise from a set of different scholarly interests—interests that became more prevalent after the 1970s-brand academia and activism that ushered in a new account of women's authorship and the intersections of gender, race, and class.

A more productive reading of Hurston's life and/or texts would begin by complicating the ostensible object of study. For there is no Zora Neale Hurston if her name is taken to be the signifier of a stable subject. She is simultaneously all and none of the things that literary critics describe. Further, "she" does not exist, as such, apart from those descriptive (and retrospective) lenses. Scholars would do well to be up front about just what we are talking about, then, in our work. Even after the poststructuralist turn that decentered "the subject" and offered ways of thinking about identity as endlessly constructed and contingent, contemporary scholarship will still talk about "her" identity being constructed—as if there is some agent standing outside doing the constructing rather than seeing "her" as something only understandable through the process and project of construction.

We are, at best, only ever engaging discourse on "Hurston" rather than some notion of *Hurston herself*. Mistakenly, archival excavations that we undertake are thought to bring us somehow closer and familiarly related to the voices being uncovered. This would explain why Alice Walker referred in a talk at Barnard College to Zora Neale Hurston and Langston Hughes as her "aunt and uncle." There is an assumed literary and ideological lineage wherein contemporary writers and scholars take on the mantle from their forebears and extend a legacy of collective ethico-political struggle. Like the foray of Henry Louis Gates Jr. into genealogical mapping in his *African American Lives*, which is heralded as a "journey into the past" on its website linked to PBS, these analytical moves suggest clear origins and identifiable chronologies. In this way, scholars fall back on essentialist rhetoric and logic in the name of progressive ideals.

In *Authentic Blackness: The Folk in the New Negro Renaissance*, J. Martin Favor talks about the emphasis in race studies on authenticating a kind of blackness thought to dwell in "the folk"—a category infused with class concerns. In his discussion of W. E. B. DuBois's column "A Questionnaire," published in *Crisis* in 1926, and its subsequent reprinting by Henry Louis Gates Jr. in the 1987 *Black American Literature Forum*, Favor emphasizes what he refers to as the "discourse of black identity"—a discourse that received boundary maintenance by black thinkers during the Harlem Renaissance and that continues to be regulated through contemporary understandings of race and identity. Noting the distinctions between "true" and "false" class strata among black Americans in the 1920s, Favor suggests, "Uniqueness lies in difference, and difference is best represented by a particular class stratum. Class becomes a primary marker of racial difference; to be truly different, one must be authentically folk. In what ways, then, does this folkness manifest itself in African American literature?" (6). Like Favor, I am wary of the critical alliances with marginalized collectives. In relation to class consciousness and racial identity, Favor notes critical moves to ally scholars and the folk they privilege, citing thinkers like Hazel Carby and Barbara Smith who seem to suggest a more authentic blackness residing in the lower class:[1] "Separated in terms of class from these critics' notions of folk, the black middle class cannot express the 'authentic' African American experience. And though most critics are, by definition, middle-class, they work themselves into a strategic alliance with folk privilege by consciously emphasizing aspects of heritage and experience that link them to the folk while downplaying their own similarities to 'buppies.' Black identity, as formulated on the class basis, requires a certain quotient of oppression; second-class status is essential to racial identity. The normative conditions of blackness derive from second-class status" (13).

Reading modern novels in relation to slave narratives provides a useful way to begin moving beyond categorical fixity in terms of both genre and identity formation. Mary Prince's *History* is one example of how the women onto whom we impose labels of "authenticity" destabilize rather than embrace such identification. Rather than believe ourselves to be scholarly benefactors of personal liberation, we should start to interrogate how our quest for the "truth" in diasporic women's experiences does not adequately account for the ways in which signs like "gender" and "work" converge and conflict with each other. A study of migration, of how these signs get reworked in different social and geographical contexts, allows for feminist and postcolonial literary scholars to begin keeping up with the narratives that have already embarked on journeys that interrogate descriptive approaches to identity and that complicate static understandings of subjectivity.

Thus, I am interested in the ways in which migration unsettles that very notion of a clear and exceptional feminized and black diasporic subject. In *Black and White Women's Travel Narratives: Antebellum Explorations* (2004), Cheryl Fish describes "mobile subjectivity" as "a fluid and provisional epistemology and subject position that is contingent upon one's relationship to specific persons, incidents, ideologies, locations, time, and space" (6–7). My project has focused on the contingencies of gender and physical labor, both of which I understand as fluctuating analytical categories that receive varying formative expectations based upon the social and physical geographies that frame the texts I have discussed. My approach rejects phenomenological approaches that place authority in experience and that speculate on personal intent or the mind-set of migrating subjects. Instead of imagining the significance of feminized subjectivity or the presumed stability of women's migration narratives,[2] this book is a call for a more sustained critique of the rhetorical and theoretical tools that literary, postcolonial, and feminist scholars use to describe women's experiences.

Specifically, my approach alters the way in which identity theorists talk about agency. A tempting move is to render authority to the ambiguous category of experience. After all, the act of a woman of color telling her story can so easily be viewed as one that grants or proves her agency. I have intended not to suggest that agency cannot exist or that it has no place in critical conversations of identity. Rather, I have meant to suggest that the manner of talking about agency as a kind of personal holy grail one finds at the end of an arduous quest is insufficient. The narratives discussed in this book show agency to be, like any other category, *an endlessly contingent thing*.

In *Authentic Blackness,* J. Martin Favor takes scholarship in an important direction by calling for a critical coalition politics, noting that since there is no such thing as the "perfect" performative text, there is use in reading alongside one another texts that dislodge the stability of identity signifiers, a practice he calls "a sort of coalition politics of reading" (152). He has the following to say, then, about the prospect of theorizing black identity:

> Do we really need a "grand unified theory" of black identity when comparing and contrasting a plurality of positions immensely instructive in its own right? If it is through coalition and an empowerment of diversity that we are to come to the destruction of discrimination, let us begin that mission by creating the largest possible space in which coalitions may be formed and diversity displayed. (152)

To this, however, I would add that we not too quickly count on neoliberal "big tent" politics to do the work for us of contesting the stability which is so often located in identity categories. Expanding the space of discourse and political action is perhaps a desirable outcome, but expansiveness is not alone sufficient as a critical method of talking about black—or, more for that matter, postcolonial or diasporic—identities. After all, to form coalitions and display diversity, decisions would have to be made about what identities to include in a particular coalition for what purpose, as well as what "diversity" means, for that matter, and what contributes to or detracts from it. Who makes those decisions, with what interests and to what ends, is just as important as the ostensible coalition or diversity "itself," for there *is no* body politic apart from the agents at work in its construction. Scholars interested in identity, narrative, and migration would be well served to keep our critical eyes on the ball. Metaphorically speaking, doing so means not looking at the ball but rather the pitcher.

The negotiations of memory and migration in the texts I have discussed help shift a critical focus on supposed truth to inescapable contexts.

Reconsidering the ways in which those of us in postcolonial literary studies might approach conversations about origins, diasporas, and identities is important if we are to take seriously the complex ways that discourses about these categories work to meet certain scholarly ends. If we stop reading migration as an exception to some geographically stable rule, and if we start having more substantive dialogue about how the rhetoric of authenticity functions ideologically for scholars emphasizing clear points of departure and return, then we might more productively discuss narratives that reveal identities shifting across spatial-social contexts. If Roland Barthes was on to something when he said "show me how you classify and I'll show you who you are," then we might think about how our portrayals of African diasporic identities say more about ourselves than about Africa or its diasporas. We might also stop looking so hard for the "authenticity" of *this* or *that* and, rather, change the subject of our discourse by looking at the ways in which people decide to *talk about* authenticity. In other words, when it comes to personal narratives, there does not exist so clearly "the subject" as there does a *discourse* on the thing we call the subject. With this distinction in mind, we can read women's migration narratives as a series of physical and textual migrations that unsettle the very notion of a cohesive diaspora and unsettle our critical strategies and theoretical certainties.

NOTES

INTRODUCTION

1. Manly served as president from 1837 to 1855. In his role as Baptist minister, he wrote the "Alabama Resolutions"—a foundational document in the decision of state Baptist conventions to withdraw from the national convention and form the Southern Baptist Convention. Manly argued that the Baptist faith would foster the humane treatment of slaves and that slavery itself is merely a natural extension and component of social stratification.

2. See *The Content of Form: Narrative Discourse and Historical Representation* (1990).

3. Much has rightly been made of feminist theory's problematic tendency to refer to a universal signifying "woman," discounting the very material effects of race and class on a woman's subjectivity. Scholars like Hazel Carby, Patricia Hill Collins, Evelynn Hammonds, Barbara Smith, and Claudia Tate, just to name a few, have aimed this critique at feminists who ignore race and class as well as race theorists who tether themselves to an essentialist and patriarchal notion of blackness and ignore feminist concerns of gender and sexuality. In "African-American Women's History and the Metalanguage of Race," for example, Evelyn Brooks Higginbotham takes a cue from Elizabeth Spelman by noting what is too often white feminism's "double standard": "White feminists . . . typically discern two separate identities for black women, the racial and the gender, and conclude that the gender identity of black women is the same as their own" (255). Implicit in white feminists' frequent separation of gender and race—if not their failure to discuss race at all—is a feminist appeal to an "authentic" experience of womanhood. Such an appeal goes against the impulses of Third Wave feminist theory that would reject what is commonly portrayed as a "Second Wave problem" (typified by thinkers like bell hooks with *From Margin to Center*)—removing oppressive institutions of patriarchy from the center

rhetorically and simply replacing them with ideas of female empowerment. Third Wave feminism would rightly argue that pointing to a center at all is a problematic beginning.

4. This feminist notion of "becoming" is key to my own study of subjects that move from place to place. Whereas the emphasis for Butler and Grosz is one largely corporeal and phenomenological, I am interested in how identities are performed and articulated when their surrounding context changes again and again. With each new societal encounter, the women in the texts I discuss imbibe different sets of expectations and evaluations imposed on their bodies and subjectivities, different definitions of tropes like "womanhood," "appropriateness," and "sexuality." Early in her narrative, Mary Prince says of her time with Betsey, the little girl to whom she belonged in Bermuda, "I was made quite a pet of by Miss Betsey, and loved her very much. She used to lead me about by the hand, and call me her little nigger. This was the happiest period in my life; for I was too young to understand rightly my condition as a slave" (187). Consistent travel and migration complicate the ability for Prince and characters like Condé's Tituba and Hurston's Janie to "understand rightly [their] condition[s]" since the condition changes in accordance with place.

5. Many feminists have begun to move forward in rethinking categorization and its effects. Rose Brewer, despite her tether to the political efficacy of categories, offers in her essay "Theorizing Race, Class and Gender" several ways that scholars and social theorists interpret race, thus exemplifying the multiplicity and heterogeneity imbedded in the very notion of "race." Then, in *Belabored Professions: Narratives of African American Working Womanhood*, Xiomara Santamarina suggests something similar on a class level, that it is "counterproductive to ground analyses of texts [on Black women workers] in traditionally discrete categories of identity such as 'working class' or 'middle class'" (167).

6. McClintock offers a nice metaphor, suggesting that "race, gender and class are not distinct realms of experience, existing in splendid isolation from each other; nor can they be simply yoked together retrospectively like armatures of Lego. Rather they come into existence *in and through* relation to each other—if in contradictory and conflictual ways. In this sense, gender, race and class can be called articulated categories" (5). At this critical crux, where inadequate classifications and individual subjects collide, women's migration narratives present a point of access that helps navigate the complex theoretical spaces of and between these forces of identity politics.

7. Exploring how identity signifiers might become confounded in diasporic contexts provides possibilities for feminist readings of texts that present specific relationships between the categories "race," "sexuality," "gender," and "class." Rather than preserving these signs as singular classifications, a much more productive approach is available when considering Laura Alexandra Harris's notion of queering categories and Rose Brewer's understanding of them as "simultaneous forces" (16).

8. Laura Alexandra Harris in "Queer Black Feminism: The Pleasure Principle" rightly suggests that problematizing a seeming category is not an end in itself: "Once a system of knowledge is in place, once gender oppression is under scrutiny, the focus should include not only disrupting the stability of the category but finding methods of making one category always a discussion of another. It just doesn't prove enough to add the themes—here's race, a bit of class, and a touch of sexuality—without allowing them to disrupt the system in ways that reconstitute it. A dialogue on race is a feminist dialogue is a class dialogue is a queer dialogue already" (25).

9. Foster's analysis focuses specifically on three autobiographies of free black women in the early and mid-nineteenth century: *The Life and Religious Experiences of Jarena*

Lee, *A Coloured Lady* (1836), *A Narrative of the Life and Travels of Mrs. Nancy Prince* (1853), and *Our Nig; or, Sketches from the Life of a Free Black* (1859).

10. Lionnet suggests, "They rewrite the 'feminine' by showing the arbitrary nature of the images and values which Western culture constructs, distorts, and encodes as inferior by feminizing them. All the texts I discuss in this book interrogate the sociocultural construction of race and gender and challenge the essentializing tendencies that perpetuate exploitation and subjugation on behalf of those fictive differences created by discourses of power" (5).

11. To put it another way, Black and Third World feminisms should not be reduced as a product of academic essentialism that would confine them to a particular set of discourses. Higginbotham notes that even these dialogues have a reductive potential that does not exempt them from the problem of glossing-over difference: "Even black women's history, which has consciously sought to identify the importance of gender relations and the interworkings of race, class, and gender, nonetheless reflects the totalizing impulse of race in such concepts as 'black womanhood' or the 'black woman cross-culturally'—concepts that mask real differences of class, status and color, regional culture, and a host of other configurations of difference" (255–56). Certainly it is likewise insufficient to try and complicate classifications like gender and labor if or while doing so with appeals to unproblematized notions of place or the body. Rather than replace one vocabulary of singularity with another, I mean to examine the ways in which specific constructions of gender and work are shaped and shifted in relation to travel and physical movement across geosocial boundaries. Especially when such movement is a result of coercion rather than an evidence of personal autonomy, "agency" becomes a fluctuating idea within varying societal constructs. Rather than insisting on a singular racial identification that falls into the rhetorical trap of making a monolith like Higginbotham warns against of "black womanhood," I would refer to Claudia Tate, who, in "Reshuffling the Deck; Or, (Re)Reading Race and Gender in Black Women's Writing," notes the problematics of categories made too singular by the presumed exclusivity of race and gender, just for two examples: "Put in terms of feminist criticism, black feminist criticism: texts of black female authority = (white) feminist criticism: texts of (white) female authority. In addition to remembering these equations in critical logic, we must be careful not to allow the racial and sexual qualifiers to lead us into regarding black feminist criticism as a form of reader-response criticism in which the so-called ideal reader arises from the social construct of the black female" (119). The same distinction Tate emphasizes regarding the context of feminist criticism should be made in literary studies as well. In this sphere, Hazel Carby's definition of black feminist criticism in *Reconstructing Womanhood* is useful. She sees it "as a problem, not a solution, as a sign that should be interrogated, a locus of contradictions" (15). The women in the texts that follow are subject to the definitions that their social contexts impose on them. Thus, "place"—as a trope with geographical but also sociopolitical and psychological significations—is key when considering not only the relationships between the spaces and the protagonists but also the ways that these women utilize various meanings of place and in their own interpersonal dialogues.

12. Scholarship has taken several important turns regarding critical conceptions of the South. Martyn Bone's *The Postsouthern Sense of Place in Contemporary Fiction* (2005) not only posits the South as a complicated product of both pastoral nostalgia and modernized economies but also contextualizes the region as a transnational space. More recently, Thadious Davis has offered to the discussion *Southscapes: Geographies of Race, Region, and Literature,* which "is invested in understanding the persistent conceptual

power of the South as a spatial object and ideological landscape where matters of race are simultaneously opaque and transparent" (2).

CHAPTER 1

1. All quotes from Mary Prince's *History* come from the 1987 reprint of the text as anthologized by Henry Louis Gates Jr. in *The Classic Slave Narratives*. This edition represents important textual migrations both geographically and ideologically as it moves into America and into mainstream conversations within African American Studies and literary theory.

2. Jenny Sharpe rightly notes that a fuller portrait of Mary Prince comes from intersecting and interrogating not only Prince's narrative but also pro-slavery documents and court proceedings regarding her manumission and character.

3. The novels I look at throughout the rest of this book are also examples of this sort of textual migration. For example, in *I, Tituba*, Condé recuperates the story of a seventeenth-century slave and repositions it within an essentialist and exclusionary feminist rhetoric that Condé interrogates even as she articulates it.

4. Kremena Todorova points to "the contemporary critical concern with authorship" as a possible reason for the sustained focus on "voice" in readings of *The History of Mary Prince* (285).

5. I follow Whitlock's reading of Prince's narrative as production. She notes, "Here is a place to examine adjacency, intimacy, and the production of identity through relationship rather than authenticity, through intersubjectivity, and through reversals of attributes that attached to gender, race and class positions there and then" (13). Whitlock presents a way to think of the *History* as cultural product even as it remains a significant addition to the genre of slave narrative.

6. One such question involves how religion and sexuality act as both coerced and strategic forces. Religio-cultural notions of feminine "appropriateness" make several important dictates in Prince's text. Her religious conversion, which allows for her English contacts and ultimate introduction to the Anti-Slavery Society, is also what provides her access to literacy. Her decidedly religious rhetoric throughout the text, then, gives her a particularly useful religious platform from which to offer a woman's critique of the institution of slavery.

7. Prince's depiction of her being sold away from Miss Betsey, the small child for whom she was bought as a gift, provides another moment of gendered and racial disruption. She writes, "The idea of being sold away from my mother and Miss Betsey was so frightful, that I dared not trust myself to think about it. We had been bought of Mr. Myners, as I have mentioned, by Miss Betsey's grandfather, and given to her, so that we were by right *her* property, and I never thought we should be separated or sold away from her. When I reached the house, I went in directly to Miss Betsey. I found her in great distress; and she cried out as soon as she saw me, Oh, Mary! my father is going to sell you all to raise money to marry that wicked woman. You are *my* slaves, and he was no right to sell you; but it is all to please her'" (189).

8. Prince extends the importance of the alliance to a familial level, stating, "Poor Hetty, my fellow slave, was very kind to me, and I used to call her my Aunt" (194).

9. In *Ghosts of Slavery*, Jenny Sharpe notes, "The slave woman acts, then, only inasmuch as she exhibits the *moral* agency of an enlightened individual. The slave narrative makes no mention of Prince attempting to gain freedom through extramarital relationships with white men" (120).

10. Barbara Baumgartner argues in "The Body as Evidence" that Pringle's inclusion of a "slanderous letter from Mr. Wood in the supplement" shifts a focus from "the disabled-turned-resistant body (Prince's portrayal) to a sexualized body (Pringle/Wood portrayal)" (262). While I believe the avoidances and elisions throughout the text are just as telling in a reading of Prince as a sexualized subject, Baumgartner provides an extremely compelling discussion of the strategic uses of corporeality in the narrative.

11. See Hortense Spillers, "Mama's Baby, Papa's Maybe: An American Grammar Book."

12. This is not to say presumptively that she does not, in fact, feel any actual shame. Rather I mean only to emphasize the place that her audience occupies imaginatively for her.

13. Thomas Pringle is an example, rebuking Mr. Wood, Captain I— and his wife, and Mr. D— for their harsh treatment of Prince: "The behavior of the slaveholder was often lacking in earthly consequences, but it could create difficulties in his moral and social acceptance by British society" (qtd. in Bracks 36).

14. Whitlock notes the way in which the narrative employs corporeal proof: "Here, as is so often the case, the body is seen to represent truth. Although what is taken from Mary's lips remains suspect, her scars on her back, her flesh, cannot lie. Skin determines the deployments of other body parts. The marks of authenticity, which abolitionist look for her, are a quite specific requirement" (23).

CHAPTER 2

1. See Houston A. Baker Jr., *Workings of the Spirit: The Poetics of Afro-American Women's Writing* (1991).

2. See Coleman Coker, "Regionalism in a Global Community" (1992).

3. Bone nods to William Gleason's socioeconomic critique of such readings: "William Gleason suggests the perils of 'nostalgia for a rural community' in Hurston scholarship when he wonders aloud: '[Does] knowing that black towns like Eatonville were in large respect labor farms for neighboring white towns that catered to wealthy northerners wintering in Florida dissipate the haze of nostalgia enveloping Hurston's youthful recollections?'" (Bone 757).

4. "The representation of the storm in *Their Eyes Were Watching God* draws upon the Lake Okechobee hurricane of 1928. On 16 September 1928, a hurricane with winds of 140 miles per hour struck Florida, having already killed hundreds of people in Puerto Rico and the Bahamas . . . The official death toll was 1,838, but this figure has been disputed by scholars who believe that up to 6,000 people died and that "four-fifths of them [were] blacks working the fertile sugar cane and bean fields near Lake Okechobee" (Bone 767).

5. Locke's review appeared in *Opportunity* in February 1939.

6. See Wright's "Between Laughter and Tears" in *New Masses,* October 5, 1937.

7. See Ralph Ellison's "Recent Negro Fiction," *New Masses,* August 5, 1940.

8. See Robert Stepto, *From Behind the Veil: A Study of Afro-American Narrative* (1979); Mary Helen Washington, foreword to *Their Eyes Were Watching God* (1990); Hazel Carby, *Cultures in Babylon: Black Britain and African America* (1999); and Gordon Thompson, "Projecting Gender: Personification in the Works of Zora Neale Hurston" (1994).

9. Jan Cooper, "Zora Neale Hurston Was Always a Southerner Too," in *The Female Tradition in Southern Literature,* ed. Carol Manning (Urbana: University of Illinois Press, 1993).

10. Bone summarizes Carby's position thusly: "Carby sees Janie's migrations 'from the southern states further south' in *Their Eyes Were Watching God* as exemplifying Hurston's discursive displacement of northward urban migration" (760).

11. He particularly critiques what he calls "Carby's overly simple model of African American migration from the rural South to the urban North" (Bone 763).

12. See Houston A. Baker Jr.'s discussion of *Their Eyes* in *Blues, Ideology, and Afro-American Literature: A Vernacular Theory* (1984). Specifically see his discussion of the way in which slavery shapes Nanny's ideologically driven wishes for her granddaughter (56–57).

13. This perception greets Janie upon her very arrival in Eatonville as Mrs. Joe Starks. Almost immediately, the townsmen argue over which of them might win her affections and over what "kind" of woman she is: "Aw, git reconciled! Dat woman don't want you. You got tuh learn dat all de women in de world ain't been brought up on no teppentine still, and no saw-mill camp. There's some women dat jus' ain't for you tuh broach. You can't git *her* wid no fish sandwich" (39).

14. Hurston describes how their relationship translates to the store: "[Janie] had her first taste of presiding over [the store] the day it was complete and finished. Jody told her to dress up and stand in the store all that evening. Everybody was coming sort of fixed up, and he didn't mean for nobody else's wife to rank with her. She must look on herself as the bell-cow, the other women were the gang" (41).

15. The issue of "good hair" is obviously at play here, with Janie's authentic blackness coming into question and her hair serving as both a conduit of access into a more privileged sector of social rank and a signifier of the exploitation she encounters at the hands of her domineering husband Joe Starks, who is primarily invested in upward mobility regarding economics and race-consciousness.

16. However, also at work in these introductory pages is the offering of another option that comes in the form of Janie, specifically her relationship with Pheoby. Janie uses Pheoby as a mediating voice between her and the community.

17. The town's gossip is evidence of this vision of Janie: "Tea Cake and Mrs. Mayor Starks! All the men that she could get, and fooling with somebody like Tea Cake!" (110).

18. Tea Cake is quick to reestablish traditional gender expectations, ensuring that he is still regarded as being able to take care of Janie: "You don't think Ah'm tryin' tuh git outa takin' keer uh yuh, do yuh, Janie, 'cause Ah ast yuh tuh work long side uh me?" (133). Janie responds with a comparison to Eatonville: "Ah naw, honey. Ah laks it. It's mo' nicer than settin' round dese quarters all day. Clerkin' in dat store wuz hard, but heah, we ain't got nothin' tuh do but do our work and come home and love" (133).

19. Bone makes a similar observation, but casts it in contradistinction to Hazel Carby's reading: "The novel does not uncritically reproduce what Carby identifies in *Mules and Men* as the 'stress on a continuity of [rural black Southern] cultural beliefs and practices with beliefs and practices in the Caribbean.' Far from it . . . Hurston's depiction of African American workers on the muck as initially aloof and condescending toward 'the Saws' and their dances suggests that she was more skeptical that Carby allows about the viability of a diasporic (or 'displaced') Southern cum Caribbean rural black folk culture. Although Janie's pioneering personal embrace of the Bahamians and their culture generates an inchoate transnational folk community, Tea Cake's conversation with Lias indicates that there are still national(ist) barriers to the growth and survival of such a community" (773).

20. Citing Thadious Davis, Jan Cooper, and Patricia Yaeger as notable exceptions, Bone refers to what David McWhirter calls possibly "southern studies' oddest and most

self-destructive feature: its strange divorce from African American literary and cultural studies" (qtd. in Bone 755). Bone notes, "Yet much recent work on Hurston by scholars working in Southern studies, whether moderately revisionist or more radically transnational, has remained disengaged from the heated debates over Hurston in African American studies. This is perplexing if one considers that Hurston's representation of the South—and of the U.S. South in relation to the Caribbean—has been a major point of contention within these debates, in which Carby's work has been central" (755).

CHAPTER 3

1. Also at stake are questions of ownership and statehood: "Willow Springs ain't in no state. Georgia and South Carolina done tried, though—been trying since right after the Civil War to prove that Willow Springs belong to one or the other of them" (4–5).

2. In the geographical and thematic contexts, *Mama Day* finds an important parallel in Julie Dash's *Daughters of the Dust* (1991). The film and subsequent book tell the story of the Peazant family, who live in a Gullah community off this same coastline shared by South Carolina and Georgia at the turn of the twentieth century. The film centers on Nana Peazant, the matriarch of the family, who, like Miranda Day, preserves the traditions and rituals of their ancestors. Inasmuch as the family has lived on the islands since being displaced as slaves, heritage and memory take on key importance within the framework of place. The film tracks the final days on the island for several members of the younger generation who are about to head north to modernity and a new way of life. There are many compelling ties to be made between *Mama Day* and *Daughters of the Dust,* including the presence of African and Afro-Caribbean themes and practices, the correlation between characters like Cocoa and Eula, and the responses to American industrialization and modern ethos. While I am unable to expand on such avenues of study in this book, *Daughters of the Dust* remains a key partner-text to *Mama Day.*

3. Ritual travels with Cocoa, too, in her comparisons of New York and Willow Springs. When she receives a package full of small gifts from the Candle Walk that Willow Springs celebrates, she regrets what she believes to be a lack of rituals in New York: "I was utterly . . . even more depressed when I got my Candle Walk package the next week. What in the hell was I doing in this city? It was cold and unfriendly. I took out the sweet orange rock Grandma had sent me and Mama Day's eternal lavender water. Seven years away from that place and December twenty-second still didn't feel right without my seeing a lighted candle" (122).

4. The effects of Ruby's spell start taking hold at almost exactly the time that the hurricane hits Willow Springs (249–50). While they both surely represent supernatural power (hurricanes are, after all, simultaneously "natural" disasters and "acts of God"), what is also at work here is Cocoa's physical relationship to place. Her body begins to deteriorate as the island itself endures the force of the storm.

5. Miranda's thoughts of the North as represented on Phil Donahue's show translate into ideas on race as well, especially regarding the show's subject matter: "On all of these 'fascinating topics' she had one opinion and that could be summed up in two words: white folks. And when they found a colored somebody to act the fool . . . she expanded it to three words: honorary white folks" (38).

6. While outside my present focus in this chapter, an interesting comparative analysis might be made of Sapphira in *Mama Day* and the matriarch in Willa Cather's *Sap-

phira and the Slave Girl on the level of performative and political manipulations in the context of slavery from two opposing power positions.

7. The concern Miranda shows here for what information is transmitted across generations, and how, resembles the matriarchal worlds found in Morrison's *Song of Solomon* and *Beloved*, in which race and history offer particular understandings of family identities.

8. This is a particularly difficult undertaking for George, who, earlier, reveals his uneasiness around Miranda's chickens: "He kinda hesitates when the chickens . . . start flocking around his feet . . . He don't seem any more comfortable inside the fence, tiptoeing around the pullets . . . And George looks about to break and run when her old brown rooster lets out a mighty crow" (194–95). When Miranda reminds him that he sees a lot of chickens in the normal course of things, just "wrapped up neat under cellophane," George's only reply is, "I think I like them better that way" (195).

9. George does refer to the difficulty of his literal trip through the west woods to meet Miranda in the other place to hear how to save Cocoa. His description of the woods changes from his initially calling them "a real pleasure" to his remembering "It was a long walk as I stumbled through the west woods, trying to step over fallen trees and around huge sections of gouged earth" (293).

10. There is an easy parallel here to Gayl Jones's *Corregidora*, in which ancestral tales of slavery help to illuminate present circumstances and questions.

11. When Miranda awakes from her vague dream/sleep state, she knows she must go uncover the well where her sister Peace died. Her understanding of her own positionality as Daughter in the Days, then, reveals itself as paired with a description of her work.

12. John Indian makes a similar appeal to performance in *I, Tituba*, which I discuss in the next chapter. When Tituba asks if they will get into trouble if discovered in the middle of their dancing and laughing with other slaves, he tells her, "They expect niggers to get drunk and dance and make merry once their masters have turned their backs. Let's *play* at being perfect niggers" (32).

13. See Tara McPherson, *Reconstructing Dixie: Race, Gender, and Nostalgia in the Imagined South* (2003) and James C. Cobb, *Away Down South: A History of Southern Identity* (2005).

14. Specifically, she tells him why their story is too complicated to tell her children. When she refers to the problems of telling her son what happened, she ironically explains, "Mama Day was right—give him the simple truth. And it's the one truth about you that I hold on to" (311). The invocation of a "simple truth" speaks to the very impossibility of the same.

15. George buys books to "figure out" how to live with a woman and is disappointed with the non-answers he finds: "Women stayed on an emotional roller coaster: between being premenstrual, postmenstrual, and menstrual, they were normal only about seventy-two hours out of each month . . . Every time you snapped at me or refused to be reasonable, it wasn't you—it was your estrogen . . . I made sure the next thing I read was written by a man. It was the same slew of depressing charts with another ongoing plea for tolerance: you were all, indeed, shrews through no fault of your own and men should try to be supportive . . . I found out very quickly that when living with a woman, the shortest distance between two points is by way of China" (141–42).

16. George attempts to approach the reductive subject of "what women want" using logic. His misogyny thus maintains the veneer of common sense: "I found out most women just didn't have Mrs. Jackson's pragmatism about the whole thing . . . And they're all waiting with some form of that inevitable question, 'What is it about me per-

sonally that turns you on?' But you're getting absolutely nowhere if you give them the truth: How can there be anything personal about you to turn me on? At this stage of the game, it's my own hormones. See, then you're a smart ass, and even one of those 'liberated' ladies will swivel around on her bar stool and find someone else to tell her what she wants to hear" (104–5).

17. In fact, it is the ritual itself that is a key part of the comfort Cocoa feels. She remembers the sayings about hair: "A ball of hair in my hands to be burned when we were through. A bird will take it and make a nest—you'll have headaches all your life. All unspoken and by rote. I felt a void when she was done" (246).

18. Miranda shares the impulse to revert to an earlier familial space. As she cares for Cocoa and notices that "it was a grown woman's body leaning over the table," she "allows herself to wish that it wasn't so, that [Cocoa had] never left to go beyond the bridge and still belonged only to them" (265).

19. Toward the end of the novel, when Abigail is dead, the call-and-response still continues: "Taking up her walking stick, [Miranda] hobbles out to the front yard and looks over at the yellow bungalow. No need to cross that road anymore, so she turns her face up into the warm air—You there, Sister?—to listen for the rustling of the trees. There's never a day so still that at least one leaf ain't moving" (312).

20. The blurring of borders between the women happens again when Cocoa tells her grandmother and great-aunt that she wants to leave Candle Walk and go back home to Abigail's house. Miranda immediately responds to her by saying, "Then we'll all go back" (307).

21. Discussing the "professional rivalry" between Miranda and Dr. Buzzard, George appeals to Miranda on the level of her service to others: "These little friendly rivalries go on in any profession. The important thing is that you're both serving the community" (196). Furthermore, Miranda notes the different work thresholds in Willow Springs versus the mainland. When she needs to fix the roof on the family home in the other place, she notes that she will have to hire workers "from beyond the bridge . . . 'cause nobody in Willow Springs would come out to the other place" (254).

22. The novel was originally published in 1986 as *Moi, Tituba, sorcière . . . Noire de Salem*.

CHAPTER 4

1. For one example, see the writings of the mid-eighteenth-century governor of Massachusetts Bay Thomas Hutchinson. Specifically, see *The History of the Province of Massachusetts-Bay, from the Charter of King William and Queen Mary, in 1691, Until the Year 1750*, vol. 2.

2. I am thinking specifically of Hayden White's groundbreaking work that sees history as having meaning only inasmuch as narrative form invests it with the present concerns and interests of those writing the histories. See especially *Metahistory: The Historical Imagination in Nineteenth-Century Europe* (1975) and *The Content of Form: Narrative Discourse and Historical Representation* (1990).

3. She is able, then, to sustain a narrative emphasis on issues of gender in a text about a woman who is effectively, in Hortense Spillers's words, "ungendered." See Spillers's "Mama's Baby, Papa's Maybe: An American Grammar Book."

4. My reading of Tituba's importance as a speaking subject is more closely aligned with that of Robert McCormick Jr., who notes the significance of "I" in the title: "Tituba

is forced to say 'I' because as a black female slave from the Caribbean who lived in the seventeenth century, she was invisible. The oft-stated goal of both Tituba's first person narration and the author herself is to resuscitate that existence" (274–75).

5. Lionnet elaborates on her approach of attempted nonintrusion: "This technique might be labeled a noncoercive feminist practice of reading, since it allows text and reader to enter a dialogue that does not follow the usual rules of linear, agonistic, and patriarchal discourses. To read noncoercively is to allow my self to be interwoven with the discursive strands of the text, to engage in a form of intercourse wherein I take my interpretive cues from the patterns that emerge as a result of this encounter—in other words, it is to enjoy an erotics of reading somewhat similar to Barthes's in *The Pleasure of the Text*" (28). I would submit that there is no such thing as a reading that is noncoercive or a text hovering in splendid isolation from its readership. While Lionnet admits that she can "never be a neutral observer," she also suggests that "our lives are overdetermined by language and ideology, history and geography" and that her purpose is "to try to investigate how that larger context may be present *in* the text" (28).

6. Baker is referring to Elizabeth Bruss's phraseology here of "autobiographical acts" from her 1976 book by the same name.

7. Specifically, Baker has in mind the detractions of Benedetto Croce and Rebecca Chalmers Burton, the former of whom notes the unavoidable egotism of the genre and the latter of whom discusses the inevitable limitations of memory.

8. Mortimer relies on "humanist and geographer" Yi-Fu Tuan, who defines "place" as rootedness and "space" as freedom in *Space and Place: The Perspective of Experience*.

9. Manzor-Coats provides an extremely useful history of the text's publication development, especially noting the audiences to which the different editions appealed. The text first appeared in France as historical fiction. Manzor-Coats states, "In the Euro-American tradition, historical novels, or better yet 'historical romances,' have a readership of mostly middle-class white women" (738). The next Folio edition was the first to be translated into English, and the cover showed a "black woman's face whose outline is achieved through variations of the colors red and orange out of what appears to be a wire fence" (738). Manzor-Coats explains, "There is no doubt that the targeted audience here is 'angry women,' more specifically 'angry black women'" (738). Finally, Manzor-Coats describes the English-language edition published in New York: "The English translation has a foreword by Angela Davis, and the foreword is clearly marked/inscribed at the bottom of the front cover. If in the French editions Condé had to validate rhetorically Tituba's voice even at the expense of reducing her own authorial position to a minimum, it seems that for the U.S. market another kind of validation needed to be made. In this case, Condé's work, relatively unfamiliar to the insular African American literary and critical tradition—a tradition that generally focuses on U.S. material—needed to be 'authorized' by several 'gatekeepers' of this tradition: thus brief remarks by Charles Johnson and Henry Louis Gates Jr. on the back cover. I read the choice of Angela Davis to write the foreword as part of this same validating and authorizing effort. Not only does the U.S. audience in general need the connection of Condé with a larger African *American* tradition, but the U.S. feminist audience specifically also seems to need Angela Davis's validating words in order to see the connections between Condé and women of African descent" (739).

10. In fact, Condé's response in an interview to why she wrote the novel was simply, "Mme Gallimard from Mercure de France asked me to write a story about a woman from the Caribbean. I accepted immediately, because it was a challenge" (qtd. in Manzor-Coats 737).

11. In *Mama Day*, Miranda is described as being able to "stand so still, she becomes part of a tree" (81). As a child, she is similarly able to "disappear into the shadow of a summer cottonwood, flatten herself so close to the ground under a moss-covered rock shelf" such that "folks started believing [she] became a spirit in the woods" (79).

12. Manzor-Coats believes that "this parodic chapter should be taken seriously, for it stages the typical power relations existing between white liberal feminists and women of color in contemporary Anglo society" (742). More important to my own focus, "It also stages incongruities of their different experiences, different along both racial and class axes" (742).

13. Only three years after the American edition of *I, Tituba* was published, another moment of intertextuality between Tituba and Hester arrived in Roland Joffe's poorly received film interpretation of *The Scarlet Letter*. In the modern filmic rendition, Demi Moore's Hester Prynne receives the services of Mituba (played by Lisa Jolliff-Andoh), a slave girl who becomes inordinately devoted to her mistress. Conveniently, "poor, mute Mituba" has no voice with which to betray Hester; however, Roger Chillingworth uses her to get to Hester and Dimmesdale. In significant ways, Roger Chillingworth's growing insanity in the film is overtly tied to his relationship with "native" rituals and traditions. At the height of his obsessive attempt to ruin his wife, Chillingworth (played by Robert Duvall) dances with a deerskin on his head and howls at the moon. His racial performance thus directly corresponds with the perception of his sanity. In a Conradesque move, the film depicts his sanity slipping away by making more frequent his interactions with the tribal Native Americans. As in *I, Tituba*, sexuality is central to the relationship between Hester and Mituba. However, the film presents this in a severely dichotomized power hierarchy. In one scene, Mituba watches as Hester seductively undresses and dwells on this image as she masturbates in the bathtub. Here, Tituba's question "Was Hester showing me another kind of bodily pleasure?" is revisited. However, this pleasure is manifested from her voyeuristic onlooking rather than "from hugging a body similar to [her] own." Perhaps this is why most reviews that bring up Mituba's role in the film at all do so with a facetious nod to what critic Caryn James calls in her *New York Times* review "one of the most ludicrous sex scenes ever." Part of what makes sexuality appear "ludicrous," however, seems to be the very presence of this unlikely sexual agent. James complains, "[Joffe] intercuts glimpses of Hester and Arthur in the grain . . . with scenes of Mituba in the bathing tub and a little red bird that fills the screen often, for no apparent reason." Mituba adds an uncanny element, apparently, because she masturbates—what critic Chris Hicks calls "her ritual"—while Hester and Arthur have sex in the granary. Discussing a different scene, Roger Ebert reveals why Mituba detracts from an otherwise sexual continuity in the film: "Hester's comely slave girl, Mituba . . . prepares her bath, and then Hester slowly luxuriates in it by candlelight, while dreaming of Arthur. It is hard to see for sure, but I think she may be indulging in the practice that the nuns called 'interfering with herself.' Meanwhile, through a convenient peephole, Mituba watches lustfully, for no other purpose than to provide the additional thrill of one attractive woman observing another one naked. Will the sin that dare not speak its name make an appearance in Massachusetts Bay? Alas, no; the prospect of interracial lesbian love, appealing as it is to today's filmmakers, would not quite fit into this story, even as revised and updated." Apart from his over-the-top euphemisms, Ebert does not entertain what he views as Mituba's "lust" as anything worth considering except in the guilty "thrill" it gives the audience. Thus, "interracial lesbian love" is a cheap convention rather than a complicated dynamic of gender, power, and race. The power dynamic between Hester and Mituba in the film is what I find most

interesting about this scene. Mituba's presence in the film serves largely as a supportive foil for Hester's own sexual desire. Her fierce loyalty is certainly not returned to any degree. Rather, she offers a portrait of a slave "staying in her place:" voiceless, loyal, and worshipping of her mistress.

14. Dukats shows, for example, that "Tituba narrativizes herself variably as mother, fetus, or newborn" (747). Furthermore, the "oppositional or revolutionary Tituba presents the other of that Tituba we have come to know, the West Indian slave who, under torture, confessed that she submitted to Satan's control and had tormented children" (747). Tituba, clearly, appears and describes herself in many different ways throughout the novel. This reveals the ambiguity out of which her voice speaks.

15. Elaine G. Breslaw offers a fascinating look at another facet of Tituba's ambiguity. She sheds light on evidence that Tituba was an Arawak Indian. While Angela Davis sees such debates as "hop[es] to stir up enmity between black and Native American women as we seek to recreate our respective histories," I believe that conversations like these are productive inroads to an interrogation of strict understandings of Tituba's identity and voice (xi).

16. Manzor-Coats suggests that this is strategic, that "In her sexual relations and lovemaking . . . Tituba constitutes herself as a desiring subject, her otherwise despised black body becoming a desirable body, a body she can enjoy" (742).

17. With "Demystifying Female Marooning: Oppositional Strategies and the Writing of Testimonios in the French Caribbean," Pascale De Souza provides a compelling look at how Caribbean texts, including *I, Tituba,* use maroon communities strategically. It allows for an intriguing understanding of Tituba as a revolutionary during her time in the maroon community at the end of the novel.

18. In both cases, maternity is significantly not a fixed or stable force of gender identification. It is a volatile context that is subject to situational ethics and concerns.

19. Benjamin Cohen uses "witch" as an unlikely term of endearment later in the text, interestingly in relationship to power hierarchies. He tells her, "Our God knows neither race nor color," and Tituba replies, "Your God even accepts witches?" (131). His tender response is, "Tituba, you are my beloved witch" (131).

CONCLUSION

1. Favor is referring to Carby's essay "The Historical Novel of Slavery" in Deborah McDowell's and Arnold Rampersad's 1989 volume, *Slavery and the Literary Imagination* and Smith as presented in Gates's "The Black Person in Art: How Should S/he Be Portrayed?"

2. In her essay "Realism, Form, Politics: Reading Connections in Caribbean Migration Narratives" (2011), Nicole Rizzuto deals with similar issues through analyses of ethnography and readership in relation to Lamming's *The Pleasures of Exile* and *The Emigrants* as well as Rhys's *Voyage in the Dark.*

WORKS CITED

Anderson, Benedict. *Imagined Communities: Reflections on the Origin and Spread of Nationalism.* London: Verso, 1983.
Andreas, James R., Sr. "Signifyin' on *The Tempest* in Gloria Naylor's *Mama Day.*" In *Shakespeare and Appropriation,* ed. Christy Desmet and Robert Sawyer. London: Routledge, 1999. 103–18.
Appadurai, Arjun. *Modernity at Large: Cultural Dimensions of Globalization.* Minneapolis: University of Minnesota Press, 1996.
Awkward, Michael. *New Essays on "Their Eyes Were Watching God."* Cambridge: Cambridge University Press, 1990.
Baker, Houston A., Jr. *Blues, Ideology, and Afro-American Literature: A Vernacular Theory.* Chicago: University of Chicago Press, 1984.
———. *The Journey Back: Issues in Black Literature and Criticism.* Chicago: University of Chicago Press, 1980.
———. *Workings of the Spirit: The Poetics of Afro-American Women's Writing.* Chicago: University of Chicago Press, 1991.
Baumgartner, Barbara. "The Body as Evidence: Resistance, Collaboration, and Appropriation in *The History of Mary Prince.*" *Callaloo* 24.1 (Winter 2001): 253–75.
Beaulieu, Elizabeth Ann. *Black Women Writers and the American Neo-Slave Narrative: Femininity Unfettered.* Westport, CT: Greenwood, 1999.
Berrian, Brenda F. "Claiming an Identity: Caribbean Women Writers in English." *Journal of Black Studies* 25.2 (December 1994): 200–216.
Blyn, Robin. "The Ethnographer's Story: *Mama Day* and the Specter of Relativism." *Twentieth-Century Literature* 48.3 (Fall 2002): 239–63.
Bone, Martyn. "The (Extended) South of Black Folk: Intraregional and Transnational Migrant Labor in *Jonah's Gourd Vine* and *Their Eyes Were Watching God.*" *American Literature* 79.4 (2007): 753–79.

———. *The Postsouthern Sense of Place in Contemporary Fiction*. Baton Rouge: Louisiana State University Press, 2005.

Bracks, Lean'tin L. *Writings on Black Women of the Diaspora: History, Language, and Identity*. New York: Garland, 1997.

Breslaw, Elaine G. *Tituba, Reluctant Witch of Salem: Devilish Indians and Puritan Fantasies*. New York: New York University Press, 1996.

Brewer, Rose. "Theorizing Race, Class, and Gender: The New Scholarship of Black Feminist Intellectuals and Black Women's Labor." In *Theorizing Black Feminisms: The Visionary Pragmatism of Black Women*, ed. Abena P. A. Busia and Stanlie M. James. New York: Routledge, 1993. 13–30.

Bruss, Elizabeth. *Autobiographical Acts*. Baltimore: Johns Hopkins University Press, 1976.

Butler, Judith. *Undoing Gender*. New York: Routledge, 2004.

Carby, Hazel V. *Cultures in Babylon: Black Britain and African America*. London: Verso, 1999.

———. *Reconstructing Womanhood: The Emergence of the Afro-American Woman Novelist*. Oxford: Oxford University Press, 1987.

Carpio, Glenda R., and Werner Sollors. "The Newly Complicated Zora Neale Hurston." *Chronicle of Higher Education,* January 2, 2011. http://chronicle.com/article/The-Newly-Complicated-Zora/125753/.

Casey, Edward S. *Getting Back into Place: Toward a Renewed Understanding of the Place-World*. Bloomington: Indiana University Press, 1993.

Clifford, James. "Diasporas." *Cultural Anthropology* 9.3 (August 1994): 302–38.

Cobb, James C. *Away Down South: A History of Southern Identity*. Oxford: Oxford University Press, 2005.

Coker, Coleman. "Regionalism in a Global Community." *Southern Reader* 8 (Spring 1992): 7.

Condé, Maryse. *I, Tituba, Black Witch of Salem*. Trans. Richard Philcox. Charlottesville: University Press of Virginia, 1992.

———. "The Role of the Writer." *World Literature Today* 67.4 (Autumn 1993): 697–99.

Cowart, David. "Matriarchal Mythopoesis: Naylor's *Mama Day*." *Philological Quarterly* 77.4 (Fall 1998): 439–59.

Daughters of the Dust. Dir. Julie Dash. Kino International, 1991.

Davis, Adrienne. "'Don't Let Nobody Bother Yo' Principle': The Sexual Economy of American Slavery." In *Sister Circle: Black Women and Work*, ed. Sharon Harley and the Black Women and Work Collective. New Brunswick: Rutgers University Press, 2002. 103–127.

Davis, Angela Y. Foreword to *I, Tituba, Black Witch of Salem*, by Maryse Condé. Trans. Richard Philcox. Charlottesville: University Press of Virginia, 1992. ix–xi.

Davis, Thadious M. "Reclaiming the South." In *Bridging Southern Cultures: An Interdisciplinary Approach*, ed. John Lowe. Baton Rouge: Louisiana State University Press, 2005. 57–76.

———. *Southscapes: Geographies of Race, Region, and Literature*. Chapel Hill: University of North Carolina Press, 2011.

De Souza, Pascale. "Demystifying Female Marooning: Oppositional Strategies and the Writing of Testimonios in the French Caribbean." *International Journal of Francophone Studies* 3.3 (2000): 141–50.

Donaldson, Susan V., and Anne Goodwyn Jones. "Haunted Bodies: Rethinking the South through Gender." In *Haunted Bodies: Gender and Southern Texts*, ed. Anne Goodwyn Jones and Susan V. Donaldson. Charlottesville: University Press of Virginia, 1997. 1–19.

Duck, Leigh Anne. "'Go there tuh *know* there': Zora Neale Hurston and the Chronotope of the Folk." *American Literary History* 13.2 (2001): 266–94.

Dukats, Mara L. "A Narrative of Violated Maternity: *Moi, Tituba, sorcière . . . Noire de Salem.*" *World Literature Today* 67.4 (Autumn 1993): 745–50.

Ebert, Roger. "Review of *The Scarlet Letter.*" *Sun Times,* October 13, 1995.

Eckard, Paula Gallant. "The Prismatic Past in *Oral History* and *Mama Day.*" *MELUS* 20.3 (Fall 1995): 121–35.

Ellison, Ralph. "Recent Negro Fiction." *New Masses* 40.6 (August 5, 1940): 22–26.

Favor, J. Martin. *Authentic Blackness: The Folk in the New Negro Renaissance.* Durham, NC: Duke University Press, 1999.

Fields, Karen E., and Barbara J. Fields. *Racecraft: The Soul of Inequality in American Life.* London: Verso, 2012.

"First Person Singular." *Essence* 3 (2004): 132.

Fish, Cheryl J. *Black and White Women's Travel Narratives: Antebellum Explorations.* Gainesville: University Press of Florida, 2004.

Foster, Frances Smith. "Adding Color and Contour to Early American Self-Portraitures: Autobiographical Writings of Afro-American Women." In *Conjuring: Black Women, Fiction, and Literary Tradition,* ed. Marjorie Pryse and Hortense J. Spillers. Bloomington: Indiana University Press, 1985. 25–38.

Gilroy, Paul. *The Black Atlantic: Modernity and Double Consciousness.* London: Verso, 1993.

Griffin, Farah Jasmine. *"Who Set You Flowin'?": The African-American Migration Narrative.* New York: Oxford University Press, 1995.

Grosz, Elizabeth. *Volatile Bodies: Toward a Corporeal Feminism.* Bloomington: Indiana University Press, 1994.

Guttman, Sondra. "'No Tomorrow in the Man': Uncovering the Great Depression in *Their Eyes Were Watching God.*" *Arizona Quarterly* 63.3 (2007): 91–117.

Hall, Stuart. "Créolité and the Process of Creolization." In *The Creolization Reader: Studies in Mixed Identities and Cultures,* ed. Robin Cohen and Paola Toninato. New York: Routledge, 2010. 26–38.

———. "Cultural Identity and Diaspora." In *Colonial Discourse and Post-Colonial Theory: A Reader,* ed. Patrick Williams and Laura Chrisman. New York: Columbia University Press, 1994. 392–401.

Harris, Joseph E., ed. *Global Dimensions of the African Diaspora.* Washington, DC: Howard University Press, 1982.

Harris, Laura Alexandra. "Queer Black Feminism: The Pleasure Principle." *Feminist Review* 54 (Autumn 1996): 3–30.

Hicks, Chris. "Film Review: *The Scarlet Letter.*" *Deseret News.* October 17, 1995.

Higginbotham, Evelyn Brooks. "African-American Women's History and the Metalanguage of Race." *Signs: Journal of Women in Culture and Society* 17.21 (1992): 251–74.

Hurston, Zora Neale. *Their Eyes Were Watching God.* 1937. New York: Perennial Library, 1990.

Ivey, Adriane L. "Beyond Sacrifice: Gloria Naylor Rewrites the Passion." *MELUS* 30.1 (Spring 2005): 85–108.

James, Caryn. "Passion, Nudity, Puritans and, Oh, Yes, That Scarlet Letter 'A'." *New York Times.* October 13, 1995.

Johnson, Barbara. "Metaphor, Metonymy, and Voice in *Their Eyes Were Watching God*." In *Zora Neale Hurston's "Their Eyes Were Watching God": A Casebook.* Oxford: Oxford University Press, 2000. 41–58.

Joseph, Philip. "The Verdict from the Porch: Zora Neale Hurston and Reparative Justice." *American Literature* 74.3 (September 2002): 455–83.

Kubitschek, Missy Dehn. "Toward a New Order: Shakespeare, Morrison, and Gloria Naylor's *Mama Day*." *MELUS* 19.3 (Autumn 1994): 75–90.

Laclau, Ernesto. *Reflections on the Revolution of Our Time*. London: Verso, 1990.

Lamothe, Daphne. "Gloria Naylor's *Mama Day*: Bridging Roots and Routes." *African American Review* 39.1–2 (2005): 155–69.

Lavie, Smadar, and Ted Swedenburg, eds. *Displacement, Diaspora, and Geographies of Identity*. Durham, NC: Duke University Press, 1996.

Li, Stephanie. *Something Akin to Freedom: The Choice of Bondage in Narratives by African American Women*. Albany: State University of New York Press, 2010.

Lionnet, Françoise. *Autobiographical Voices: Race, Gender, Self-Portraiture*. Ithaca, NY: Cornell University Press, 1989.

———. *Postcolonial Representations: Women, Literature, Identity*. Ithaca, NY: Cornell University Press, 1995.

Locke, Alain. Review of *Tell My Horse*, by Zora Neale Hurston. *Opportunity*, February 1939, 38.

———. Review of *Their Eyes Were Watching God*, by Zora Neale Hurston. *Opportunity*, June 1, 1938.

Manzor-Coats, Lillian. "Of Witches and Other Things: Maryse Condé's Challenges to Feminist Discourse." *World Literature Today* 67.4 (Autumn 1993): 737–44.

McClintock, Anne. *Imperial Leather: Race, Gender and Sexuality in the Colonial Contest*. New York: Routledge, 1995.

McCormick, Robert H. Jr. "Return Passages: Maryse Condé Brings Tituba Back to Barbados." In *Black Imagination and the Middle Passage*, ed. Maria Diedrich, Henry Louis Gates Jr., and Carl Pederson. Oxford: Oxford University Press, 1999. 271–81.

McPherson, Tara. *Reconstructing Dixie: Race, Gender, and Nostalgia in the Imagined South*. Durham, NC: Duke University Press, 2003.

Meisenhelder, Susan. "False Gods and Black Goddesses in Naylor's *Mama Day* and Hurston's *Their Eyes Were Watching God*." *Callaloo* 23.4 (Autumn 2000): 1440–48.

Miller, Shawn. "'Some other way to try': From Defiance to Creative Submission in *Their Eyes Were Watching God*." *Southern Literary Journal* 37.1 (Fall 2004): 74–95.

Minor, Kyle. "Review of *The Dew Breaker*." *Antioch Review*, September 22, 2004.

Mitchell, Katharyne. "Different Diasporas and the Hype of Hybridity." In *Critical Geographies: A Collection of Readings*, ed. Harald Bauder and Salvatore Engel-Di Mauro. Praxis (e)Press, 2008. 257–77.

Mortimer, Mildred. "A Sense of Place and Space in Maryse Condé's *Les derniers rois mages*." *World Literature Today* 67.4 (Autumn 1993): 757–62.

Mudimbe, V. Y. *The Invention of Africa: Gnosis, Philosophy, and the Order of Knowledge*. Bloomington: Indiana University Press, 1988.

Mudimbé-Boyi, Elisabeth. "Giving a Voice to Tituba: The Death of the Author?" *World Literature Today* 67.4 (Autumn 1993): 751–56.

Mullin, Michael. *Africa in America: Slave Acculturation and Resistance in the American South and the British Caribbean, 1736–1831*. Chicago: University of Chicago Press, 1994.

Naylor, Gloria. *Mama Day*. New York: Vintage, 1988.

Newman, Judie. "'Dis Ain't Gimme, Florida': Zora Neale Hurston's *Their Eyes Were Watching God*." *Modern Language Review* 98.4 (October 2003): 817–26.
Paquet, Sandra Pouchet. "The Heartbeat of a West Indian Slave: *The History of Mary Prince*." *African American Review* 26.1 (1992): 131–46.
Paterson, Kathryn M. "Gloria Naylor's North/South Dichotomy and the Reversal of the Middle Passage: Juxtaposed Migrations within *Mama Day*." In *Middle Passages and the Healing Place of History: Migration and Identity in Black Women's Literature*, ed. Elizabeth Brown-Guillory. Columbus: The Ohio State University Press, 2006. 76–95.
Potter, Andrew. *The Authenticity Hoax: How We Get Lost Finding Ourselves*. New York: HarperCollins, 2010.
Prince, Mary. *The History of Mary Prince, A West Indian Slave, Related by Herself*. 1831. In *The Classic Slave Narratives*, ed. Henry Louis Gates Jr. New York: Mentor, 1987. 183–238.
Pryse, Marjorie Lee, and Hortense J. Spillers, eds. *Conjuring: Black Women, Fiction, and Literary Tradition*. Bloomington: Indiana University Press, 1985.
Puhr, Kathleen M. "Healers in Gloria Naylor's Fiction." *Twentieth Century Literature* 40.4 (Winter 1994): 518–27.
Richardson, Alan, and Debbie Lee. *Early Black British Writing: Olaudah Equiano, Mary Prince and Others*. New York: Houghton Mifflin, 2004.
Rizzuto, Nicole. "Realism, Form, Politics: Reading Connections in Caribbean Migration Narratives." *Comparative Literature* 64.4 (Fall 2011): 383–401.
Rodgers, Lawrence R. *Canaan Bound: The African-American Great Migration Novel*. Urbana: University of Illinois Press, 1997.
Santamarina, Xiomara. *Belabored Professions: Narratives of African American Working Womanhood*. Chapel Hill: University of North Carolina Press, 2005.
Scarlet Letter, The, directed by Roland Joffé (Burbank, CA: Buena Vista Pictures, 1995), DVD.
Sharpe, Jenny. *Ghosts of Slavery: A Literary Archaeology of Black Women's Lives*. Minneapolis: University of Minnesota Press, 2003.
———. "'Something Akin to Freedom': The Case of Mary Prince." *Differences: A Journal of Feminist Cultural Studies* 8.1 (1996): 31–56.
Spillers, Hortense J. *Black, White, and In Color: Essays on American Literature and Culture*. Chicago: University of Chicago Press, 2003.
———. *Comparative American Identities: Race, Sex, and Nationality in the Modern Text*. New York: Routledge, 1991.
———. "Mama's Baby, Papa's Maybe: An American Grammar Book." 1987. In *African American Literary Theory: A Reader*, ed. Winston Napier. New York: New York University Press, 2000. 257–79.
Stanford, Ann Folwell. *Bodies in a Broken World: Women Novelists of Color and the Politics of Medicine*. Chapel Hill: University of North Carolina Press, 2003.
Stepto, Robert B. "Ascent, Immersion, Narration." In *Modern Critical Interpretations: Zora Neale Hurston's "Their Eyes Were Watching God,"* ed. Harold Bloom. New York: Chelsea House, 1987. 5–8.
———. *From Behind the Veil: A Study of Afro-American Narrative*. Urbana: University of Illinois Press, 1979.
Storhoff, Gary. "'The Only Voice Is Your Own': Gloria Naylor's Revision of *The Tempest*." *African American Review* 29.1 (Spring 1995): 35–45.
Tate, Claudia. "Reshuffling the Deck; Or, (Re)Reading Race and Gender in Black Women's Writing." *Tulsa Studies in Women's Literature* 7.1 (1988): 119–32.

Thomas, Sue. "Pringle v. Cadell and Wood v. Pringle: The Libel Cases over *The History of Mary Prince.*" *Journal of Commonwealth Literature* 40.1 (2005): 113–35.
Thompson, Gordon E. "Projecting Gender: Personification in the Works of Zora Neale Hurston." *American Literature* 66.4 (December 1994): 737–63.
Todorova, Kremena. "'I Will Say the Truth to the English People': *The History of Mary Prince* and the Meaning of English History." *Texas Studies in Literature and Language* 43.3 (Fall 2001): 285–302.
Traub, Valerie. "Rainbows of Darkness: Deconstructing Shakespeare in the Work of Gloria Naylor and Zora Neale Hurston." In *Cross-Cultural Performances: Differences in Women's Re-Visions of Shakespeare,* ed. Marianne Novy. Urbana: University of Illinois Press, 1993. 150–64.
Tucker, Lindsey. "Recovering the Conjure Woman: Texts and Contexts in Gloria Naylor's *Mama Day.*" *African American Review* 28.2 (Summer 1994): 173–88.
Washington, Mary Helen. "'I Love the Way Janie Crawford Left Her Husbands': Zora Neale Hurston's Emergent Female Hero." In *Zora Neale Hurston's "Their Eyes Were Watching God": A Casebook,* ed. Cheryl A. Wall. New York: Oxford University Press, 2000. 19–26.
White, Hayden. *The Content of Form: Narrative Discourse and Historical Representation.* Baltimore: Johns Hopkins University Press, 1990.
———. *Metahistory: The Historical Imagination in Nineteenth-Century Europe.* Baltimore: Johns Hopkins University Press, 1975.
Whitlock, Gillian. *The Intimate Empire: Reading Women's Autobiography.* New York: Cassell, 2000.
Whitt, Margaret Earley. *Understanding Gloria Naylor.* Columbia: University of South Carolina Press, 1999.
Wright, Richard. "Between Laughter and Tears." Review of *These Low Grounds,* by Waters Edward Turpin, and *Their Eyes Were Watching God,* by Zora Neale Hurston. *New Masses,* October 5, 1937, pp. 22, 25.
Wynter, Sylvia. "Unsettling the Coloniality of Being/Power/Truth/Freedom: Towards the Human, After Man, Its Overrepresentation—An Argument." *New Centennial Review* 3.3 (2003): 257–337.

INDEX

African American literary theory, ix, 141, 148n1
African American Lives (Gates), 141
African-American Women's History and the Metalanguage of Race (Higginbotham), 145n3
African diaspora, 4, 74, 116, 120–21, 137; discourses on, 8; feminist readings of, 4–5; identification within, 22, 144; memory in, 28, 121; postcolonial readings of, 4–5, 143–44; scholarly analysis of, 13–14, 21, 142–44; voice of, 30
agency, 12, 24, 30–31, 74, 113, 142–43, 147n11
agenda: authorial, 19, 29; editorial, 24, 29; in *I, Tituba*, 112–13, 115–16, 118–19, 124
American South. *See* South, the
Anti-Slavery Society, 5, 10, 23–26, 29, 34, 42, 148n6
Antigua, 25–27, 32–33, 35, 42, 46
Augustine of Hippo, 16
Authentic Blackness: The Folk in the New Negro Renaissance (Favor), 6, 141, 143

authenticity, 6, 8, 13–14, 17–22, 25, 47, 52, 144; black, 6, 141–42; claims of, x, 5–7, 24; definition of, 53; destabilization of, 7, 15; discussions about, 24, 144; experiential, 21; in *History of Mary Prince*, 23–25, 28, 30–31, 36, 44–47; in *I, Tituba*, 111, 113, 115–17, 126, 136; personal, 30; rejection of, 18; subversion of, 15, 18, 28; in *Their Eyes*, 52, 58, 69, 77; women's, 23
Autobiographical Acts: The Changing Situation of a Literary Genre (Bruss), 154n6
Autobiographical Voices: Race, Gender, Self-Portraiture (Lionnet), 10–11, 16, 116
autobiography, 12, 37, 38, 116; black, 11–12, 146n9; in colonial and postcolonial culture, 28; conventional definition of, 28
Away Down South: A History of Southern Identity (Cobb), 152n13
Awkward, Michael, 66–67, 139–40

Bagley, Meredith, xi

163

Bahamas, 43, 74, 149n4
Baker, Houston, x, 12, 50, 59, 116–17, 149n1, 150n12, 154n6–154n7
Baumgartner, Barbara, 149n10
Barbados, 111, 119–20, 122–23, 125, 128–31, 133, 135
Barthes, Roland, 144
Behind the Veil: A Study of Afro-American Narrative (Stepto), 149n8
Beidler, Phil, x
Belabored Professions: Narratives of African American Working Womanhood (Santamarina), 146n5
Bell, Bernard W., 112
Beloved (Morrison), 91, 129, 152n7
Bermuda, 23, 31–32, 43, 45
Berrian, Brenda F., 29
Between Laughter and Tears (Wright), 149n6
bildungsroman, 53, 138
Black American Literature Forum (Gates), 141
Black and White Women's Travel Narratives: Antebellum Explorations (Fish), 133, 142
Black Person in Art: How Should S/he Be Portrayed, The (Gates), 156n1
Black, White, and In Color: Essays on American Literature and Culture (Spiller), 12
blackness, 6–7, 99, 141–42, 145n3, 150n15
Blackwell, Linda Patterson, xi
Blues, Ideology, and Afro-American Literature: A Vernacular Theory (Baker), 150n12
bodies, 8
Body of Evidence, The (Baumgartner), 149n10
Bolden, Tony, x
Bone, Martyn, 50–51, 54–56, 58, 73–74, 76, 147n12, 149n3, 150n10–50n11, 150n19–50n20
Bracks, Lean'tin, 28–29, 33, 45–47, 149n13
Breslaw, Elaine, 19, 111, 156n15
Brewer, Rose, 146n5, 146n7
Brown, William "Boysey," 1–4, 76
Brown v. Board of Education, 138–39

Bruss, Elizabeth, 154n6
Burton, Rebecca Chalmers, 154n7
Butler, Judith, 8, 146n4

Canaan Bound (Rodgers), 123
Carby, Hazel, 51–52, 55–56, 141, 145n3, 147n11, 149n8, 150n10–50n11, 150n19, 156n1
Caribbean, the, 6, 11, 14–18, 21, 52, 55, 109–10, 139, 150n20; in *History of Mary Prince*, 23, 30–31, 33, 42, 47; in *I, Tituba*, 111, 113, 115, 117, 119, 121–22, 126, 156n17; in *Mama Day*, 79, 104, 109; in *Their Eyes*, 51, 71–75, 77
Carpio, Glenda R., 138–40
Casey, Edward, 82, 88
Cather, Willa, 151n6
character, 6, 15, 23–24, 26, 31, 34–36, 41–43, 54
Christianity, 36, 40, 46, 104, 132
Chronicle of Higher Education (Carpio and Sollors), 138
class, ix, 8–9, 13, 37–38, 136, 140–42, 146n5–46n6, 146n8; in *Their Eyes*, 53, 60, 61, 63–70, 72–73, 75–77, 150n13–50n15, 150n17, 150n19
Classic Slave Narratives, The (Gates), 5, 24, 148n1
Cleveland, James, 79
Clotel (Brown), 4
Cobb, James C., 152n13
Coker, Coleman, 51, 149n2
Collins, Patricia Hill, 145n3
Comparative American Identities: Race, Sex and Nationality in the Modern Text (Spillers), 12–13
Condé, Maryse, 13, 16, 19, 21, 39, 101, 110–36, 148n3, 154n9–54n10
Conjuring: Black Women, Fiction, and Literary Tradition (Spillers), 12
Content of Form: Narrative Discourse and Historical Representation, The (White), 145n2, 153n2
Cooper, Jan, 55, 76, 149n9, 150n20
Corregidora (Jones), 152n10
counternarrative, 2
Crawford, Janie, 14, 17, 49–77, 110,

122, 138. See also *Their Eyes Were Watching God*
Crawford, William J., 1
Créolité and the Process of Creolization (Hall), 6
creolization, 6, 13, 20, 111; in *I, Tituba* 111
Crisis (Du Bois), 141
Croce, Benedetto, 154n7
Crooms, Sandy, xi
Culture on the Edge, xi
Cultures in Babylon: Black Britain and African America (Carby), 149n8
Cyphers, Tara, xi

Dash, Julie, 151n2
Daughters of the Dust (Dash), 151n2
Davenport, Alex, xi
Davis, Adrienne, 44
Davis, Angela, 113, 154n9, 146n15
Davis, Thadious, 15, 147n12, 150n20
Day, Miranda, 78–80, 82, 84–86, 88–95, 98, 100, 103–6, 109, 122, 151n2, 151n5, 152n8, 152n11, 155n11. See also *Mama Day*
De Souza, Pascale, 156n17
Demystifying Female Marooning: Oppositional Strategies and the Writing of Testimonios in the French Caribbean (De Souza), 156n17
Deutsch, David, xi
Different Diasporas and the Hype of Hybridity (Mitchell), 20–21
diasporas: community, 9; geosocial, 9
'Don't Let Nobody Bother Yo' Principle': The Sexual Economy of American Slavery (Davis), 44
Donaldson, Susan V., 94–95
Douglass, Frederick, 12, 32, 116–17
Du Bois, W. E. B., 138, 141
Duck, Leigh Anne, 51, 53, 64
Dukats, Mara L., 126, 129, 156n14
Dust Tracks on a Road (Hurston), 116

Early Black British Writing (Richardson and Lee), 24–25
Ebert-Wagner, Kristen, xi

Eckard, Paula Gallant, 79
Ellison, Ralph, 52, 149n7
Emancipation Bill, 24, 30
Emigrants, The (Lamming), 156n2
England, 24, 26–27, 30, 32–33, 35, 42
Environment and Planning D: Society and Space (Mitchell), 20
Erevelles, Nirmala, ix
Everglades, 50–51, 54–56, 67, 70–76
(Extended) South of Black Folk: Intraregional and Transnational Migrant Labor in 'Jonah's Gourd Vine' and 'Their Eyes Were Watching God,' The (Bone), 50, 54–56

family, 28, 39; in *Mama Day*, 78, 85, 88–93, 95–96, 98, 105, 153n18
Favor, J. Martin, 6, 141–43, 156n1
Female Tradition in Southern Literature (Manning), 149n9
feminism, 9–10, 20, 31, 48, 128, 145n3, 147n11; and race, 145n3, 147n11
femininity, 9, 34, 61, 147n10
feminist hero, 17, 50, 53–54, 62, 110, 118
feminization, 40
Ferguson, Moira, 30–31
Fields, Barbara, 114
Fields, Karen, 114
Fish, Cheryl, 133, 142
Foster, Frances Smith, 7–8, 10–12, 146n9
Frantom, Christina, xi
From Margin to Center (hooks), 145n3

Gates, Henry Louis Jr., 5, 24, 141, 148n1, 154n9
gender, 5, 7–10, 13, 15–17, 20, 43, 47, 110, 137–38, 140, 142, 146n6; in *History of Mary Prince*, 26–27, 30–34, 36–41, 44, 148n6; in *I, Tituba*, 112–115, 120, 124–25, 127–29, 132–33, 135; in *Mama Day*, 82, 88, 91, 93–96, 99–106, 108–9; in *Their Eyes*, 50–72, 76–77, 150n18
Ghosts of Slavery (Sharpe), 44–45, 148n9
Ginzberg, Lori D., 133
Giving a Voice to Tituba: The Death

of the Author? (Mudimbé-Boyi), 115–116
Gleason, William, 149n3
Glissant, Edouard, 10–11
Grant, Joan, 30
Great Migration, the, 14, 17, 55–56, 74
Griffin, Farah Jasmine, 14
Grosz, Elizabeth, 8, 146n4
Guttman, Sondra, 53, 67, 69–70, 75

Hall, Stuart, 6
Hammonds, Evelynn, 145n3
Harlem Renaissance, 138–39, 141
Harris, Laura Alexandra, 136, 146n7–146n8
Heartbeat of a West Indian Slave, The (Paquet), 29
Heremakhonon (Condé), 116
Higginbotham, Evelyn Brooks, 94, 145n3, 147n11
hip hop, 6
histoire Romanesque, 117
historical accuracy, 4, 18–19, 67, 111, 120, 136
Historical Novel of Slavery, The (Carby), 156n1
history, 2, 4; as fiction, 4
History of Mary Prince, A West Indian Slave, Related by Herself, The (Prince), 5, 13–18, 21, 23–48, 79, 110, 112, 126, 136–37, 142, 148n1, 148n7; as autobiography, 37; authenticity of, 23–25, 28, 30–31, 36, 44–47; categorizations of author, 29–30, 32, 34–36, 41–42; confrontations and power struggles in, 45, 149n13; cultural context of, 27–29, 31, 36, 47; familial bonds in, 39; gender in, 26–27, 30–32, 34, 36–41, 44, 148n6; impact of patronage and editing on, 26, 29, 31–32, 36, 41, 45, 149n12; migrations in, 31–33, 45, 48; narrative of, 23–34 38, 40–41, 43–48, 148n5, 149n14; omissions from, 25–26, 41, 44, 46–47, 149n10; place in, 23, 26, 29, 32, 35–36, 41–43, physical abuse in, 39, 45–47; race in, 30, 36–39, 46–47; as reflective of working slave women's experience, 33; representation of ideal femininity, 34–35, 37, 40, 42, 44–46; representation of the Caribbean, 23, 30–31, 33, 42, 47; role of geographic and societal shifts in, 27–28; self in, 25, 30–31, 33, 38; sexuality in, 26, 32–33, 41–42, 44–46, 148n9, 149n10; slavery/freedom dichotomy in, 33; voice in, 23, 25–31, 36–38, 44–47, 148n4; women's relationships in, 26, 36–40, 148n8; work in, 27, 31–33, 36, 40–44
History of the Province of Massachusetts-Bay, from the Charter of King William and Queen Mary, in 1691, Until the Year 1750, vol. 2 (Hutchinson), 153n1
home, 14; in *I, Tituba*, 115, 120, 122–23; in *Mama Day*, 82–83
hooks, bell, 145n3
Hughes, Langston, 51–52, 141
humanism, 11
Hurston, Zora Neale, 13, 16–21, 49–77, 79–80, 115–16, 138–40; critical assessment of, 138–41, 149n3, 150n20
Hutchinson, Thomas, 153n1
hybridity, 13, 20–22

I, Tituba, Black Witch of Salem (Condé), 13, 18–19, 21, 25, 28, 38–39, 88–89, 101–2, 106, 110–36, 148n3, 152n12, 153n22, 154n9; authenticity of, 111, 113, 115–17, 126, 136; authorial agenda of, 112–13, 115–16, 118–19, 124; Caribbean represented in, 111, 113, 115, 117, 119, 121–22, 126, 156n17; creolization in, 111; criticism of, 112–13, 115, 117, 119; freedom represented in, 112; gender in, 112–15, 120, 124–25, 127–29, 132–33, 135; history in, 112, 114–15, 118–22, 124, 134; history as fiction in, 112, 114, 119, 122; home represented in, 115, 120, 122–23; identity in, 112, 115, 122, 124, 126, 153n4; maternity in, 115, 129–31,

156n14, 156n18; memory in, 119–20, 134; migration in, 112, 117–18, 120–24, 126, 135, 146n4; narrative of, 112–13, 116, 118–22, 124, 136, 153n4; oppression in, 112, 121; place in, 111, 120, 125; power represented in, 113–15, 117, 120–21, 128, 133; Puritanism in, 113, 133; race in, 111–12, 114, 121, 124–25, 132, 156n15; rape in, 126; self in, 117, 118, 121–22, 126; sexuality in, 115, 117, 120, 124–29, 134, 155n13, 156n16; slavery in, 112–13, 120–22, 124, 127–30, 135–36, 155n13; voice of, 112–13, 115–16, 118, 120, 126, 128, 133, 135, 156n14; witchcraft in, 111–14, 117, 120–21, 130–35, 156n19; womanhood in, 112, 115, 117, 120, 124, 128–30, 134; women's relationships in, 115, 120, 123–25, 128, 134, 136; work in, 112–13, 115, 120, 124, 129, 131, 133, 135

'I Will Say the Truth to the English People': 'The History of Mary Prince' and the Meaning of English History (Todorova), 30

identity, 12–13, 140, 143; black, 12, 141–43; changing of, 9, 144; discourses on, 9; in *History of Mary Prince*, 26, 28–30; in *I, Tituba*, 112, 115, 122, 124, 126, 153n4; impact of migration on, 19–20, 156n4; in *Mama Day*, 79, 82–83, 89, 94, 102, 109; surrounding African diasporas, 22, 138, 143, 146n7; in *Their Eyes*, 49, 53–55, 58, 61–62, 73–74, 77

Imperial Leather: Race, Gender and Sexuality in the Colonial Contest (McClintock), 9

Intimate Empire, The (Whitlock), 28, 36–38, 46

Jacobs, Harriet, 129
Jacobs, Steve, xi
Jamaica, 43
James, Daniel, 32
Joffe, Roland, 155n13
Johnson, Barbara, 53–54, 66, 140
Johnson, Charles, 154n9
Jonah's Gourd Vine (Hurston), 56, 58
Jones, Anne Goodwyn, 94–95
Jones, Gayl, 112, 152n10
Joseph, Philip, 68, 77
Journey Back: Issues in Black Literature and Criticism, The (Baker), 12, 116–17

Kane, Sarah, xi
Kyriakoudes, Louis, 50

labor, 5, 9–10, 13, 17, 19, 27, 31, 43, 47, 58, 67, 110, 147n11; benevolent, 133; migrant, 73–75; racial differences in, 76; sexual, 32–33, 44–45. *See also* work
Laclau, Ernesto, 137
Lamming, George, 156n2
Last Magi, The (Condé), 117
Le Discours Antillais (Glissant), 10–11
Lee, Debbie, 24–25
Les derniers rois mages (Condé). See *Last Magi, The*
Li, Stephanie, 112
Life and Religious Experiences of Jarena Lee, A Colored Lady, The (Lee), 147n9
Lionnet, Françoise, 10–11, 16, 116–17, 147n10, 154n5
Litchfield, Malcolm, xi
Locke, Alain, 52, 140, 149n5

Mama Day (Naylor), 13–14, 17, 21, 25, 38–39, 57, 77–111, 114–15, 134, 151n2, 152n8, 152n15–52n16, 153n17, 154n21; Caribbean representation in, 79, 104, 109conjuring in, 80, 88, 91, 98, 103–4; criticism of, 80; displacement in, 79–80, 88; family in, 78, 85, 88–93, 95–96, 98, 105, 153n18; gender in, 82, 88, 91, 93–96, 99–106, 108–9; healing in, 80, 85, 89–92, 97–99, 104, 106; home in, 82–83; identity in, 79, 82–83, 89, 94, 102, 109; legend in,

78–79, 81, 85, 88–89, 92, 94–95, 106; maternity in, 100, 106; migration in, 79–80, 85, 89; oppression in, 79; place in, 81–83, 85–88, 90–97, 99, 101–5, 107–8, 151n4; power represented in, 79, 91, 100–1, 151n6; race in, 80–81, 85–86, 93–94, 96, 99, 103, 105, 109–10, 151n5; realness in, 79–80, 83–85, 90, 95–99, 102–3, 107, 109, 152n14; representation of the South, 79–80, 86, 88, 94–96, 99, 102–3, 105, 108–10; self in, 85, 89–90, 98, 102; slavery in, 78, 81–82, 88–89, 93–94, 99–100, 102, 109–10; travel in, 82–83, 85, 96, 109, 151n3, 152n9; voice of, 78, 81, 101; womanhood in, 80, 82, 93, 96, 99–103, 105–6; women's relationships in, 104–5, 153n19–53n20; work in, 80, 82, 88–90, 93, 95, 101, 104–9

Mama's Baby, Papa's Maybe: An American Grammar Book (Spillers), 12, 149n11, 153n3

Manly, Basil Sr., 2, 145n1

Manora, Yolanda, x

Manzor-Coats, Lillian, 118, 126–7, 154n9–54n10, 155n12, 156n16

Martin, Craig, xi

Martin, Lindsay, xi

Marxism, ix

masculinity, 9–10, 62, 95, 106, 108

maternity: in *I, Tituba*, 115, 129–31, 156n14, 156n18; in *Mama Day*, 100, 106

Mauritius, 43

McClintock, Anne, 9, 146n6

McCormick, Robert Jr., 153n4

McCutcheon, Russell, x–xi

McDowell, Deborah, 156n1

McElya, Micki, x

McPherson, Tara, 5–6, 51, 152n13

McWhirter, David, 150n20

Meisenhelder, Susan, 66

Metahistory: The Historical Imagination in Nineteenth-Century Europe (White), 153n2

migration, 5, 7–10, 13–14, 16–17, 19, 22, 26, 28, 47, 74, 142–44; and destabilization of freedom, 33, 50; in *History of Mary Prince*, 31–33, 45, 48; in *I, Tituba*, 112, 117–118, 120–24, 126, 135, 146n4; impact on identity, 19–20; in *Mama Day*, 79–80, 85, 89; narrative of, 38, 144; repression manifested in, 26; role in subject formation, 27; in *Their Eyes*, 50–59, 63–64, 67, 70, 73, 146n4, 150n10–50n11; and travel, 54–59, 62–63, 71, 77, 82–83, 96, 109, 151n3, 152n9; via slavery, 14, 39. *See also* Great Migration, the

Miller, Monica, xi

Miller, Shawn, 62, 77

Mitchell, Angelyn, 112

Mitchell, Katharyne, 20–21

Moi, Tituba, sorcière . . . Noire de Salem (Condé). See *I, Tituba, Black Witch of Salem*

money, 9, 23, 41, 68, 73

Morrison, Toni, 91, 112, 114, 129, 152n7

Mortimer, Mildred, 117, 154n8

motherhood. *See* maternity

Mudimbé-Boyi, Elisabeth, 115–16, 118–19

Mules and Men (Carby), 150n19

Mullen, Michael, 33

Murphy, Tim, ix

Mykle, Robert, 74

narrative, 2, 12, 21, 116, 143; accuracy of, 25, 143; as an author's responsibility, 19; as a product of patronage and editing, 26, 28, 31; authenticity of, 6, 20, 44, 46–47, 110, 137, 144; by women of color, 9, 25, 29, 142–43; of the Caribbean, 117; first-person, 12, 38; gender and self, 19–20, 31, 34, 136; historical, 2; in *History of Mary Prince*, 23–34, 38, 40–41, 43–48, 148n5, 149n14; in *I, Tituba*, 112–113, 116, 118–22, 124, 136, 153n4; liberatory, 112; master, 12; mock slave, 19, 112; neoslave, 112; parameters of, 14; personal, 2, 6, 144; revision of, 18, 50; shaped

by intended audience, 26, 117; slave, 10–12, 15–16, 18–19, 21, 23, 25, 28–30, 110–11, 142; subjectivity of, 22, 25, 31, 38; travel in, 9, 54, 56–59, 71, 142; women's, 5, 9, 117
Narrative of the Life and Travels of Mrs. Nancy Prince, A (Prince), 147n9
Narrative of the Life of Frederick Douglass (Douglass), 12, 116–17
Narrative of Violated Maternity, A (Dukats), 126, 129
nation, 8, 10, 14, 21, 51, 115, 123, 151n1
Naylor, Gloria, 13, 17, 21, 57, 77–110, 115
New Essays on 'Their Eyes Were Watching God' (Awkward), 66–67, 139–40
New Masses (Wright and Ellison), 149n6–149n7
New Southern Studies, 51
Newly Complicated Zora Neale Hurston, The (Carpio and Sollors), 138–39
Newman, Judie, 59, 73
Nietzsche, Friedrich, 4, 16
Notices of Brazil (Walsh), 43

Of Witches and Other Things: Maryse Condé's Challenges to Feminist Discourse (Manzor-Coats), 118
Ohio State University Press, The, xi
Opportunity (Locke), 52, 149n5
oppression, 19, 33, 38–39, 47, 79, 112, 121
origin, 13–14, 21–22, 82, 89, 111, 121–23, 141, 144
Our Nig; or, Sketches from the Life of a Free Black (Wilson), 147n9

Paquet, Sandra Pouchet, 25, 29–30
Parable of the Sower (Butler), 91
Phillips, Joseph, 25, 42
place, 14, 41–43, 53–54, 58, 60, 69–70, 73–74, 79, 81, 117, 147n11; in *History of Mary Prince*, 23, 26, 29, 32, 35–36, 41–43; in *I, Tituba*, 111, 120, 125; in *Mama Day*, 81–83, 85–88, 90–97, 99, 101–5, 107–8, 151n4; in *Their Eyes*, 53–54, 58, 60, 69–70, 73–74
Pleasure of the Text, The (Barthes), 154n5
Pleasures of Exile, The (Lamming), 156n2
political right, 20
Postcolonial Representations: Women, Literature, Identity (Lionnet), 117
Postsouthern Sense of Place in Contemporary Fiction (Bone), 147n12
power: in *History of Mary Prince*, 45, 149n13; in *I, Tituba*, 113–15, 117, 120–21, 128, 133; in *Mama Day*, 79, 91, 100–1, 151n6; in *Their Eyes*, 53, 57, 64–69, 72, 74
Pratt family, 2
Prince, Mary, 5, 10, 13–19, 21, 23–48, 50, 79, 100, 107, 110–12, 115–18, 121, 124, 127, 135, 137, 139, 146n4, 148n1–48n2. See also *History of Mary Prince, A West Indian Slave, Related by Herself, The*
Pringle, Mary, 47
Pringle, Thomas, 25–27, 31, 34–36, 41–44, 46–47, 100, 149n10, 149n13
Prismatic Past in 'Oral History' and 'Mama Day,' The (Eckard), 79
progressivism, 6, 12, 20, 100, 137–38, 141
Projecting Gender: Personification in the Works of Zora Neale Hurston (Thompson), 54, 149n8
Prynne, Hester, 39–40, 113, 123–26, 128, 130, 155n13
Puritanism, 113, 133

Queer Black Feminism: The Pleasure Principle (Harris), 146n8
Questionnaire, A (Du Bois), 141

race, ix, 7–10, 13, 15, 21, 30, 36–39, 47, 110, 136–37, 140–41, 146n5–46n6; feminism and, 145n3, 146n8; in *History of Mary Prince*, 30, 36–39, 46–47; in *I, Tituba*, 111–12, 114, 121, 124–25, 132, 156n15; in *Mama*

Day, 80–81, 85–86, 93–94, 96, 99, 103, 105, 109–10, 151n5; in *Their Eyes*, 59–60, 65, 68, 75–77, 150n15
racecraft, 114
Ramey, Steven, x–xi
Rampersad, Arnold, 156n1
Realism, Form, Politics: Reading Connections in Caribbean Migration Narratives (Rizzuto), 156n2
Recent Negro Fiction (Ellison), 149n7
Reclaiming the South (Davis), 15
recognition, 2
Reconstructing Dixie: Race, Gender, and Nostalgia in the Imagined South (McPherson), 5–6, 51, 152n13
Reconstructing Womanhood (Carby), 147n11
recuperation, 4–5, 7–8, 11, 19, 80, 117–18, 140, 148n3
Reflections on the Revolution of Our Time (Laclau), 137
regional designations, 15, 137
Regionalism in a Global Community (Coker), 149n2
Reshuffling the Deck; Or, (Re)Reading Race and Gender in Black Women's Writing (Tate), 147n11
Rhys, Jean, 156n2
Richardson, Alan, 24–25
Riley, Denise, 37–38
Rizzuto, Nicole, 156n2
Rodgers, Lawrence R., 123
Rowe, John Carlos, 56
Rudolph, Jack, 1–4, 76

Salem witch trials, 18, 111, 134
Salt Eaters, The (Bambara), 91
Santamarina, Xiomara, 146n5
Sapphira and the Slave Girl (Cather), 151n6
Scarboro, Ann Armstrong, 121
Scarlet Letter, The (Jotte), 155n13
Schulte, Pete, xi
self, 12–13, 15, 20, 154n5; in *History of Mary Prince*, 25, 30–31, 33, 38; in *I, Tituba*, 117, 118, 121–22, 126; in *Mama Day*, 85, 89–90, 98, 102; in *Their Eyes*, 54, 56, 63

Sense of Place and Space in Maryse Condé's 'Les derniers rois mages,' A (Mortimer), 117
sexuality, 8–10, 14, 31–33, 136, 146n4; in *History of Mary Prince*, 26, 32–33, 41–42, 44–46, 148n9, 149n10; in *I, Tituba*, 115, 117, 120, 124–29, 134, 155n13, 156n16
Sharpe, Jenny, 25–27, 31–32, 39, 44, 148n2, 148n9
slavery, 1, 10, 15, 26–27, 32; apology for, 1–2; as metaphor, 75; at University of Alabama, 1–4; authority on, 47; Caribbean versus North American, 33; corruptive nature of, 39, 43; freedom from, 33; and gender, 36, 39, 44, 46–47; histories of, 4, 16, 19, 30, 43; in *I, Tituba*, 112–13, 120–22, 124, 127–30, 135–36, 155n13; impact on black womanhood, 13, 59; in fiction, 88–89, 99, 110–12; labor of, 41, 43–44; in *Mama Day*, 78, 81–82, 88–89, 93–94, 99–100, 102, 109–10; maternity in, 129; physical abuse in, 46–47; relationship between treatment and obedience, 39, 100; self-definition within, 33; sexual exploitation in, 23, 42–46; spirit of, 43; symbol of, 36; and transatlantic slave trade, 4, 24; use of narrative against, 29
Slavery and the Literary Imagination (McDowell and Rampersad), 156n1
Smith, Barbara, 141, 145n3, 156n1
Smith, Leslie Dorrough, xi
Sollors, Werner, 138–40
'Something Akin to Freedom': The Case of Mary Prince (Sharpe), 25–26, 32, 39, 44, 112
Song of Solomon (Morrison), 114, 152n7
South, the, 2, 12, 16–17, 21, 51, 55, 74; compared to American North, 15, 55; identity of, 15; in *Mama Day*, 79–80, 86, 88, 94–96, 99, 102–3, 105, 108–10; mobility in, 50; nostalgia for, 51, 54, 58, 102, 147n12, 149n3; racism in, 76; representations of, 18, 52, 58, 72; in *Their Eyes*, 51, 56, 58, 72, 77; womanhood in, 21

Southern Studies, x, 51, 55, 150n20
Southscapes: Geographies of Race, Region, and Literature (Davis), 147n12
space, 117
Space and Place: The Perspective of Experience (Tuan), 154n8
Spelman, Elizabeth, 145n3
Spillers, Hortense, 12–13, 44, 149n11, 153n3
Stanford, Ann Folwell, 80
Strickland, Susanna, 19, 36–38, 44, 46–47, 112
Sula (Morrison), 114
Supplement to 'The History of Mary Prince' (Pringle), 26–27, 36, 40–44, 46, 100, 149n10
Stephen, George, 27
Stepto, Robert, 52, 149n8

Tate, Allen, 138
Tate, Claudia, 145n3, 147n11
Tell My Horse: Voodoo and Life in Haiti and Jamaica (Hurston), 51–52
Their Eyes Were Watching God (Hurston), 13–14, 16–18, 25, 38–39, 49–77, 79, 102, 106, 109–11, 114, 138, 149n4, 149n8; authenticity of, 52, 58, 69, 77; autonomy in, 50; Caribbean represented in, 51, 71–75, 77class represented in, 53, 60–61, 63–70, 72–73, 75–77, 150n13–50n15, 150n17, 150n19; criticism of, 52; gender in, 50–72, 76–77, 150n18; identity in, 49, 53–55, 58, 61–62, 73–74, 77; liberation in, 50, 55–56, 59, 66, 70; love in, 49, 55–56, 59–60, 66; migration in, 50–52, 54–59, 63–64, 67, 70, 73, 146n4, 150n10–50n11; ownership of narrative, 50; place in, 53–54, 58, 60, 69–70, 73–74; power represented in, 53, 57, 64–69, 72, 74; race in, 59–60, 65, 68, 75–77, 150n15; self in, 54, 56, 63; social and geographical context of, 50; South represented in, 51, 56, 58, 72, 77; travel in, 54, 56–59, 62–63, 71; voice of, 52–53,
62, 69, 77; womanhood in, 58–59, 62–65, 67–68, 70–74, 77; women's relationships in, 50, 57–58, 66, 69, 75, 150n14, 150n16; work in, 50–61, 63–68, 70–72, 74–77
Theorizing Race, Class and Gender (Brewer), 146n5
Thompson, Gordon E., 17, 52, 54, 58, 76, 149n8
Todorova, Kremena, 30, 148n4
Touna, Vaia, xi
tourist sites, 5–6
Trost, Ted, x
Tuan, Yi-Fu, 154n8
Tucker, Lindsey, 80
Turk's Island, 31–32, 45

Understanding Gloria Naylor (Whitt), 79
Undoing Gender (Butler), 8
University of Alabama, ix–x, 1–2; "African American Heritage Tour" at, 4; Gender and Race Studies at, 2; graves at, 2–3, 5, 76; "Recovering Black Women's Voices and Lives" symposium at, 4; Religious Studies at, 2; slavery at, 1–3

Vanderbilt University, x
voice, 12, 15, 18–19, 21, 28–29, 47, 52, 110; autonomy of, 26–28, 36; in *History of Mary Prince*, 23, 25–31, 36–38, 44–47, 148n4; in *I, Tituba*, 112–113, 115–116, 118, 120, 126, 128, 133, 135, 156n14; in *Mama Day*, 78, 81, 101; qualitative uniqueness of, 25, 28–30; as representative of a larger group, 28–30; in *Their Eyes*, 52–53, 62, 69, 77
Voice of Freedom: Mary Prince, The (Ferguson), 30
Volatile Bodies (Grosz), 8
volatile collectivity, 37–38
Voyage in the Dark (Rhys), 156n2

Wade, Elizabeth, xi
Wade, Sapphira, 18, 78–79, 81–82,

88–90, 92–93, 99–100, 102–3, 106, 110, 134, 151n6
See also Mama Day (Naylor)
Walker, Alice, 140–41
Walsh, Robert, 43
Walter, Kirk, xi
Warren, Robert Penn, 138
Washington, Booker T., 138
Washington, Mary Helen, 52, 149n8
West Indies, 24–25, 38, 42
White, Hayden, 4, 153n2
White, Heather, x
white supremacy, 13, 38, 75, 94
Whitener, Bonnie, xi
Whitlock, Gillian, 27–28, 31–32, 36–38, 46–47, 148n5, 149n14
Whitt, Margaret Earley, 79
"Who Set You Flowin'?": The African-American Migration Narrative (Griffin), 14
Wind Done Gone, The (Randall), 4
witchcraft, 18, 39, 99, 111, 114; in *I, Tituba*, 111–14, 117, 120–21, 130–35, 156n19
Wright, Richard, 51–52, 140, 149n6
Writings on Black Women of the Diaspora: History, Language, and Identity (Bracks), 28
womanhood, 10, 13, 19, 146n3; black, 13, 147n11; in *History of Mary Prince*, 34–35, 37, 40, 42, 44–46; in *I, Tituba*, 112, 115, 117, 120, 124, 128–30, 134; in *Mama Day*, 80, 82, 93, 96, 99–103, 105–6; Southern, 21, 39; in *Their Eyes*, 58–59, 62–65, 67–68, 70–74, 77
women's relationships: in *History of Mary Prince*, 26, 36–40, 148n8; in *I, Tituba*, 115, 120, 123–25, 128, 134, 136; in *Mama Day*, 104–5, 153n19–53n20; in *Their Eyes*, 50, 57–58, 66, 69, 75, 150n14, 150n16
Wood, John, 25–27, 32–36, 41–44, 46, 149n10, 149n13
work, 7, 9–10, 15–16, 19, 21, 30–32, 36, 43–44, 50, 137, 142; in *History of Mary Prince*, 27, 31–33, 36, 40–44; in *I, Tituba*, 112–113, 115, 120, 124, 129, 131, 133, 135; in *Mama Day*, 80, 82, 88–90, 93, 95, 101, 104–9; in *Their Eyes*, 50–61, 63–68, 70–72, 74–77; women's, 39–41, 50–51, 53–54, 57, 59–60, 70–72, 77, 106, 113, 131. *See also* labor
Workings of the Spirit: The Poetics of Afro-American Women's Writing (Baker), 149n1

Yaeger, Patricia, 58, 150n20
Young, Robert, ix

Zora Neale Hurston Was Always a Southerner Too (Cooper), 149n9

www.ingramcontent.com/pod-product-compliance
Lightning Source LLC
Chambersburg PA
CBHW020802160426
43192CB00006B/409